Gender and Dance in

Gender and Dance in Modern Iran: Biopolitics on stage investigates the ways dancing bodies have been providing evidence for competing representations of modernity, urbanism, and religiosity throughout the twentieth century.

Focusing on the transformation of the staged dancing body, its space of performance, and spectatorial cultural ideology, this book traces the dancing body in multiple milieus of performance, including the Pahlavi era's national artistic scene and the popular café and cabaret stages as well as the commercial cinematic screen and the post-revolutionary Islamized theatrical stage. It links the socio-political discourses on performance with the staged public dancer in order to interrogate the formation of dominant categories of "modern," "high," and "artistic," and the subsequent "othering" of cultural realms that were discursively peripheralized from the "national" stage. Through the study of archival and ethnographic research as well as a diverse literature pertaining to music, theater, cinema, and popular culture, it combines a close reading of primary sources such as official documents, press materials, and program notes with visual analysis of films and imageries, as well as interviews with practitioners. It offers an original and informed exploration into the ways performing bodies and their public have been associated with binary notions of vice and virtue, morality and immorality, commitment and degeneration, chastity and eroticism, and veiled-ness and nakedness.

Engaging with a range of methodological and historiographical methods, including postcolonial, performance, and feminist studies, this book is a valuable resource for students and scholars of Middle East history and Iranian studies, as well as gender studies and dance and performance studies.

Ida Meftahi is Visiting Assistant Professor in contemporary Iranian culture and society at the Roshan Institute for Persian Studies, University of Maryland. Her interdisciplinary historical research transcends the studies of gender, dance, theater, cinema, public entertainment, and performative politics.

Iranian Studies

Edited by: Homa Katouzian, University of Oxford and
Mohamad Tavakoli, University of Toronto.

Since 1967 the International Society for Iranian Studies (ISIS) has been a
leading learned society for the advancement of new approaches in the study
of Iranian society, history, culture, and literature. The new ISIS Iranian Studies series published by Routledge will provide a venue for the publication of
original and innovative scholarly works in all areas of Iranian and Persianate
Studies.

Gender and Dance in Modern Iran

Biopolitics on stage

Ida Meftahi

Routledge
Taylor & Francis Group

LONDON AND NEW YORK

First published 2016
by Routledge
2 Park Square, Milton Park, Abingdon, Oxon OX14 4RN

and by Routledge
711 Third Avenue, New York, NY 10017

First issued in paperback 2017

Routledge is an imprint of the Taylor & Francis Group, an informa business

British Library Cataloguing in Publication Data
A catalogue record for this book is available from the British Library

Library of Congress Cataloging in Publication Data
Names: Meftahi, Ida.
  Title: Gender and dance in modern Iran : biopolitics on stage / Ida
Meftahi.
  Description: New York, NY : Routledge, [2016] | Series: Iranian studies; 32
  Identifiers: LCCN 2015030803| ISBN 9781138804043 (hardback) | ISBN
9781315753294 (ebook)
  Subjects: LCSH: Dance–Iran–History. | Gender expression–Iran–History.
  Classification: LCC GV1697 .M44 2016 | DDC 792.8/09550904–dc23
LC record available at http://lccn.loc.gov/2015030803

ISBN 13: 978-0-8153-4883-2 (pbk)
ISBN 13: 978-1-138-80404-3 (hbk)

Typeset in Times New Roman
by Taylor & Francis Books

To my life partner Arash
My mother Surayya
And my dance mother Farzanah

Contents

List of figures

Acknowledgment

This book was developed from my doctoral dissertation which I completed in September 2013 at the University of Toronto's Department of Near and Middle Eastern Civilizations. This project would have never materialized without the tens of interviewees, performers, and scholars who have courageously shared their knowledge, lived experiences, and artistry and selflessly helped me along this path. They shall remain anonymous; nevertheless, I am eternally indebted to them.

I would like to express deep gratitude to my doctoral supervisor Professor Mohamad Tavakoli-Targhi for his patience, guidance, energy, creativity, his sheer insightfulness, and his exceptional gift for instilling critical thinking and the problematization of cultural and academic stereotypes in my work. I credit Professor Selma Odom, who supervised my research at the master's level, with inciting my interest in dance studies and initiating my academic career as I continue to benefit from her ongoing support and selfless guidance. My appreciation goes to Professor Stephen Johnson for his unconditional support and encouragement, and for generously sharing his immense knowledge and experience, as well as for keeping my academic life connected to the world of performance studies. To Professor James Reilly I am deeply grateful for going above and beyond the call of duty as a committee member—he also helped me expand my academic horizon beyond Iran during the several semesters that I was his teaching assistant. I extend my gratitude to Professor Amir Hassanpour, who oversaw the initial years of my doctoral research during which I drew much energy from his ability to instill in me a spirit of resistance; I thank him for all his encouragement, which continues to this day.

From Professor Afsaneh Najmabadi, in addition to much inspiration from her pioneering scholarship, I have also received invaluable feedback from her reading of my dissertation as the external examiner on my committee. I look forward to benefiting from her mentorship in the future. Professor Shahrzad Mojab was not only an influential member of my defense committeem, I have also been inspired by her academic integrity and courage to engage with topics which require a sincere dedication to social justice. Professor Rivanne Sandler's experience and knowledge of Iranian women's literature added a fresh perspective to my defense. I also benefited from her commentary during the defense, as it further enhanced my dissertation. I would also like to thank Professors Anthony Shay, Fatemeh Keshavarz, Ahmet Karamustafa, Karin Van Nieuwkerk, Modesto Amegago, Darcey Callison, Mary Jane Warner, Houshang Chehabi, and Bruce Barton for reading sections of my work and providing insightful comments.

My uncle, Dr. Moussa Ghaninejad, was my pathway into a vast number of archives, and without his unconditional help I could not have succeeded in this research. Film scholar Abbas Baharloo generously granted me access to his personal archive and shared his invaluable knowledge of Iranian cinema, which was instrumental in shaping the fourth chapter of my dissertation. Pioneering ethnomusicologist Professor Sasan Fatemi shared his unpublished research and extensive knowledge on the *mutribi* sphere. I am indebted to Dr. Elahé Omidyar Mir-Djalali and the Roshan Cultural Heritage Institute for providing me with a generous fellowship for 2011–2012 that facilitated my archival research.

As an Institute of Arts and Humanities 2013–14 post-doctoral fellow at the Pennsylvania State University, I greatly benefited from the ingenuity and generosity of Professor Michael Bérubé, whose directorship has created the most welcoming environment for interdisciplinary research. Professor Jonathon Brockopp kept my connection to the History Department while adopting me as part of the Middle East Studies community. I am also indebted to Drs. Lauren Kooistra, Nina Safran, Janet Lyon, Paula Droege, Hoda El Shakry, and Craige Eley for their friendship and care.

Since fall 2014, the Roshan Institute for Persian Studies at the University of Maryland has been the most invigorating home for my academic adventures. Dr. Fatemeh Keshavarz supports my academic dreams in teaching exciting courses in Iranian history and pursuing new spectrums of research combining history and digital humanities. I extend gratitude to Professor Ahmet Karamustafa for his wisdom and perceptiveness to the field of history. My Roshan Institute colleagues and friends, Dr. Nahal Akbari Sanah, Dr. Ali Abbasi, Matthew Thomas Miller, Susan Moinfar, Samar Ali Ata, and Nazanine Beryanvand have greatly smoothened my transition to the University of Maryland with their warmth, insight, and enthusiasm.

I am deeply indebted to Nadir Rajabpur, Haideh Akundzadeh, Nejad Ahmadzadeh, Mohammadreza Darvishi, Dr. Hamid Amjad, Mr. Shahbazi, Arezu Afshar, Mahshad Mokhberi, Farshid Saffari, Nesta Ramezani, Sara Reyhani, and Drs. Salehpour, Azizi, and As'adi.

My colleague Shabnam Rahimi-Golkhandan took time out of her busy schedule to read several drafts of my dissertation. I benefited greatly from her comments, energy, and passion. My friend and colleague Farzanah Hemmasi mentored me along my academic path since the day we met, and I foresee decades of fulfilling collaborations in our future. I am thankful to my performance studies colleagues Shelly Liebembuk, Paromita Kar, and Samantha Mehra for reading different versions of my dissertation and providing useful feedback. I am thankful to Faegheh Mobarhan, Azar Masumi, Seika Boye, Ali Kamran, Maryam Nabavinejad, Shayan Mashatian, Babak Taati, Arnavaz Danesh, Janet Alexanian, Yashar Salek, Maral Salek, Faegheh Mobarhan, Hossein Bioukzadah, Heather Rastovac, Art Babyants, Fethi Karakechili, and Mercedeh Tariverdi for their tremendous help and support. Finally, if it were not for the camaraderie and support of my colleagues at the University of Toronto Department of Near and Middle Eastern Civilizations— Golbarg Rekabtalaei, Hamid Rezaeiyazdi, and Arshavez Mozaffari—my doctoral journey would have been a solitary one.

This note of acknowledgements would not be complete without a mention of my life partner Arash Bateni. He has provided a supportive and caring home in which I received the love and energy needed to complete this project, and his humor, understanding, and overwhelming support helped me tremendously along the way. I also would like to thank my parents, my beloved brother, and my extended family for their tremendous support.

1 Introduction

This transdisciplinary historiographical study offers a narrative of corporeality in modern Iran centered on the transformation of the staged dancing body, its space of performance, and its spectatorial cultural ideology. It analyzes the ways in which dancing bodies have provided evidence for competing representations of modernity, urbanity, and Islam throughout the twentieth century. This book focuses particularly on three theatrical Iranian dance genres (as discourses) which emerged in the twentieth century. These include the "national dance" (*raqs-i milli*) of the Pahlavi era (1925–79); cabaret dancing of the post-1940 era (onstage and on cinema screens); and the post-revolutionary genre called "rhythmic movements" (*harikat-i mawzun*).[1] Each genre is studied as an artistic product conditioned by multiple social, cultural, political, economic and ideological factors (see Figures 1.1–1.3).

Exploring the socio-historical milieu of performance, this book investigates the (contending) discursive constructions of the dancing body and its audience. At the same time, it historicizes the formation of dominant cultural categories of "modern," "high," and "artistic" in Iran and the subsequent "othering" of cultural realms that were discursively peripheralized from the "national" stage. This is enhanced by close analysis of the three contending modern vernacular social discourses: (1) the national(ist) discourse, which was aimed at educating the nation and achieving national arts, (2) the anti-obscenity discourse of the press with religious orientations, which I will refer to as Islamic discourse, and (3) the Marxist-inspired discourse of performing arts and mainly the theater. All of these discourses intersected in reacting to the intrusion of female sexuality into public space and the emergence and commercialization of mixed gender forms and sites of urban popular entertainment. Within this analysis is a parallel discussion throughout the book on the historicization of the ways notions of "degeneration" (*ibtizal*) and "eroticism" (*shahvat*) have been constructed, reconfigured, and deployed in the twentieth-century context as moral and aesthetic criteria applied to the performing body.

This book further explores the ideological applications of the cultural categories for conditioning the aesthetics and ethics of the dancing body onstage, as well as the audience's taste. This includes the impetuses behind the

Figure 1.1 A national dancer in the late 1940s
The studio for the revival of classical arts of Iran, souvenir program, undated.

Figure 1.2 A Cabaret dancer; Rawshanak Sadr in *Jahil va Raqqasah* (The Jahil and
the dancer, 1976)
Ida Meftahi's Personal Archive.

Figure 1.3 Rythmic Movements, Farzanah Kabuli in Epic of the Rock Revolution, 2000
Photo by Omid Salehi.

selection of cultural motifs from ancient symbolism, literature, folklore, and mysticism and religious rituals, as well as the use of European art forms in the construction of new virtuous "national(ist)" or "Islamic" performing bodies. Other factors that I consider in this study include the shifting dynamics of the body in public space as they relate to urban transformations, the state's top-down implementations in establishing various institutions, the competing conceptions of discipline and regulatory systems as pertaining to public space, and the bio-economy of the dancing body in relation to the income of the performance venues.

According to the socio-historical context of performance, the onstage performer in each genre has constituted a differing dancing self through choice of movement, posture, appearance, and behavior, as well as gender performativity and relations. Therefore, this project required multi-method data gathering and analysis from both pre- and post-revolutionary eras. The types of data used for this study encompassed textual, narrative, visual, and that based on participant observation (conducted in dance classes, rehearsals, and performances), all of which complemented different aspects of each other.

Discourse analysis on dance, the performing arts, and popular culture was conducted through usage of a diverse range of twentieth-century periodicals with various ideological stances, literature pertaining to theater, music, and cinema, as well as governmental documents and program notes. Additionally, academic literature pertaining to music, theater, cinema, and popular culture was consulted. Furthermore, a large pool of cinematic productions was studied for narrative analysis.

I extracted vital information about the work conditions of cabaret dancers of the Pahlavi era from interviews I held with the performers who worked in such settings.[2] My examination of the post-revolutionary period also involved interviews with practitioners who have been constantly redefining and re-creating their genres to work around the unwritten regulations of the post-revolutionary stage enforced by theater authorities whose disciplinary gaze (not to discount the other senses) has sought to prevent sexual stimulation and immoral thoughts in the audiences.

The visual data deployed for this study included images of dance, video footage of theatrical performances, and cinematic productions. To interpret the visual data of performance, I focused on visual codes and elements such as theme, costume, posture, gesture, movement vocabulary, pace, use of space, lighting, props, and music to develop a framework of criteria that could explain the semiotics and aesthetics of the staged body in multiple milieus of performance. In examining the dancing body onstage, in addition to movement and semiotic analysis and representational study, I also draw on the recent scholarship on affect, feeling, and emotion, to further explore the sensorial experience of performers and audiences.[3] This multi-faceted approach not only deepened my historical study of the body, movement, and embodiments of "vice" and "virtue" in the Iranian socio-cultural context; it also helped to shed light on the regulatory mechanism of the post-revolutionary stage, one which scrutinizes the semiotics of bodies as well as their "feeling technology."

This study raises a number of theoretical, historiographical, and choreographical issues concerning dance, the body, subjectivity, and biopolitics, and their interplay with nationalism in Iran. Focusing on the female body on the theatrical stage, I draw on several Foucauldian notions including biopower, biopolitics, the effects of the correctional gaze, and technologies of the self.[4] In light of Joan W. Scott's emphasis on the significance of gender as a category for historical analysis, as well as Judith Butler's gender performativity as a regulatory regime, I explore the various ways in which gender identity is constructed on the Iranian theatrical stage.[5] Informed by feminist and postmodernist subject, agency and self, I reconstruct the Islamic concept of self in an effort to explain the transformation of dance in twentieth-century Iran. I explore the genres of national dance and rhythmic movements as "invented traditions," deployed to promote two competing conceptions of Iran as a modern nation.[6] In my analysis of the cabaret dancer on stage and in film, I employ Erving Goffman's conceptions of "front-stage" and "offstage" to analyze the ways the characteristics of "corruption" and "sexual perversion" associated with the cabaret dancer's daily life were transformed into a bold performance of sexuality, signified by her costume, movements, behavior, and relationship with her audience.[7] Furthermore, in unpacking the corporeal aspects of "degeneration" (*ibtizal*) and "eroticism" (*shahvat*) as aesthetic criteria applied to performing bodies, I deploy the notion and theories of affect to explore the emotional impact and the visceral and sensory experience of the audience.

In the area of dance and performance, I rely on pertinent scholarship to explore the significance of the staged performing body, and its potential capacity to project ideologies and constructed identities, ideal bodies, and relations through its appearance, actions, and aesthetics, as well as its interaction with the audience.[8] Theories articulating gender identity on stage are of particular importance with regard to the dancing body on the Iranian stage, especially in the area of the ways in which gender, as a visual marker in a theatrical context, is being constructed and often used for cultural conditioning and reinforcing the status quo.[9]

Conducting the first historiographical study on dance in Iran, I dealt with a number of predicaments throughout this project, forcing me to both broaden the scope of my research and deal with unpredicted but fundamental questions in the area of cultural studies in Iran. A primary problem was a lack of documents on the subject as well as the understudied status of dance and other forms of performance that involved the dancing body. These prevented a more precise periodization of the genres and trends explored in the ninety-year span this book covers.

As I show throughout this study, as a consequence of diverging political attitudes towards modernity, cultural evaluation, and moralization, as well as concerns with sexuality, the historical narratives of performance, even those provided by the secondary literature, have been intertwined with rumors, myths, and speculations. Furthermore, the discursive bifurcation of culture as "high," "elite," "modern," "literate," "intellectual," and even "secular,"—as opposed to the "popular," "low," "traditionalist" ("unmodern" or "ante-modern"), "illiterate," "degenerate," and "religious,"—has been deeply embedded in the socio-political discourses. The uncritical treatments of these notions in the academic narratives further added to the challenges I encountered in this inquiry.

Furthermore, the oral, improvisational, and liminal nature of the forms of performance prevalent in popular realms and their associations with social corruption and prostitution, have resulted in their neglect and dismissal by scholars as immoral and thus unworthy.[10] This was especially the case with regards to the interconnected spheres of urban popular culture of the Pahlavi era, including the *mutribi* scene, the café and cabaret milieus, the theatrical setting of Lalehzar post-1950, and the commercial cinema genre *film-i farsi*. Constituting a "negative space" in Iranian cultural history, these cultural realms have not only been regarded negatively, but have also been actively kept absent from Iranian historiography, resulting in their systematic omission from historical accounts. In particular, the cabaret dancer has served as a "stop sign" at which scholars have cut off their inquiries rather than entering into the "emotive" realm of her performance. Likewise, the dominance of these cultural categories and the inaccessibility of the performers associated with these realms to the written discourse have made them silent subjects in historical narratives.

A historical overview of the major performances and performance spheres

This section aims to contextualize the performances discussed in relation to the dance genres explored in the book. It first introduces a number of performances that have been categorized as folk, ritualistic, and/or traditional and have been presumed to have existed prior to the twentieth century. Then it moves on to explore the dance practices that emerged in twentieth-century Iran with the creation of urban public theatrical spaces as well as sites of sociability, including balletic performances, European social dancing, and cabaret dancing. Lastly, it introduces the dance practices of the post-revolutionary era.

A number of movement scenes have been assumed to have existed prior to the twentieth century. A major group of them are the dances with ethnic ties and regional genealogies that have usually been identified as "folk dances" (*raqs-i mahalli*). These include dance practices prevalent in Azerbaijan, Gilan, Kurdistan, Khurasan, Baluchistan, and many other regions. These dances have been regularly practiced on private and public occasions such as weddings and familial gatherings, where people dance to celebrate.[11] Some of these practices include stylized combat, such as stick dances (*chub-bazi*) from Luristan and Baluchistan.[12]

Additionally, a number of folk games have featured dance and other movements, such as *dig bah sar* (pot on head) of Maku.[13] In addition to folk dances of many regions that have been practiced in heterosocial spaces, women's theatrical games (*bazi-ha-yi namayishi*) have also included dancing.[14] Furthermore, several shamanistic rituals have involved distinctive rhythms and movements, such as the healing ceremonies of *zar* and *guati* in southern Iran. Another style, now known as Persian or Iranian solo improvised dance, refers to a widely practiced dance form that has been prevalant in different areas of Iran and the Persianate world.[15] The general presumption with regard to folk dances and ethnic rituals has been that they have had timeless existence, and thus it has been impossible to trace them historically.[16]

Another ritualistic movement form is *sama'*, or Sufi dance, which has received enormous attention in the press and in scholarly publications, mostly in relation to Persian poetry and especially with the thirteenth-century poet Mawlana Jalalulddin Rumi. A general trend in these writings has been to link the genealogy of whirling dervish ceremonies—which are performed in Turkey today by Mevlevi-order dervishes—to Iranian mysticism described in Persian poetry.[17] However, what is practiced by Sufi orders in different regions of Iran today (including the Qadiriyah and Naqshbandiyah dervishes in Kurdistan and Baluchistan) mostly involves swaying, swivelling, and self-flagellation, as opposed to the structured ceremony of Turkish dervishes.

Other movements and themes which have been specially deployed in the post-revolutionary genre of rhythmic movements are borrowed from theatrical genre *ta'ziyah* as well as the Muharram mourning processions for the deaths of the Third Shi'i Imam Husayn and seventy-two of his companions in 680 AD in Karbala on the day of 'Ashura, the tenth of Muharram. Genealogically, *ta'ziyah* has often traced back to the mourning ritual processions which began in the tenth century, but it was during the Safavid dynasty (1501–1722), which established Shi'i Islam as the state religion in Iran, that the Muharram rite received royal encouragement. During this era, a number of performative forms of publicizing Shi'ism, including the dramatic narrations of the life, deeds, suffering, and death of Shi'i martyrs, became prevalent.[18] Scholars speculate that it is through the combination of corporeal elements within the ritual processions, and the historical and imaginary narrative forms, that *ta'ziyah* has found its current shape.[19] The main theme of *ta'ziyah* has been the siege of Karbala, but the focus has been on individual heroes around whom separate plays have been written, often by unknown authors.

The "golden age" of *ta'ziyah* has been regarded as the Qajar era (1794–1925), especially that of the Nasir al-din Shah (1831–1896), when it was professionalized as a theatrical form.[20] The occasional entrance of Qajar kings into the religious narratives, as well as the implementation of comedic elements into the performances, prompted a negative response from the clergy.[21] In the early twentieth century, the intelligentsia also are said to have joined the opponents of *ta'ziyah*, a genre which to them manifested a ceremony that caused and exhibited Iran's backwardness. This secularist-nationalist ethos was then echoed by Reza Shah Pahlavi state that, in 1928, banned the form in urban spaces.[22] *Ta'ziyah* was then marginalized to being performed in rural areas.[23]

Gradually, by the 1960s and 1970s, *ta'ziyah* received attention from scholars, artists, and the Pahlavi state. This was partly due to a nativist movement in the 1960s known as "return to the self," as well as the international overtures towards the form. In the same vein, after the Revolution of 1979, not only did (secular) directors and scholars continue valorizing *ta'ziyah* as the national theatrical form, but religious theater since then became a constituent of the government's cultural programming.

Genealogically traceable to those of the Safavid era, the *mutribi* ("minstrel") is another major performance form, which involved music, acting, and dancing.[24] In his ground-breaking work on *mutribi* music, the ethnomusicologist Sasan Fatemi has categorized the musical troupes active from the Safavid to the Pahlavi era principally as either groups of women who performed in homosocial private events, or troupes chiefly consisting of men who performed for male (or mixed) audiences in public and private settings, including the court. In the Safavid era, female dancers accompanied the *mutrib*s for public performances, while in the Qajar era, mainly transvestite male adolescent dancers (*bachchah-raqqas*) performed dance publicly. Regardless of their sex, the public dancing bodies performing for male audiences were commonly associated with overt sexuality and prostitution.[25]

Numerous accounts, including Iranian memoirs and European travelogues, have described viewing musical performances accompanied by dance. The boy dancers often created astonishment in European travelers who were viewing their performance of sexuality with a heteronormative gaze, as reflected in several of their travelogues.[26] In the Qajar era, many *mutribi* troupes settled in larger cities and primarily in the capital, Tehran.[27] Qajar kings were especially interested in *mutribi* performances and some of the most important musicians and actors resided in their courts. In the late Qajar era especially, the acting component of *mutribi* troupes became stronger, making it a venue for the creation of the blackface performance of *siyah-bazi* that is today considered one of the two most important "traditional" theatrical forms of Iran.[28] As these performances were often performed on a stage set up by planks placed on small pools in houses for celebrations, they were called *ruhawzi* or *takhtah-hawzi* (literally, "on the pool").

Serving as the main professional performing artists of their time, the *mutribi* actors known as *taqlidchi* (literally, "imitators") were also employed to act in the European plays of the late Qajar era, which were initiated by modernist intelligentsia who considered theater to be a school for morality. In this interaction, the *taqlidchi* actors also started to adapt European plays to their own style and conditions, labeling them as *tiyart* (instead of *ti'atr*). In that era, several of Molière's plays were adapted by *taqlid* ("imitation") practitioners, with characters renamed and the plots relocated to Iranian contexts.[29] Until the late Qajar era, Tehran's *mutribi* troupes used to gather in certain coffee houses (*qahvah-khanah*s).[30] Then, it is often speculated that as part of first (Reza Shah) Pahlavi's ordering of the public sphere, *mutrib*s were pushed away from *qahvah-khanah*s, and consequently went to open the early *shadimani* ("joyfulness") agencies (*bungah-i shadimani*).[31]

Starting around the late nineteenth and early twentieth centuries, *mutrib*s found a new "performance" rival: the elite nationalist-modernist performing arts community which staged romantic musicals and European-style plays, through which they sought to advance and educate the nation. These theatrical productions were concentrated in the Lalehzar district in Tehran. Built in the Qajar era, the creation of Lalehzar Street is often linked to one of the trips of the Qajar ruler Nasir al-din Shah to Paris.[32] For about four decades, "the street" was the main venue for the modernist cultural endeavours of the nationalist art scene, where several active amphitheaters resided next to printing houses and cinemas as well as restaurants and cafés in the area.

Numerous plays, operettas, and variety shows were staged in the Lalehzar venues, which expanded from the Grand Hotel's proscenium stage in the early twentieth century to a dozen theaters by the 1940s. Non-Muslim female dancers with ballet training were also recruited to the scene to perform in the operettas with nationalist themes or as part of variety shows. Gradually, several dance classes and companies started in Tehran, leading to the creation of a professionalized dance scene in Tehran and the emergence of the new dance genre, national dance (*raqs-i milli*), that fused Iranian vernacular movements and themes with ballet.

In addition to the theatrical stage, cafés and cabarets were other venues of performance. Emerging in the late nineteenth and early twentieth century, Iranian café culture was a product of urban modernity, and a site of socializing where people sought to experience and embody new mediums. By the 1930s, a number of café-chantants with musical performances (of both European orchestras and high-end Iranian music) surfaced in Lalehzar Street and the new "northern" Tehran areas. During the Second World War, allied soldiers were also audience members of these cafés, including a café on Lalehzar Street where Polish dancers performed.[33]

With the opening of affordable "modern" café-chantants during the 1940s in the Lalehzar area, different classes of society intermingled while enjoying presumably stylized versions of *mutribi* music.[34] Theater historian Bahram Bayza'i described these performances as a mixture of *taqlid* and *mutrib*'s interpretations of European-style dance and music which emulated "foreign" films, the performers often adorned with sailor clothing, frocks, and Mexican hats. Their audience, he pronounces, were the "night vigilantes of the new civilization" (*shabzindahdaran-i farangi-ma'ab*).[35] Particularly after 1950, cafés with performances by the *mutribi* troupe members boomed in different areas of Tehran, including Lalehzar Street.[36] Known as *saz-va-zarbi* or *saz-zan-zarbi* cafés for their vernacular music, these venues gradually became dominated by male audiences from a range of backgrounds.

Also associated with Tehran's nightlife were the cabarets constructed as "classy" in relation to the cafés. The dancers who performed in these venues offered a different repertoire than that of the national dancing scene: often coming from a *mutribi* or foreign background or with no training in dance, these performers were hired to depict a sexually stimulating dancing body onstage. The recruitment of cabaret dancers to the theater scene of Lalehzar after 1950, as well as Iranian commercial cinema, contributed financially to these private-sector venues while also creating controversies around cabaret dancers.

In addition to cabaret dancing, a variety of (modern) European social dances (*raqs-ha-yi mudirn-i urupa'i*), including samba, rumba, swing, tango, cha-cha, and the waltz, were practiced in the sites of leisure (see Figures 1.4–1.5). Several dance classes also taught these forms in Tehran.[37] Those who practiced these dances were often deemed *mutajaddid* ("modern"), whereas these practices caused controversy in many sectors of society, including the religiously oriented press.[38] While a reason for their negation was the close proximity of men and women in public, the joining of the US and British soldiers to these venues after the Anglo-Soviet invasion of Iran in 1941 further prompted these sensitivities.[39] The social dancing trend became a part of the popular culture in the 1960s and 1970s, to be practiced in venues associated with the nightlife.

In contrast to the dancing bodies of the popular scene were the national dancers, who with the opening of state-sponsored schools and companies especially after 1950, found a permanent venue of performance. While creating a dignified image for dance and a platform for development of artistic dance forms in Iran, the reception of these performances was limited to dignitaries and distinct audiences. These endeavors were interrupted by the Revolution of 1979.

As a consequence of the Revolution of 1979 that prohibited a range of performance forms, dance practices went underground to familial and friendly gatherings, and community settings. Dance education also had to be concealed and held in home-based studios, private-sector gyms, and kindergartens. Within a few years, however, a renamed version of national dance, "rhythmic movements" (*harikat-i mawzun*), returned to the theater stage, with mainly religious, "revolutionary" (*inqilabi*), or mystical themes. The choreographers and performers in these productions were often the performers with the major dance companies prior to the revolution, most of whom were also involved in dance education in post-revolutionary era.

The strategy of renaming dance also set the ground for the classification of folk dances as "ritualistic" (*a'ini*), to be performed by local or urban-based groups in various folk and ritualistic festivals and state-sponsored celebrations on public stage or in spaces such as parks. The majority of these performances had been male-based, and occasionally involved women or younger girls in minor roles.[40]

Within the three decades after the revolution, the dance scene has grown enormously. The genres of dance taught in underground classes have been

Figure 1.4 Social dancing cartoon
"Coordination on the dance floor, a photo from a recent soirée," *Tihran-i Musavvar*, 1333/1954.

updated to include international trends such as salsa, flamenco and hip-hop, as well as a range of vernacular performing arts. While some dance classes have been advertised in the community press, educational videos by male instructors have become available for sale in stores (see Figure 1.6).[41] Break dancing, which started as an underground youth culture in the 1980s, has also been renamed "professional aerobics" (*ayrubik-i hirfah'i*) to appear in public.

Figure 1.5 Social dancing in discothèque in 1970s
Ida Meftahi's Archive.

In fact, its recognition and governmentalization as a sportive field by the Organization of Physical Education (Sazman-i Tarbiyat-i Badani) has paved the way for official break dance classes, as well as dance competitions, in several cities around the country.[42]

On the theatrical stage, the *harikat-i mawzun* scene has grown as a new generation with post-revolutionary dance training has joined the scene as choreographers and directors.[43] Furthermore, a new genre of movement-based theatrical performance has surfaced since 2000 out of the physical theater scene. Recognized by some as "contemporary dance" (*kantimpurari dans*), or some other alternative terms, this genre has been showcasing tormented Artaudian bodies onstage, ones that have not just been aesthetically divergent from *harikat-i mawzun*, but that exercise greater onstage freedom in terms of gender performativity and relations.[44] With the trending of performance art, especially, the gallery spaces have also become venues for these types of performances.

In addition to public stagings of dance, carnivalesque situations, such as the international success of the National Soccer Team, have been bringing people to celebrate on the streets by dancing.[45] While the post-revolutionary dance scene appears to be thriving, due to the sensitivities towards the dancing body

Figure 1.6 Dance class advertisement which emphasizes the athletic aspects of ballet
        and hip-hop
Payk-i Tihran, nos. 20–21, Azar 1388/December 2009, 16.

and depending on the day-to-day politics, it is important to note that these practices have been subject to scrutiny and controversies and may lead to penalty
for the practitioners or the responsible authority who allowed them to happen.

A more in-depth discussion of these themes follows and is divided into
seven additional chapters. Chapter 2 examines the biopolitics of the invention
of an ideal female dancer for the national(ist) stage of the Pahlavi era.
Chapter 3 focuses on performing arts in the leftist discourses and practices in

the 1940s and explores the marginalization of *mutrib*s and their dancers as the counter ideals of a new Iran and their exclusion from the many historical narratives of Iranian theater. Chapter 4 sheds light on the milieus of performance of the female cabaret dancer of the popular urban entertainment scene. Chapter 5 explores the dance genres and offstage performances that crossed over to cinema with a main focus on the cinematic depiction of the cabaret dancer in film. Chapter 6 investigates the disciplinary discourse of the Islamic periodicals of the Pahlavi era, while comparing them to their contemporaneous Marxist-inspired theater and nationalist and art discourses. Chapter 7 examines the emergence of post-revolutionary rhythmic movements in light of the Islamic Republic's bio-ideology. And Chapter 8 concludes the book by retrospectively comparing and contrasting the contending notions and genres of dance throughout the twentieth century while exploring the dancing bodies and subjects in relation to their spaces of performance.

Notes

1 This study is limited to the theatrical stage in Tehran, and mostly focuses on female performing bodies. Moreover, as it deals with twentieth-century genres of theatrical dance, folk dances and rituals are outside the scope of this book. They are mostly mentioned in this study in relation to their deployment in the discussed theatrical genres.
2 Due to social and political sensitivities to the topic, I have used aliases to refer to the majority of interviewed artists throughout this book. All interviews were conducted by me in Persian and all translations thereof are mine.
3 In analyzing the dancing body in each genre and describing the vernacular movements, I have deployed the effort-shape system; the interpretation of my analysis requires a knowledge of the system. See Cecily Dell, *A Primer for Movement Description: Using Effort-Shape and Supplementary Concepts* (New York: Dance Notation Bureau Press, 1977).
4 Michel Foucault, "Biopower," in *The Foucault Reader*, M. Foucault and P. Rabinow, eds (New York: Pantheon Books, 1984), 257–89; Michel Foucault, "Technologies of the Self," in *Technologies of the Self: A Seminar with Michel Foucault*, L. H. Martin, H. Gutman, and P. H. Hutton, eds (Amherst: The University of Massachusetts Press, 1988), 16–45; Michel Foucault, "Governmentality," in *The Foucault Effect: Studies in Governmentality*, G. Burchell, C. Gordon, and P. Miller, eds (Chicago, IL: University of Chicago Press, 1991), 87–104; Michel Foucault, "The Eye of Power," in *Power/Knowledge: Selected Interviews and Other Writings, 1972–1977*, ed. C. Gordon (New York: Pantheon, 1980), 146–65.
5 Joan W. Scott, "Gender: A Useful Category of Historical Analysis," *American Historical Review* 91, no. 5 (December 1986): 1053–75; Judith Butler, *Gender Trouble: Feminism and the Subversion of Identity* (New York: Routledge, 1990).
6 Eric Hobsbawm and Ranger Terence (eds), *The Invention of Tradition* (Cambridge: Cambridge University Press, 1983).
7 Erving Goffman, *The Presentation of Self in Everyday Life* (New York: Doubleday Anchor Books, 1959).
8 Jane C. Desmond, "Engendering Dance: Feminist Inquiry and Dance Research," in *Researching Dance: Evolving Modes of Inquiry*, S. H. Fraleigh and P. Hanstein, eds (Pittsburgh, PA: University of Pittsburgh Press, 1999), 309–33; Jill Dolan, "Gender Impersonation on Stage: Destroying or Maintaining the Mirror of Gender Roles,"

---

in *Gender in Performance: The Presentation of Difference in the Performing Arts*, ed. L. Senelick (Hanover, NH: University Press of New England, 1992), 3–13.

9 Helen Gilbert and Joan Tompkins, *Post-Colonial Drama: Theory, Practice, Politics* (London: Routledge, 1996); Laurence Senelick, ed., *Gender in Performance: The Presentation of Difference in the Performing Arts* (Hanover, NH: University Press of New England, 1992), xii.

10 The performances of the café and cabaret cultures could be categorized among dance, music, and theater, and also as relating to gender and sexuality studies.

11 For a description of folk dances in Iran, see Mansureh Sabitzadah, "Raqs dar iran: Anva' va vizhigi-ha" [Dance in Iran: Types and characteristics], *Mahoor Musical Quarterly* 6, no. 24 (Summer 2004): 99–115; Robyn C. Friend, "Modern Persian dance," in *Encyclopedia Iranica*, vol. 6, fascicle 6, ed. E. Yarshater (Costa Mesa, CA: Mazda), 641–5.

12 The famed ethnomusicologist Muhammad-Reza Darvishi has explored these dances in an unpublished book manuscript: see Muhammad-Reza Darvishi, "Bazi-ha va raqs-ha-yi a'ini-i iran" [Ritualistic games and dances of Iran], n.d.

13 For more on these practices, see Surayya Qizil-Ayaq, *Rahnama-yi bazi-ha-yi iran* [A guide to traditional Iranian games] (Tehran: Daftar-i Pazhuhish-ha-yi Farhangi, 1379/2000).

14 See Furuq Yazdan Ashuri and Javad Insafi, *Namayish-ha-yi zananah'i iran* [Women's performances in Iran] (Tehran, Intisharat-i Rabi'ah, 1388).

15 See Anthony Shay, *Choreophobia: Solo Improvised Dance in the Iranian World* (Costa Mesa, CA: Mazda, 1999).

16 Late nineteenth-century images of some of these performances are available in the photographic records by Antoin Sevruguin. Antoin Sevruguin (Nineteenth Century). Photograph of Musician and Dancer. Stephen Arpee Collection of Antoin Sevruguin Photographs, Smithsonian Institution, Freer/Sackler Gallery of Art.

17 For an example, see Abulqassim Tafazzuli, *Sama'* (Tehran: Intisharat-i Zaryab, 1382/2003); Arezoo Afshar, "Pazhuhishi bar raqs-ha-yi 'arifanah, sama'" [A study of mystic dances, Sama'], (master's thesis, Azad University of Tehran, Department of Arts and Architecture, 1383/2004), 158–207.

18 These include the prospering of the performative *rawzah khani* ("recitation"), *shamayil-gardani* ("showing around portraits"), *manaqib-khani* ("adoration"), *maddahi* ("eulogy"), and religious *naqqali* ("recounting"). See Muhammad-Husayn Nasirbakht, *Naqshpushi dar shabihkhani* [Wearing the character in Shahbihkhani] (Tehran: Intisharat-i Namayish, 1386/2007), 12.

19 Bahram Bayza'i, *Namayish dar Iran* [Theater in Iran], 5th edn. (Tehran: Intisharat-i Rawshangaran va Mutali'at-i Zanan, 1385/2006), 120.

20 Khosrow Shahriari, *A Different Approach to a Unique Theater: Taziyeh in Iran* (Sweden: Kitab-i Arzan, 2008), 33.

21 Majid Sarsangi, *Muhit-i ti'atri va rabitah'i bazigar va tamashagar-i namayish-i dini* [The theatrical space and the relationship between performer and the audience in religious theater] (Tehran: Intisharat-i Afraz, 1389/2010), 310.

22 Farrokh Gaffary, "Evolution of rituals and theater in Iran," *Iranian Studies* 17, no. 4 (Autumn 1984): 361–89, 371.

23 Sarsangi, *Muhit-i ti'atri*, 312.

24 See Sasan Fatemi, "Mutrib-ha az Safaviyah ta mashrutiyat" [Mutribs from Safavid age until the constitutional movement], *Mahoor Music Quarterly* 12, no. 3 (Summer 2001); Ardeshir Salehpour, *Taranah'i namayish-ha-yi pishpardahkhani dar iran, 1320–1332* [The lyrics of the *pishpardahkhani* in Iran, 1941–53] (Tehran: Namayish, 1388/2009), 120. A variety of traveling performers, including jugglers, puppeteers, and animal trainers, also fall into the classification of *luti* and had close socio-cultural associations with *mutrib*s as well as comedians and buffoons (*lawdah* and *muzhik*).

25   See Rudi Matthee, "Prostitutes, courtesans, and dancing girls: Women entertainers in Safavid Iran," in *Iran and Beyond, Essays in Middle Eastern History in Honor of Nikki R. Keddie*, Rudi Matthee and Beth Baron, eds (Costa Mesa, CA: Mazda, 2000), 121–50; Mahdi Qara'iyan, "Tarikhchah'i akhlaq-i jinsi-i iranian dar dawrah'i Qajar" [Sexual ethics in Qajar Iran], (Master's thesis, 1389/2010), 33–63.

26   For examples of such accounts, see Charles James Wills, *The Land of the Lion and the Sun: Modern Persia* (London: Ward, 1891); Jean Baptiste Feuvrier, *Trois ans à la cour de perse* (Paris: F. Juven, 1900), 254.

27   Bayza'i, *Namayish*, 159.

28   Ardeshir Salehpour, *Taranah'i*, 128.

29   *The Misanthrope, The Flying Doctor*, and *The Forced Marriage* are among Molière's plays that were adapted to *mutribi* style. For more on this, see Hiva Guran, *Kushish-ha-yi nafarjam: Sayri dar sad sal ti'atr-i iran* [Futile efforts: A journey in one hundred years of theater in Iran] (Tehran: Intisharat-i Agah, 1981), 82–5.

30   Bayza'i, *Namayish*, 174; Ahmad, "Yadigaran-i hunar-i qadim" [Memories of the old art], *Sinama*, Mihr 1339/October 1960, 91.

31   Salehpour, *Taranah'i*, 437. Quoting Mansoureh Ettihadieh, Salehpour asserts that the regulations for public spaces imposed in 1930 banned the regular performances in the coffee houses, and the admission of traveling entertainers to these public spaces; I was not able to locate that information in Ettihadieh's book. Mansoureh Ettihadieh, *Inja tihran ast* [This is Tehran] (Tehran: Nashr-i Tarikh-i Iran, 1377/1998), 146.

32   For instances of such an assertion, see Salehpour, *Taranah'i*, 358.

33   Sasan Fatemi, *Jashn va musiqi dar farhang-ha-yi shahri-i iran* [Festivity and music in the urban musical cultures], (Tehran: Mahoor Institute of Culture and Arts, 1393/2014), 205.

34   Fatemi, "Jashn," 198.

35   Bayza'i, *Namayish*, 199.

36   Fatemi, "Jashn," 198.

37   "Kilas-i raqs tavassut-i madmazil Ojik" [Mademoiselle Ojik's dance class], *Itti-la'at*, 15 Azar 1316/6 December 1937, 7; "Kilas-i raqs-i madmazil Klara" [Mademoiselle Klara's dance class], *Saba* 7, no.4, 4 Urdibihisht 1328/24 April 1949, 16.

38   Surur Afkhami, "Man bara-yi suing mimiram, shuma chitur?" [I die for Swing, How about you?], *Taraqqi* 8, no. 16, 28 Shahrivar 1329/19 September 1950, 11, 21.

39   Jalal Ni'matullahi, "Tihran miraqsad" [Tehran is dancing], *Kaviyan* 2, no. 10, 22 Day 1329/12 January 1951, 6–7, 22; 6.

40   These include events organized by Iran's Cultural Heritage, Handcrafts, and Tourism Organization (Sazaman-i Miras-i Farhangi, Sanayi'-i Dasti va Gardish-gari) as well as the International Nawruz Festival (Jashn-i Jahani-i Nawruz) (1390/2011) and the annual International Ritual and Traditional Theater Festival (Jashvarah'i Baynulmilali-i A'ini-Sunnati).

41   "Bashgah-i rak, markaz-i takhassusi-i amuzish-i balah va hiphap" [Rock studio, the specialist studio of ballet and hip-hop], *Payk-i Tihran*, nos. 20–21, Azar 1388/December 2009, 16; "Amuzish-i harikat-i hamahang va in'itafi, hip-hop, jaz, salsa, khususi va guruhi" [Public and private teaching of harmonious and supple movements, hip-hop, jazz, salsa], *Payk-i Tihran*, Shahrivar 1388/September 2009, 20. Instances of instructional videos include Navid Farah Marzi's VCDs, "Amuzish-i harakat-i mawzun" [Rhythmic movements training], 1386/2007; Utlar Dance DVD "Amuzish-i harakat-i mawzun-i azari" [Instruction of Azeri rhythmic movements], 1383/2004.

42   Currently, it is a subcategory of "Fitness and Aerobics" (*amadagi-i jismani va ayrubik*) of the Federation of Public Sports (Fidrasyiun-i Varzish-ha-yi Hama-gani), under the newly established Ministry of Sports and Youth (Vizarat-i Varzish va Javanan-i Iran); see www.isfaf.ir/dit_fl.asp?news=453 (accessed 10 June 2013).

43 Some of these active choreographers include Sa'id Dakh, Behzad Javdanfar, and Idah Abutalibi.
44 Some of these alternative terms include "form physical theater" (*fizikal ti'atr-i furm*) and "contemporary movements" (*harikat-i mu'asir*). See, for instance, Helia Qazi-Mirsa'idi, "Sag-Sukut, nukhustin ti'atr-i bakhsh-i khususi" [Dog-Silence, the first private-sector play], *KhabarOnline*, 7 Tir 1388/28 June 2009, www.khabaron line.ir/detail/11595/culture/theater (accessed 10 October 2015).
45 Mahdi Rustampur, "Raqs va shadi dar khiaban-ha-yi iran ba'd az su'ud bah jam-i jahani" [Dance and rejoice in the streets of Tehran following (soccer team's) ascent to the World Cup], *RadioFarda*, 1 Tir 1392/22 June 2013, www.radiofarda.com/ content/f8-world-cup-qualification-celebration-in-iran/25021109.html (accessed 10 June 2013).

2 The invention of an ideal female national dancer in twentieth-century Iran*

Hailed as "ancient" (*bastani*), "authentic" (*asil*), "traditional" (*sunnati*), and "classic" (*kilasik*), the Iranian "national dance" (*raqs-i milli*) emerged in the creative performing arts sphere of Tehran in the early twentieth century. In the decades to follow, this genre became an artistic means to showcase the narratives of the nation through dancing bodies. Offering a genealogy of this choreographic genre, this chapter explores *raqs-i milli* as an artistic medium whose trajectory encompasses innovative experiments with concepts, nuances, movements, and aesthetics drawn from the "repository of Iranian national culture" throughout the twentieth century.[1] Moreover, it examines the female national dancer as a performative subject of the nationalist stage, embodying the characteristics of the modern Iranian woman.

In the aftermath of the Iranian Constitutional Revolution (1905–09), the newly established public sites of sociability brought together performing artists not only from various parts of Iran but also from the southern regions of the Russian Empire, mainly the Caucasus. With the Russian Revolution of 1917 and its consequent dispersion of ethnic and cultural Russians to Iran, Tehran's artistic scene developed into a cosmopolitan center for experimentation in the performing arts. The mingling of these diverse peoples in the public sites of entertainment allowed Iranian musical and performing arts conventions to come into close contact with their counterparts from other places. It was this cohabitation of performing arts and artists that provided the creative spaces for the shaping of modern Iranian "national" music, dance, and theater. It also paved the way for female performing bodies to appear on the modern theater stage, and to replace and consequently eliminate the cross-dressing male performer, *zanpush*, and the transvestite *bachchah-raqqas* (see Figure 2.1 for a picture of a Qajar-era *mutribi* troupe featuring a *bachchah-raqqas*) from the "national" stage. In the period following, each of these disciplines, including dance, became professionalized in their own way. They all, however, share continuity with their early years of emergence.

Looking at the dancing body of the nationalist theatrical stage of twentieth-century Iran, this chapter first provides a historical overview in roughly two periods: from the early 1920s to the mid-1940s, when most dance

Figure 2.1 Bachchah raqqas (top center) in a Qajar-era mutribi ensemble
Freer Gallery of Art and Arthur M. Sackler Gallery Archives, Smithsonian
Institution.

performances were part of the theatrical scene; and from the mid-1940s
through the 1970s, when an independent public dance scene was developed.[2]
The chapter goes on to examine the nationalist biopolitics that regulated the
stage and its staged dancing subjects.[3] It also explores the prevailing trends in
the discourse of dance in Persian periodicals of the Pahlavi era. Focusing
primarily on the female subject of the national dance through a comparative
perspective, this chapter investigates the ways her regulated female performativity defamiliarized both the image of *raqqas*—the contemporaneous dancer
of the popular cabaret scene—and the male *bachchah-raqqaqs*—the boy-
dancer of previous eras. Finally, this chapter addresses how the female performer of this invented genre embodied the ideas, aesthetics and ethics of
Iranian nationalism and modernity.

The dancing bodies of early nationalist plays and musicals

There is evidence of non-vernacular dance performances in the newly developed Iranian performing arts scene of the early twentieth century. These
dances were either performed as an element of the variety show concerts
popular in that era, which included short musical, theatrical, and cinematic
presentations; or they were a component of operettas, the musical theater

genre that combined music and poetry with singing, acting, and dancing.[4] The majority of these privately funded performances occurred in the area of Lalehzar Street and, in particular, on the stage of the Grand Hotel.

Gaining popularity in Iran during the 1910s, most of the earlier operettas were performed by touring companies from Azerbaijan, Armenia, and Georgia (comprising the southern region of Caucasus). The most popular operettas performed in Iran in that era included the works of the Azerbaijani composer Uzeyir Hajibeyov (1885–1948), such as *Arshin Malalan, Asli va Karam*, and *Mashhadi 'Ibad*, as well as the Armenian *Upira-yi Anush* and Oscar Wilde's *Salomé*. Although the newly introduced operetta genre was widely seen and well received for its entertainment factor, the unfamiliarity of the language was an obstacle to its reception by the Persian-speaking audiences in the capital, Tehran. This in turn induced these troupes to translate their work into Persian.

Within a few years, Iranian playwrights were similarly compelled to compose operettas in Persian, often based on romantic historical and nationalist narratives. This choice of theme was due to the general nationalist-modernist theater environment, which had been developing during the decades after the Constitutional Revolution. Being largely inspired by European dramatic traditions and seeking to educate and mobilize the public, these new theatrical trends distinguished themselves from the pre-existing vernacular Iranian performance traditions of *ta'ziyah* and *taqlid*. Among the famous early operettas of this era are *Parichihr va Parizad* (1921), by Reza Kamal (aka Shahrzad), and *Rastakhiz-i Salatin-i Iran* (The resurrection of Persian kings, 1921), by Mirzadah'i Ishqi, both of which have historical and romantic plots. Produced in Iran by touring companies from regions of the newly formed Soviet Union, these operettas often featured dancers. These included *Kavah'i Ahangar* (The blacksmith Kavah, 1921), by the Azerbaijani troupe Sharifzadah, and *Kaykhusraw* (1920), by Monsieur Ruba.

While this newly emerged theater community strived to present modern ideas to the Iranian nation through its artistic productions, it was faced with a variety of restrictions, including against the casting of women. Traditionally, in the Iranian forms of *ta'ziyah* and *taqlid*, the cross-dressing *zanpush* men portrayed the female roles. The new modes of theater, however, required women to act for themselves.[5] For instance, in the early stagings of 'Ishqi's important nationalist operetta, *Rastakhiz-i Salatin-i Iran*, in which he criticized Iran's backwardness for its gender regulations, the two female leading roles were played by men.[6] The problem of casting women was partially resolved in the 1920s by the recruitment of non-Iranian or non-Muslim (mostly Armenian) women to the Iranian stage, since this was generally not considered controversial.

As historical accounts of performing arts indicate, a number of dance styles were performed with these musical performances. Some are clearly identified as ballet or "Caucasian" (*qafqazi*), and some were vaguely labeled as "Asian" (*asiya'i*) or "European" (*urupa'i*), "oriental" or "Eastern" (*sharqi* or *mashriqi*), and "new" (*jadid*) or "old" (*qadim*).[7] Presumably, some of these "nonindigenous" dances adopted Iranian elements when they emerged as the genre *balah'i irani* ("Iranian ballet") or accompanied Iranian traditional music.[8]

The majority of Iran's early dance performers were new immigrants from different regions of the Soviet Union. These include Monsieur Ruba, introduced as an artist from the Russian Imperial Ballet, Gul Sabah Khanum, Madmoiselle Asiya (Qustaniyan), Mademoiselle Marie, and Suri Khanum. While actively dancing in the theatrical context of the time, these performers were commonly identified as *aktur* and *aktris* ("actor" and "actress"), and not *raqqas*, which was the regular term in use to denote a dancer. Later, the Iranian-Armenian Madame Aqabayov joined this cosmopolitan scene, becoming the most celebrated star of the operettas in the 1920s and 1930s. Aqabayov's role in *Parichihr va Parizad* was significant in creating her fame and acclaim, to the extent that offstage she became known as Madame Pari, meaning "fairy." Her progressive-minded male audiences praised her performance in her diverse acts, ranging from her Bizet-inspired Karmin (*Carmen*, 1923) to Parichihr, an idealized Persian princess and the beloved of the Sasanid King Anushirvan.

In these historical plays and operettas, the dancing bodies enacted interchangeable roles, ranging from the entertaining and seducing of kings—such as King Anushirvan of the Sasanid era (AD 224–651) to Shah Abbas of the Safavid—to participating in reconstructions of ancient Iranian rituals. Performing seductive oriental dances for the king—as by Salomé in *Haft-hijab* (The dance of the seven veils)—was a recurring scene in the historical plays, seemingly inspired by the several stagings of *Salomé* starring Aqabayov.[9] An early instance of the staged reconstruction of an ancient ritual in the form of dance is found in the operetta *Kavah'i Ahangar* (The blacksmith Kavah, 1921), in which A'in-i Jam—an ancient Iranian ritual—was staged.[10]

Ali Nasr, the pioneering figure who founded Iran's first official theater school—the Foundation for Acting College (Bunyad-i Hunaristan-i Hunarpishigi)—in the 1930s on Lalehzar Street, had especially deployed dance in the productions of his earlier company Comédie Iran (Kumidi-i Iran) in the 1920s. Monsieur Ruba and Madame Aqabayov, who were known for their dancing skills, were both members of this company for a time.[11]

Ali-Naqi Vaziri, one of the most influential musical figures in early twentieth-century Iran and a promoter of Iran's national music, also endeavored to combine theater and music, founding the Musical Club (Kulup-i Musikal) in 1923. Viewing theater as "a site for critiquing people's habits" and "a 'university' [*danishgah*] for arts and ethics with no entrance exam for its audience," Vaziri sought the creation of theatrical institutions that "could boldly remind the Iranian nation of its missteps."[12] Vaziri identified opera as the assembly of five art forms, namely, music, dance, painting, poetry, and theater, staging several productions with the Kulup-i Muzikal between 1923 and 1930. Most of these works, including *Raw'ya-yi Majnun* (Majnun's dream), *Dukhtar-i Nakam* (The discontented girl), and *Gul-rukh* (The flower face), incorporated dance scenes.[13] Also among these works, *Raw'ya-yi Hafiz* (Hafiz's dream), staged in 1925, is of particular significance, as, in the play, the fourteenth-century poet Hafiz fantasizes about his beloved's dance. Pari Aqabayov was reportedly the leading star in most of Vaziri's works.[14]

In the scripts of his musical plays, Vaziri often employed the verses of classical Persian poets such as Firdawsi (940–1020), Nizami (1141–1209), and Hafiz (1325–89). His musical drama *Juda'i* (*Separation*), performed in 1928, especially sought to instill patriarchal sensibility in his audiences, urging the men to attend military service.[15] Displaying musical scenes of marching and dancing, the staging of this play was concurrent with the Iranian government's enforcement of mandatory military service.

Dancing bodies continued to enact themes of nationhood and nationalism up until the first Pahlavi era (1925–41), when such subject matter was not only supported by the government but also enforced as a criterion for public performances.[16] The nationalist "Moral Plays" (*namayish-ha-yi akhalqi*) constituted the other popular genre of the era that often included dance. These plays were known to be a medium for moral censure, using "recreation" and "amusement" to direct their audiences to virtue and correct social vice or "old-fashioned" habits, such as drug addiction, alcohol consumption, gambling, and the prevention of girls' education.[17]

The Barbud Society (Jami'ah'i Barbud), founded in 1926 by the eminent musician Ismail Mihrtash (1904–1980), was another collective that staged (nationalist) musicals. Aiming to showcase the Iranian "national arts," the company staged operettas such as *Layli va Majnun, Khayyam*, and *Khusraw va Shirin* (also titled as *The Sasanid Princess*).[18] In their major 1930 production of *Shab-i Hizar va Yikum* (The night of one thousand one), written by Reza Kamal (Shahrzad), Madame Pari appeared as the principal ballet dancer along with a troupe of Caucasian dancers.[19]

In addition to the above-mentioned artists, Madame Allahverdiov, along with her troupe, was also engaged in dance performance in the 1930s, appearing in the operettas *Layli va Majnun* (Layli and Majnun) in 1932; *Raqs-i Firishtagan* (Dance of angels) in the musical *Firishtah* (Angel) in 1934; and *Bihisht* (Heaven) in 1937, as well as the ballet *Jashn-i Gul-ha va Shadi-i Parvanah-ha* (The festivity of flowers and the jollity of butterflies), in 1935.[20] Madame Hamberson also danced in the theatrical productions of *Layli va Majnun*, and *Rustam va Suhrab* (Rustam and Suhrab, 1934) at the Firdawsi Millennium. Moreover, Madame Cornelli's students danced in the plays *Taj-i Iftikhar* (Crown of pride) and *Sulayman va Bilqays* (Sulayman and Bilqays) in 1932, as well as in the annual celebration of Cornelli's ballet studio in 1932 and 1935.[21]

A number of newly founded governmental theatrical institutions also served as platforms for teaching dance in the 1930s and 1940s, aiming to improve actors' movement skills and their public appearance. For instance, Madame Escampie taught dance at the Foundation for Acting College (on Lalehzar Street), and Madame Cornelli taught at the Municipal Opera (Upira-yi Baladiyah). In the meantime, nationalist periodicals of the time widely promoted physical education for Iranian women, introducing dance as a suitable exercise that could be executed in the confines of their home.[22]

Some of the aforementioned non-Muslim dancers also appeared in the newly emerging Iranian film industry of the time. For instance, the Armenian-born Asiya Qustaniyan, who also acted in the 1933 silent film *Haji Aqa Aktur-i sinama* (Haji Aqa the cinema actor), performed a ballet-influenced Iranian dance that is perhaps the earliest visual account of this hybrid form. Madame Escampie also danced in *Tufan-i Zindigi* (The turmoil of life) in 1948.

By the mid-1940s, the number of operettas decreased. Particularly after state-enforced unveiling of women in 1936, female Muslim performers gradually joined the theatrical sphere primarily as actors, but not yet as dancers. Concurrently, an independent dance scene emerged, prompted by the wave of immigrants from the Soviet countries who specialized in dance. These changes resulted in a growing distance between the three disciplines of dance, music, and theater. This diversification of performing arts genres and the gradual shift towards professionalization can be observed in the play *Ilaha-yi Misri* (The Egyptian goddess), which was performed by Muslim actresses, while the ballet was performed by Madame Allahverdiov's troupe.[23] Most presentations of dance after 1945 were directed by dance artists and choreographers and were exclusively characterized as "dance performances."

National(ist) theatrical dances

While from the early twentieth century ethnically diverse dance artists were using Iranian themes in their choreographies, the first major dance project that heavily portrayed itself as being in the service of enhancing Iranian national arts was Nilla Cram Cook's Studio for the Revival of the Iranian Classical Arts (Istudiyu-yi Ihya-yi Hunar-ha-yi Iran-i Bastan), founded in 1946. Recruiting a few young ballet-trained women of mixed or non-Muslim background, as well as several men, Cook sought to revive and restore the seemingly "forgotten ancient art of Iranian dance."[24] In her choreographic attempts to reconstruct and revitalize Iranian dance, Cook was inspired by ancient Iranian visual imagery—drawing on the orientalist scholar Arthur Pope's (1881–1969) manuscripts on Persian arts—as well as folklore, Persian poetry and mythology, and Zoroastrian and Islamic rituals, including the *sema* of the Mevlevi dervish orders.[25]

A former employee of the US embassy in Tehran, who collaborated with the Iranian state as an inspector for theater and cinema, Cook withdrew from both occupations with the hope of establishing a national institution for the performing arts in Iran. Although she did not succeed in that ambition, Cook attracted the support of the royal family, with Princess Shams Pahlavi becoming the patron of Cook's dance project. Her studio's first performances were in 1947 at the Rex Cinema Theater and in the garden of the US embassy in the presence of the prime minister, Ahmad Qavam.[26] Only a few years after its creation, her troupe toured in Turkey, Greece, Italy, Egypt, Iraq, Syria, India, and Lebanon.[27] Besides "restoring Iranians' sense of pride in their own

culture," according to the former company dancer and author Nesta Ramazani, Cook's other agenda was to break the barrier set up between public
dancing and "women of good families," a project that claimed to contribute
to the process of modernization in Iran.[28]

Cook's nationalist creations at times aligned with the state, as exemplified
by her 1947 production *Ardeshir Babakan*, which revolved around the founder of the pre-Islamic Sasanid Empire. Inspired by "Achaemenid art and
Zoroastrian ritual and symbolism," this piece recounted a fairy tale concerning five (mythic) angels who urged Ardeshir Babakan to save Iran.[29] Presenting the Sasanid king as the hero of ancient Iran who restored Zoroastrianism
and "rebuilt" Iran from destruction, the piece implied a parallel between
Ardeshir Babakan and the Pahlavis, who were purportedly the modern-day
saviors of Iran. The program notes to Cook's company's performance in the
1940s highlight this particular nationalist venture by quoting from the pre-
Islamic kings Darius and Babakan in the captions to the program's images of
posed dancers. There, a Babakan the cover reads "Oh! Angel of the earth!
Awake our nation from this sleep" (see Figures 2.2 and 2.3 for images of this
company's production).[30]

Cook's other works include *Gurd-afarid*, inspired by a story in the *Shahnamah* and movements of *zurkhanah*; *Majnun va Lalah* (Majnun and the
tulip), inspired by Nizami Ganjavi's *Layli va Majnun*; *Prayer of Darius*,
inspired by a Luristan goddess figure of five thousand years and Magi, the fire
priest; and the *Dance of the Rose and Nightingale*, inspired by a poem by
Hafiz.[31] Cook's troupe also presented folk dances, including Gilani, for which
the dancers wore the regional costumes of the time.[32]

In addition to Cook's company, the two famous Armenian dance artists of
the 1950s and 1960s, Madame Yelena and Sarkis Djanbazian, also produced
works on such themes. Settling in Iran as part of later waves of immigrants
from the Soviet Union, both Yelena and Djanbazian opened dance schools in
Tehran, where they taught ballet, as well as dances from various regions of
the Soviet Union and Eastern Europe. They gradually added Iranian national
dances to their repertoires, and later, in the 1960s, the Iranian regional folk
dances. *Gul-i Shiraz* (The flower of Shiraz) is one of Yelena's choreographies
that is inspired by the life of the poet Hafiz.[33]

The influential Sarkis Djanbazian was also an advocate of dance as a
"national" Iranian art form. Claiming to establish Iran's first song and dance
group, his company performed ballet-influenced Iranian "characteristic" and
folk dances along with his European classical repertoire. Seeing himself as a
liberator of the "national art form of dance" from its vulgar position within
the "cheap entertainment scene," Djanbazian aimed to revive Iranian ancient,
national, and folk dances by staging them on *pointe*, thereby depicting them
in a manner easily accessible for a wider "international audience."[34] In addition to live performances, Djanbazian's troupe performed balletic dances in a
number of cinematic productions of the 1950s, including *Khabha-yi Talai'i*
(Golden dreams, 1950) and *Dukhtari az Shiraz* (A girl from Shiraz, 1954).

Figure 2.2 Haideh Akhundzadeh in the 1940s
The studio for the revival of classical arts of Iran, souvenir program, undated.

The Iranian-born and European-trained Lili Lazarian also had a ballet academy in Tehran, where she taught various styles of dance, from ballet to tango and paso-doble. Lazarian also choreographed ballet-based Iranian dances including *Qalb-i Madar* (The mother's heart), based on a poem by Iraj Mirza (1874–1926); *Yatim* (The orphan), based on Parvin I'tisami's (1907–41) poem; and the ballet *Takht-i Jamshid* (Persepolis).[35]

Figure 2.3 Haideh Akhundzadeh (*left*) and Nesta Shahrokh (aka Ramazani)
The studio for the revival of classical arts of Iran, souvenir program notes, undated.

The Iranian National Ballet Company—known as the Iran Ballet Academy at its foundation—was established in 1956 by two protégés of Cook, Haideh Akhundzadeh (née Ahmadzadeh) and Nejad Ahmadzadeh, as Iran's first major government-funded dance company in Iran. Besides functioning as a ballet company, this institution was meant to stage Iran's "ancient and folk" dances and to "visualize Iran's literature and history."[36] Supported by the Ministry of Culture and Arts, the company aimed not only to entertain the court and public but also to present the national arts of Iran to visiting foreign dignitaries.[37]

The Iranian repertoire of the company included works such as *Gurd-afarid*, inspired by the Iranian epic poem *Shahnamah* by Firdawsi; *Miniyatur-ha-yi Irani* (Iranian miniatures), based on dancing figures prevalent in that style of painting (see Figure 2.4); *Dilbaran* (Sweethearts, 1969); and *Raw'ya* (The dream, 1969), a fictional story set in the Safavid court; and *Ru-nama*, all of which combined the gestural vocabulary of Iranian dance with basic ballet movements. While in most of the company's European classical ballet repertoire the lead dancers were guest artists recruited from abroad, in their milestone production of *Bijan va Manijah* (1975), based on a love story from *Shahnamah*, the soloists were native Iranians. Between 1963 and 1970, the company traveled internationally to perform their national folk-music, song,

Figure 2.4 Miniyatur-ha-yi Irani (Iranian miniatures) by the Iranian National Ballet
　　　Rudaki Hall
Souvenir program, October 1970.

and dance repertoire in countries such as Afghanistan, Pakistan, Italy, the
Soviet Union, Poland, Morocco, Japan, and Canada.[38]

The staging of national dances to showcase Iranian arts and culture
nationally and internationally soon became the responsibility of the Iran
National Folklore Organization (Sazman-i Milli-i Fulklur), a large state-
funded company created in 1967 which aimed "to safeguard the nation's
treasures in ethnic dances, music and ceremonies."[39] The company dancers
were trained in the three-year program of the College of National and Folk
Dances (Hunaristan-i Raqs-ha-yi Milli va Mahalli), which was an institution
dependent on the Folklore Organization. The students of this college were
recruited from various cities through an audition advertised in the press.

Besides their dramatized folk dances, the company created and staged a
wide range of national dances, including the choreographic reconstruction of
the Safavid and Qajar court dances, as well as the narrative-based *Haft-
Paykar* (Seven beauties, 1972) that portrayed the Sasanid king Bahram's love
story inspired by the verses of thirteenth-century poet Nizami Ganjavi (see
Figures 2.5–2.6). More balletic productions of this company included
Simurgh (Pheonix), which featured an angel who fought the wicked Ahriman,
and the Iranian literary love legends including the *Candle and Butterfly* and

Figure 2.5 Zarb va Zangulah, a production by the National Folklore Organization
A page from the program notes of the company in the 1970s.

Figure 2.6 Haft Paykar, a production by the National Folklore Organization in the
          1970s
Company's souvenir program.

Rose and Nightingale.[40] The company had occasional productions that
underlined the state's politics as exemplified by the trilogy *Naft-i Shu'lihvar*
(Burning oil), *Naft-i Siyah* (Black oil), and *Naft-i Sifid* (White oil). Denoting
the Shah's White Revolution that was launched in 1963, while undermining
the controversies surrounding the nationalization of oil and the overthrow of
former Prime Minister Muhammad Musaddiq in a 1953 coup d'état, the
piece framed petroleum as a "national product" saved from foreign hands by the
Iranian king:

> Oil, this national and empowering treasure of our homeland has been stolen
> for years to color the foreigners' [dinner] table. With the leadership, ingenuity,
> wisdom and hard work of the Shah, a page was turned in history. And
> now it begins a happy life, hopefulness and 'great civilization' for Iran.[41]

The National Dance Company regularly performed in Rudaki Hall, Iran's
most prestigious concert stage founded in 1967, and presented Iranian dance
to visiting politicians and dignitaries. The company toured internationally to
England, Turkey, Pakistan, and the United States to showcase Iranian culture
(see Figure 2.7–2.8).[42]

Figure 2.7 Program note of the National Folklore Organization in the 1970s
Ida Meftahi's personal archive.

The Pars National Ballet (Balah'i Milli-i Pars), founded in 1966, also
selected themes from classical Iranian literature, labeling the performances as
"national ballet." These included *Mard-i Parsa va Khishtzan* (The devout
man and the bricklayer), based on a poem by Sa'adi (twelfth to thirteenth
centuries), and *Shaykh-i San'an va Dukhtar-i Tarsay* (Shayk San'an and the
Christian maiden), based on the verse of Attar (1145–1221).

In the process of the professionalization of dance as an artistic field, the
term *raqsandah* was employed to demarcate and distinguish the high status of
trained national dancers from those contemporaneous performers of popular
entertainment, with the latter working in the settings of cabarets and cafés,
and derogatorily labeled as *raqqas* and *raqqasah* (discussed in Chapter 3 and
Chapter 4). The negative associations with these last terms increased after the
1950s due to the development of Tehran's nightlife industry in which the

Figure 2.8 Farzanah Kabuli, the lead dancer of the company in Kuhkiluyah National Folklore Organization's souvenir program, 1976.

Iranian cabaret dancer, with seemingly "unrestrained" sexuality, was the key attraction, bringing multitudes of (male) audiences to the cabarets, restaurants, and vernacular Iranian musical cafés (known as *kafah*).

The *raqqas* also became the main dancing persona of Lalehzar theaters, replacing the national dancers as the now governmentalized "national stage" moved to other areas, mainly the prestigious Rudaki Hall. Her image also dominated the widely seen commercial film industry of *film-i farsi*, replacing the ballet-trained dancing bodies which were formerly featured on the screen. The popular private-sector entertainment and cinema industries largely relied on the bioeconomy of dancing bodies which saved them from bankruptcy by selling overt performances of sexuality. The relatively small "national art" stage of the late Pahlavi period, conversely, was a site for enacting the bioideology of nationalism to limited and select audiences, autonomously from and regardless of its box-office sales.[43]

Figure 2.9 Heather Rastovac performing at Seattle Turk Festival, 2007
Photo by Julia Bruk.

Though the position of dance significantly changed after the Iranian Revolution of 1979, the "national dance" style of choreography continues to thrive to this day. Referred to with various labels—ranging from "classical Persian dance" and "Iranian ballet" to "contemporary" and "traditional" dance—similar notions of choreography are prevalent in the Iranian diasporic communities, where national heroes and characters such as Arash, Rustam, and Gurd-afarid embodied by diversely trained dancing bodies occasionally stir a sense of "national pride" in Iranian audiences (see Figure 2.9 for a performance of classical Persian dance in the US).[44] In post-revolutionary Iran, a renamed and reformed style of movement-based performance known as "rhythmic movements" (*harikat-i mawzun*) has become a medium of stage dances with genealogical relations to *raqs-i milli*, echoing similar themes and movements of the pre-revolutionary national dances.

The biopolitics of the nationalist stage and the emergence of multiple dancing subjects

The dancing body of the nationalist theatrical stage of twentieth-century Iran can be further analyzed in light of the biopolitics that concerned the stage. As previously mentioned, the newly developed performance scene of theater and music in the city of Tehran did not include female performers; instead, transvestite *zanpush* performers enacted the female roles. Nevertheless, the modernist environment of theater, which sought a new ordering of the society, was not content with the "ambiguous" performance of sexuality of the *zanpush* men. Writing in October 1914, the author and theater critic Khan Malik Sasani affirmed this frustration:

> I have to note that until women act in theater, we won't achieve a satisfying result. We have to learn from Istanbul to utilize Armenian and Jewish women, so that "odd" (*nukhalah*) men won't be performing the delicate female roles.[45]

Similar assertions are made by other writers, including Mortiza Mushfiq Kazimi, who in an article in the journal *Iranchahr*, published in Berlin, criticized the situation of theater in Iran claiming that "the (Iranian) audience are addicted to feminine dance of young [men] in woman's costume," as women are absent from performances.[46] While within a few years a number of Armenian and emigre non-Muslim actresses took on female roles in many plays, these grievances persisted in the media until 1930. A critic reflected on *Firishtah'i Umid* (The angel of hope), a play that promoted women's education, advising the directors to first try to hire (the non-Muslim) "Madames" and only turn to hiring the "improper" *zanpush* in the event that these women acted deceitfully or misbehaved.[47]

Khan Malik's description of a *zanpush* as "an odd man," and the emergence of female actors replacing the "odd" *zanpush* in the early twentieth-century new theater in Iran can be analyzed in light of Afsaneh Najmabadi's argument on the heteronormalization of the public space as a product of the process of "achieving modernity" in Iran.[48] In her pioneering historiographical study, Najmabadi asserts the irrelevance of the gender binary of men and women in the pre-twentieth-century Iranian context, wherein separate visible gender categories such as *amrad* and *mukhannas* mingled in the public space in Iran.[49] She argues that through the interactions between Iranians and Europeans (especially during the nineteenth century), Iranian society became self-conscious about the presence of European spectatorship that misinterpreted some of their public everyday homosocial behaviors as markers of their homosexuality and thus backwardness. This spectatorship resulted in the erasure of some of those "effeminate masculinities," leading to the existing gender binary of man/woman that has been normalized in modern Iranian society. This heteronormalization is preeminently evident on the modernist theatrical stage of Iran, from which the transvestite *zanpush* was eliminated because he embodied these previous "effeminate" behaviors and so did not match the image of a modern individual and a representative of contemporary society.

Yet while in the early twentieth century several non-Muslim actresses from diverse ethnic backgrounds joined the modernist theatrical milieu of cosmopolitan Tehran to replace the *zanpush*, the female presence on the public stage was especially heightened by the presence of the Iranian-Armenian performer Madame Aqabayov. Aqabayov was praised for her performance in various plays, including her role in *Parichihr va Parizad*. For her performance in the operetta *Ilahah* (The goddess), in which she enacted the goddess of flowers, Madame Pari was described by a newspaper contributor as "an angel of heaven having no stain on her whiteness."[50] While her non-Muslim religious background gave her access to the public stage, Pari Aqabayov also owed part of her success to her training in opera and ballet in Europe, which gave her a unique quality and novel bodily skills.

The level to which Madame Pari was praised and the position of non-Muslim "other" female performers as the locus of the gaze of their predominantly Muslim audiences is quite comparable to the historian Mohamad Tavakoli-Targhi's description of the ways in which European (*farangi*) women were seen by late eighteenth- and early nineteenth-century Persian travelers to Europe.[51] Describing the (European) "other" women as fairies, these travelers, unaccustomed to public display of female beauty, saw the unveiled body of European women as markers of "developed" countries. Viewed as cultured and educated, European women became the "future" ideal of Iranian women. In a similar situation, the staged performing body of these non-Muslim "other" women was the subject of its male audience's gaze: in a theatrical sphere where the ideas of modernity and nation were largely being experimented with, the non-Muslim female performers' bodies were seen as the future and the "ego ideal" for the Iranian woman.

The presence of *zanpush* was not the only gender-related dilemma of the early twentieth-century modernist artistic milieu. While the presence of non-Muslim women on the public stage became established in the late Qajar era, there remained a severe resistance to Muslim women's presence in the public theatrical space, not only as performers but also as spectators. Similar sensitivities also existed towards public performance for female-only audiences.[52] These pressures were not exclusively social, as the state too showed caution against allowing female performers to enter the country. A number of documents of the late Qajar's police office (Idarih'i Nazmiyah) indicate that the government hesitated to issue a visa to a Muslim actress from Baku, Azerbaijan, to enter Iran in 1926.[53] When they at last issued a conditional visa, Nazmiyah stated the following to the department of foreign affairs:

> Due to religious conventions and regulations as well as the current situation of the society, Muslim women, regardless of their nationality, are not permitted to perform in public concerts, but their performance in women-only gatherings would not be too problematic.[54]

Similar restrictions on Muslim women's participation in the artistic sphere of a state-sponsored institution are evident in the letters exchanged in 1923 between the editor of the newspaper *Shafaq-i Surkh* and Qamar-al-Muluk, a reader of the newspaper. Criticizing the newly founded Academy of Music (Madrasah'i 'Ali-i Musiqi) for its policy of not accepting Muslim women, Qamar-al-Muluk argued that if learning music was considered problematic according to Islam, then men should also be barred from music education. Pointing to the incapability of progressive-minded Iranian modernists—namely, Ali-Naqi Vaziri, the founder of the Academy of Music, and the poet and playwright Mirzadah'i Ishqi—to emancipate women, she claimed that the women of her era are less welcome in public social activities than their predecessors who could attend mixed gatherings, including the traditional *ta'ziyah* and *rawzah*.[55] The editor of the newspaper responded to Qamar-al-Muluk with the following:

> Teaching music to women by men is not very "seemly" (*zibandah*) in our society, and the cause for the imposed limitations of men and women's mixed gatherings is the corrupt behavior of men and the frivolousness of some women.[56]

A similar approach is also evident in the advertisement of a play in 1928 by Comédie Iran, which announced that unchaste women and dissolute men would not be admitted to the venue.[57] The issue of public order can be read in light of Near Eastern studies scholar Cyrus Schayegh's discussion on social "hygiene" in early twentieth-century Iran.[58] The anxiety about the escalating corruption in the newly urban public social sphere marked the sites of popular entertainment as sensitive and volatile spaces that required the regulation of their participants. Despite the initial resistance towards performances arranged for female audiences, during and after the 1930s, women's associations organized moral plays in which the ideal modern Iranian women were showcased on stage while blaming "old-fashioned customs."[59]

While up to the 1930s and 1940s the majority of dance performances were performed by non-Muslim women, nationalist periodicals gradually adopted a favorable attitude towards dance by encouraging their female readers to dance in the confines of their home. This attitude was in keeping with the nationalist concern for Iranian women's physical health, viewed as the prerequisite for a progressive nation. The central assertion was that only a healthy and educated mother could raise healthy and educated children.[60]

Promoting the importance of sports and physical education for a healthy nation, the periodicals emphasized the effects of physical exercise on women's mental and physical health, regularly referencing women's activities in the "progressive" (*mutaraqqi*) countries.[61] In particular, due to the idealization and positive relationship with Germany in that era, the women of Germany and their athletic and artistic activities were used by the nationalist periodicals to exemplify a successful nation that supposedly shared the same "Aryan" race with Iranians. Dance was viewed in this context as an especially suitable physical exercise for women, a prevalent practice in those progressive countries, thus becoming a signifier for the actual practice and embodiment of "modernity."[62]

Another instance of dance-related nationalist endeavor was the staging of folk dance. The regional folk dances of Iran, with their strong ties to various Iranian ethnicities, were re-articulated in the nationalist framework as an "authentic" element of Iran's national culture. Relying on a purist premise that the folklore of rural areas of Iran remained untouched by "Arab/Islamic invasion"—because of their remoteness from urban centers and the difficulty reaching their originary sphere of performance—these cultures were perceived as having true practices of the Aryan race that needed to be investigated.[63] The state also urged this position, promoting both folkloric studies as well as public performance of folklore and regional performing arts.

While there is evidence of the staging of folk dance in Tehran in the 1940s, it was from the 1950s onward that these performances received further urban staging interest and were reported in the periodicals.[64] The Pahlavi government was especially invested in presenting these dances in governmental public spaces, including garrisons, factories, and schools all around the country, even in the most conservative cities, such as Yazd and Qom.[65] Framed under the general label of "folk dance," the dances of various ethnicities of Iran, including Azeris, Kurds, Gilaks, and Baluchi, became a regular component of official celebrations in larger festivals such as the Festival of Culture and Arts (Jashn-i Farhang va Hunar)—organized as a set of performances, lectures, and exhibitions in various cities around the country (1969–78)—and Jashnvarah'i Farhang-i 'Ammah (Folklore Festival, 1978).

While the official groups—such as the National and Folk Dance Group of the National Ballet of Iran and the Iran National Folklore Organization—showcased these dances in Iran and abroad, local dance groups were frequently sent by the Ministry of Culture from various regions of the country to other cities, often far away from their place of origin, to present dance as a key component of the national culture. Although reframing folk dance as an element of "Iranian national culture" tended to ignore the folk dances' ethnic affiliations, in comparison to other aspects of ethnic cultures—particularly languages, which have been often disguised in official public displays—the nationalist policies towards dance were not repressive but rather supportive, promoting them as part of the national commodity culture.[66]

Nationalism and prevailing trends in discourse on dance in the press

Three main trends emerged in the discourse on dance published in the Pahlavi period, which arguably can be traced back to observations on the choreographic approaches of national dance and the ways dancing bodies were presented on stage.

A primary inclination—stimulated by the prevailing literary nationalism—was to suggest that Persian poetry was a genuine Iranian inspirational source and a national cultural repository for all performing art forms. Drawing on Persian poetry and literature has been offered as a particularly optimal solution in revitalizing Iranian dance to a high art form. Nilla Cram Cook, for instance, asserted:

> If the dance has fallen from the position of national dignity it once held and is now the province of café entertainers of low order, it is because it has been divorced from poetry. Reunited to it, it could fill once more a sacred office.[67]

In a similar approach, Hasan Shirvani, a regular commentator on music and theater, and later the head of Tehran's Opera Bureau, suggested a combination of Persian poetry, music, and dance in lieu of a pure national performing art form in an account published in the monthly *Namayish*.[68] Shirvani's suggested hybrid resonates closely with early twentieth-century Iranian operettas.

Abdullah Nazimi, the founding director of the aforementioned Pars National Ballet, in an interview with *Talash*, contended that the only solution to elevate the art of dance in Iran was to pay attention to national dance and national ballet. Nazimi maintained that Iran's rich poetic narratives would be better suited for Iranian ballet productions than the content borrowed from the classical (European) ballet.[69] In a more recent account, an informant of the dance scholar Anthony Shay identified the frequent use of literary and historical themes in Iranian dance productions as a "green card to dance" and a "legitimate way of validating dance."[70]

Another dance-related tendency in the press discourse was to offer historical narratives for dance(s) of Iran. Based on archeological and literary evidence as well as European travelogues, several journalists and scholars attempted to contemplate the way Iranian people danced in ancient and medieval times. Written in the twentieth century and dealing with a past as distant as two millennia ago, these accounts were often highly romanticized. One of the earliest and most widely cited historical accounts that deployed archeological evidence was "The History of Dance in Iran," by Yahya Zoka' (1924–2001). Exploring dance in prehistoric and ancient Iran, this article was published several times prior to the revolution and still receives pseudo-scholarly attention.[71]

Nilla Cram Cook also composed an account that discussed various historical sources to trace back dance in Iran including pre-Islamic architecture:

> These principles of design, which made Persepolis, the Athens of Asia, and have lived on, in essence, through so many eras of Persian art, are the birthright of the Persian dance. If it has been claimed that the "Greek dance," as imagined or reconstructed from sculpture and paintings, is the "natural dance," which indeed it is, the same claim could be advanced for the Iranian dance, as imagined or reconstructed from Achaemenid Art. The Iranian dance, springing from such a tradition, has as much right to plastic freedom and natural grace as Greek.[72]

In her 1949 article, Cram Cook related the prejudices against dance in the Middle East to the loss of its religious and national association.[73] In fact, Cram Cook's presumption of the high status of religious dances in pre-Islamic Iran is one shared by others.[74]

The Paris-based choreographer and performer Medjid Rezvani, who compiled the first book-length account on dance in Iran, in 1962, repeatedly asserted the high status of dance in ancient Iran. Assuming a religious significance for dance in the Achaemenid era (550–330 BC), Rezvani claimed that the kings were frequent participants in those ceremonies. Arguing a Persian genealogy for Greek dances, Rezvani questioned the tendency of Iranian scholars to look for theater roots in Greece. He maintained that in the Sasanid era, learning dance and music was mandatory for the princes and princesses, who held the highest social status. He also declared that Iranian dancers were globally recognized for their skills during the Sasanid era. A choreographer himself, Rezvani illustrated a dance scene of the Persian princess Roxana, which he presumed had balletic manifestations.[75]

There are a number of writings about dance in the Safavid and Qajar periods, some of which portray idealized images of the Iranian dancer of the past. An interesting example is *Shahid-i Shiraz* (The witness of Shiraz, 1962) a semi-fictional travelogue by Khan Malik Sasani, who employed an unspecified historical document to shed light on Iranian dance in the Safavid era. In his account of a *bazmi* (festive) dancer, Sasani offers the following description:

> The dancer must be young, very beautiful, and pleasant, with a fit and proper body, large eyes, and a face like a flower; she should delicately follow the

rhythm of the music and feel it; she should dance like the reflection of the winter clouds on waves of the sea; she must be confident.[76]

Providing nineteen movements, each with a poetic label such as "butterfly" (*parvanah*), "flame" (*shu'lah*), and "message" (*payam*), Sasani introduced the ultimate task of a dancer as the bending back and picking up of a needle with her eyelid. Employing the term *"raqs-i milli"* (national dance), the famed Iranian musician Ruhullah Khaleqi also inquired about dance in his historical study of music in Iran. Referring to several paintings and travelogues to examine dance in the Qajar era, he introduced a number of prominent (female) performers from the early decades of the twentieth century.[77]

Ballet was a major focus of the discourse on dance in the periodicals until the late 1970s. While balletic performances were common from the 1920s onwards, the concept of ballet was not yet a topic for lengthy discussions in distinction to theater and music. The emblematic appearance of the goddess Anahid as a winged angel on pointe shoes standing beside a railroad, as the logo of the weekly *Nahid* in 1923, was one of the first visual manifestations of ballet in the media (see Figure 2.10). Another early mention of ballet is found in the famous speech given by Ali-Naqi Vaziri at the College of Music (Madrasah'i 'Ali-i Musiqi) in 1925 where he introduced theater as an educational medium and operetta as a medium for visualizing history and pointed to ballet as a form of opera.[78]

Figure 2.10 The logo of the weekly *Nahid*, 1920s

Writings about ballet, ballet dancers, and ballet companies surfaced during and after the 1930s, when dance developed into a professionalized discipline. In the Persian periodicals, ballet received the most attention of all dance forms, and perhaps more than the vernacular dances of Iranian origin. While the majority of the ballet-related accounts were translations from European languages, a few Iranian authors also attempted to introduce and promote this art form. The poet and writer Hushang Irani, for instance, began his article on ballet by introducing this dance as "the most organized form of arts, [which] can exhibit the pulse of creation with its full appearance."[79]

The periodicals had urged the need for a national ballet company before the creation of such a company in 1956. An early instance of this is Sarkis Djanbazian's account of the significance of dance as an art form supported in all "progressive" (*mutaraqqi*) countries of the world. Djanbazian especially emphasized the necessity of having an Iranian ballet-trained national company capable of presenting the concepts and innovations of "the old and new Iran."[80] The Iranian scholar Ehsan Yarshater later backed Djanbazian by introducing him as the most appropriate individual in Iran to undertake this project.[81]

The creation of an Iranian ballet to perform national narratives was primarily discussed by those who sought to justify the government's investment in this "imported" art form. The discussion of ballet's capacity to serve as a "progressive" medium for visualizing Iran's history and culture remained in the periodicals until the Revolution of 1979. An example of such writing reads: "The same as in the United States and other developed countries, ballet in Iran has national characters and qualities, in addition to its classical forms and techniques.[82] To some others, including the cultural critic Jalal Sattari, Pahlavi's investment in ballet and opera appeared as a pretentious and futile attempt which "tended to pride 'us' in the eyes of foreign guests."[83]

National dancer in a comparative perspective

To appear authentic, modern, and artistic, while sharing cultural elements, the female national dancer distantiated herself from the concurrent cabaret dancer of the popular entertainment scene and the *bachchah-raqqas*, the sexualized male adolescent dancer of earlier eras who shared similarities in gender performativity to the *zanpush*.[84] An important transformation placed upon the dancing body in the twentieth century took place through a change in the performance venue, marked by a departure from the traditional setting, *hawz* (staged on a surface prepared by setting wooden planks over a small pool), to the European-style proscenium stage of the prestigious Grand Hotel of Lalehzar Street in the 1920s and Rudaki Hall in the 1960s.[85] According to the journalist Farrokh Safavi, this spatial transition helped elevate Iranian dance to a high art form.[86]

The costume—the most obvious signifier for framing the performing body—also greatly differed in these genres. The covered body of a national dancer looked distinctly different from the transgressive, "semi-naked" female cabaret dancer, who dressed to expose and accentuate her hips and breasts. The national dancer was often fully covered with vivid, stylized vernacular clothing, primarily inspired by Persian miniature paintings. The costumes of *bachchah-raqqas* were quite similar to the female costumes of the Qajar era, featuring long sleeves and light colors. To appear feminine, the male *bachchah-raqqas* had to grow their head hair, shave their facial hair, and put on makeup.[87]

In further distinction between national dance and popular dance, the popular urban music of Tehran, often accompanied by explicit lyrics, while playing in cabarets and most probably also serving as the accompaniment to the dance of *bachchah-raqqas*, never accompanied the "elite" national dancers. Instead, these dancers performed to traditional Persian music, regional folk music, and sometimes contemporary and classical European music.

The behavior of the national dancers also stood out against the transgressive *bachchah-raqqas* and cabaret dancer. The confident performance of sexuality expressed by a cabaret dancer marked her as immoral. Conceivably the *bachchah-raqqas* also experienced a similar backlash. Yet between these two genres the difference in gender played a major role. While the charming, delicate, and sexual gestures of the *bachchah-raqqas*, such as blinking, and "raising a single eyebrow" (*abru bala andakhtan*), which connoted bisexual/drag behavior to modernists, were performed by males, the cabaret performances were danced by female dancers.[88] In contrast, both male and female dancers of *raqs-i milli* were quite physically fit, healthy, confident, joyful, and active, and displayed a sense of pride in behavior. Men depicted a greater degree of "masculinity" in their moves whereas the women's movements displayed controlled femininity and charm.

While using movements from Iranian dances—mainly the popular solo improvised dance—the often "ballet-influenced" national dancer moved in a stylized manner that contrasted with the dance of both a cabaret dancer and *bachchah-raqqas*. In addition to choreographic units derived from the solo improvised dance, national dance also borrowed from the movement vocabulary of Iranian regional folk dances and rituals. Depending on the proficiency and the background of the performers and choreographers, the movements could also be more polished or influenced by ballet. For instance, while wrist rotations were a common element in all these forms, in the national dances of the National Dance Company, the arms were further extended.

The discussed genres share the rotation of wrists, triplet steps, and some movements of arms. The most important movement in characterizing their difference, however, is the *qir*—the free-flow rotations of hips causing a psychological state of elation in the performer—as well as the shimmy-like movements of shoulders. These movements were exaggerated by both cabaret dancers and *bachchah-raqqas*, but were not absorbed into national dance.[89] Arguably, the elimination of these gestures was an intentional removal of signifiers of transgressive sexuality and a distinguishing of the form from the ante-modern aesthetics of *ruhawzi* dance of *bachchah-raqqas* and cabaret dancers. This process of "de-*qir*ing" was interpreted by Abdullah Nazimi as leaving out the essence of Persian dance.[90] While female national dancers share some movements with the cabaret dancer and *bachchah-raqqas*, male performers of national dance do not use feminine movements in their dances, as their dances have been "hyper-masculinized."[91]

Inventing national dance and an ideal female modern dancing subject

By exploring the characteristics of the national dancer through a historical perspective and in relation to nationalist trends and biopolitics, national dance can arguably be viewed as an invented genre which was constructed to meet the demand for a national high art form and to showcase an ideal national body on stage.

Relying on the notion of the "invented tradition," as described by Eric Hobsbawm and Terence Ranger, *raqs-i milli* can be viewed as a nationalist construct which borrows heavily from literary texts, historical imaginations, folk culture, and ancient symbols to create a dance that resonated with the expectations of modern Iran.[92] Furthermore, the staged female national dancer is a multifaceted character who internalizes the advocated virtues of the nationalist biopolitics and discourse.

She is an invented ideal female subject who combines charm with chastity in her behavior and internalizes ballet while claiming authenticity with her Iranian dance movements, themes, clothing, and music. Her healthy. athletic body is well versed in the physical training of both vernacular Iranian dances and ballet. With her heterosexual performance of femininity, which is markedly distinct from the "vague" sexuality of the *zanpush* and *bachchah-raqqas*, she re-emphasizes the gender binary of modern Iran on stage. Her controlled femininity distantiates her from the transgressive sexuality of the *raqqas* of the popular cabaret stage. She often looks like the ideal woman described in Persian classical literature, with attributes such as large eyes, youth, a beautiful face, and a physically fit body—all aesthetic qualities portrayed in Persian literature. She depicts an idealized—even ancient—past, internalizing contemporary ideas that were commonly offered by the nationalist outlets.

Her corporeal "modernity" typecasts various modes of the mythic ideal Iranian woman, such as the heroine in *Gurd-afarid*, the Persian princess in *Haft-Paykar*, the chaste beloved in *Layli va Majnun*, and the pure angel in numerous productions throughout the twentieth century, from early productions of Cram Cook to many post-revolutionary religious rhythmic movements. The female national dancer is the ultimate bodily staging of the Iranian woman: one who embodies the aesthetics of "modernity" in her ballet-trained, stylized, fit, and "chic" body. She is authentic for her Iranian movements and clothing, and her female sexuality is regulated in her graceful feminine charm as she performs narratives of the nation for her audiences to witness and to emulate.

Notes

* A slightly different version of this chapter was published in *Oxford Handbook on Dance and Ethnicity*, ed. Anthony Shay and Barbara Sellers-Young (Oxford: Oxford University Press, 2016).
1 Together with *raqs-i mahalli* (regional folk dance), the term *raqs-i milli* (national dance) was often deployed to refer to the two main categories of Iranian dance. While the category of folk dance clearly refers to the diverse existing regional folk dances with ethnic ties, "national dance" is an ambiguous genre that is also interchangeably referred to as "ancient dance" (*raqs-i bastani*), "Iranian classical dance" (*raqs-i kilasik-i irani*), "Iranian ballet" (*balah'i irani*), "characteristic dance" (*raqs-i karaktiristik*), and, sometimes, "Iranian traditional dance" (*raqs-i sunnati-i irani*). While all these terms have different connotations, most of them denote Iranian culture or history. For their part, "Iranian ballet," "classical" (*kilasik*), and "characteristic" (*karaktiristik*) dance have obvious balletic implications.
2 Despite the influence of vernacular ideas and themes, here I discuss a dancing body largely inspired or shaped by non-Iranian disciplines of dance, mainly the classical ballet.
3 I use *biopolitics*, originally a Foucauldian term, in origin, to refer to politics, power dynamics, and social conditions within the theatrical milieu that governed the stage, shaping or reshaping the performers' bodies. By its original definition, biopolitics submits to the ways modern states control the population through subjugating their bodies in everyday life. See Michel Foucault, "Right of Death and Power over Life," in *The Foucault Reader*, ed. Michel Foucault and Paul Rabinow (New York: Pantheon, 1984), 262.
4 See, for example, "Dar Salun-i grand hutil" [At the Grand Hotel Venue], *Iran*, no. 1116, 28 Hamal 1301/18 April 1922, 4; reprinted in Mas'ud Kouhestani-Nejad, ed., *Guzidah'i asnad-i namayish dar iran, az inqilab-i mashrutiyat ta 1304* [Selected records of drama in Iran, from the Constitutional Revolution to 1925], vol. 2 (Tehran: Intisharat-i Sazman-i Asnad-i Milli-i Iran, 1381/2002), 268.
5 For a description of *zanpush*, see Khosrow Shariari, *Kitab-i namayish: Farhang-i vazhah-ha, istilah-ha va sabk-ha-yi namayishi* [The book of theater: A glossary of terminology, expressions and performance genres] (Tehran: Intisharat-i Amirkabir, 1365/1986), 136.
6 Parviz Mansouri and Hasan Shirvani, *Fa'aliyat-ha-yi hunari dar panjah sal shahanshahi-i Pahlavi* [Artistic activities in the fifty years of the Pahlavi Dynasty: Theater, music, opera, and dance] (Tehran: Intisharat-i Vizarat-i Farhang va Hunar, 2535/1976), 209.
7 See, for instance, "Ti'atr-i namus" [The honour play], *Rahnama*, no. 183, 28 Zihajjah 1338/12 September 1920, 4, reprinted in Kouhestani-Nejad, *Guzidah'i asnad-i namayish dar iran, az inqilab-i mashrutiyat ta 1304*, 236–7.
8 "Kunsirt-i bashukuh-i 'ali" [Excellent performance], *Iran*, no. 1611, 16 Juza' 1303/5 June 1924, 4; "Namayish-i 'ali, mirza murad ya pisar-i mashhadi 'ibad, upirit dar chahar pardah" [Excellent performance, Mirza Murad or the son of Mashhdi 'Ibad, operetta in four scenes], *Iran*, no. 968, 8 Sunbulah 1300/31 August 1921, 4.
9 "Talar-i madrasah'i aramanah" [The venue of the Armenian school], *Iran*, no. 834, 20 Jumadi al-avval 1339/9 February 1921, 4; "Namayish-i ba shukuh" [Glorious performance], *Iran*, no. 1020, 29 'Aqrab 1300/21 November 1921, 3.
10 "Kavah'i Ahangar" [The blacksmith Kavah], *Iran*, no. 907, 15 Juza' 1300/3 June 1921, 4.
11 "Bisharat" [Good news], *Iran*, no. 824, 16 Jumadi al-avval 1339/26 January 1921, 4.
12 Ali-Naqi Vaziri, "Sukhanrani dar madrasah'i 'ali-i musiqi" [The lecture at the College of Music], Tir 1304/July 1925, reprinted in *Zindigi va asar-i Ali-Naqi*

Vaziri [Life and the works of Ali-Naqi Vaziri], ed. Vahid Ayoubi (Tehran: Intisharat-i Kitabsaray-i Nik, 1385/2006), 9.

13 Ayoubi, *Zindigi va asar-i Ali-Naqi Vaziri.*

14 In addition to Pari Aqabayov, Mademoiselle Mahin, a Muslim, was reported to have been dancing in one of his 1930s productions.

15 Ayoubi, *Zindigi va asar-i Ali-Naqi Vaziri*, 34.

16 Ali Mir Ansari and Sayyad Mehrdad ziaii "Pishguftar" [Introduction], in *Guzidah'i asnad-i namayish dar iran, az 1305 ta 1320* [Selected records of drama in Iran, 1926–41], Ali Mir Ansari and Sayad Mehrdad Ziaii, eds (Tehran: Intisharat-i Sazman-i Asnad-i Milli-i Iran, 1381/2003), 23.

17 "Dar ti'atr-i sirus avvalin ti'atr-i milli" [In Cyrus Theater, the first national theater], *Ittila'at*, 17 Azar 1308/ 8 December 1929, 3.

18 Abulqasim Jannati-Ata'i, *Bunyad-i namayish dar iran* [The Theater Foundation in Iran] (Tehran: Kitabkhanah'i Ibn-i Sina, 1333/1954), 74.

19 Behruz Qaribpur, *Ti'atr dar iran* [Theater in Iran] (Tehran: Daftar-i Pazhouhish-ha-yi Farhangi, 1384/2005), 15.

20 Mansouri and Shirvani, *Fa'aliyat-ha-yi hunari*, 212, 232.

21 Mansouri and Shirvani, *Fa'aliyat-ha-yi hunari*, 212, 222.

22 For example, see "Varzish va ziba'i: ta'sir-i raqs dar ziba shudan" [Sports and beauty: The beatifying effect of dancing], *Mihrigan*, 27 Shahrivar 1316/18 September 1937, 20.

23 Ali-Asghar Azarakhshi, "Vizarat-i ma'arif, idarah'i intiba'at" [Ministry of Culture, the office of publications], 29 Urdibihisht 1317/19 May 1938, in *Guzidah'i asnad-i namayish dar iran, az 1305 ta 1320*, 253.

24 Fakhri Nazimi, "Namayish-hayi istudiu-yi ihya-yi hunar-ha-yi bastani-i iran" [Performances of the studio of revival of ancient arts of Iran], *Jahan-i-Naw*, Tir 1327/June 1948, 169–70.

25 Nesta Ramazani, *The Dance of the Rose and the Nightingale* (Syracuse, NY: Syracuse University Press, 2002).

26 Ali-Pasha Saleh, "The Persian Studio," *Iran and the U.S.A.*, April 1947, 14–16; "A Cultural Relations Reception and Program," *Iran and the U.S.A.*, July and August 1947, 1–5; 1.

27 Mansouri and Shirvani, *Fa'aliyat-ha-yi hunari*, 233.

28 Nesta Ramazani, "A Meeting of Cultures: Writing My Memoir," *Middle East Critique* 17, no. 3 (2008): 293–308; 299, 301.

29 Saleh, "The Persian Studio," 14–16.

30 "Istudiyu-yi ihya-yi hunar-ha-yi iran-i bastan" [The studio for the revival of classical arts of Iran], souvenir program notes, undated.

31 See Nilla Cram Cook, "The Theatre and Ballet Arts of Iran," *Middle East Journal* (October 1949): 406–20; 406; Ramazani, *Dance of the Rose and the Nightingale*, 414–17; *Zurkhanah* is a vernacular Iranian martial arts form.

32 "Da'vat-i Sifarat-i Amrika" [Invitation of the US embassy], *Sukhan*, 1324/1945, 794.

33 "Hargiz faramush nimikunam" [I will never forget], *Ittila'at-i Banuvan*, no. 209, 11 Urdibihisht 1340/1 May 1961, 4, 65.

34 Iraj Nabavi, "Ustad janbazian" [Master Djanbazian], *Afarin*, 5 Aban 1333/27 October 1954; "Jashn-i hunaristan-i balit-i tihran" [Tehran Ballet School recital], *Saba*, 17 Khurdad 1329/7 June 1950, 21.

35 Janet Lazarian, *Danishnamah'i iranian-i armani* [Encyclopedia of Iranian Armenians] (Tehran: Markaz-i Baynalmilali-i Guftigu-yi Tamaddun-ha and Hirmand, 1382/2003), 450.

36 "Man bihtarin dastah'i balit ra az iran bah dunya khaham firistad" [In a few years I will send the best ballet troupe from Iran to the world], *Ittila'at-i Mah*, Tir 1336/July 1957, 26; Pari Abasalti, "Kumpani-i raqs" [The dance company], *Ittila'at-i Banuvan*, 14 Farvardin 1340/3 April 1961, 4.

37 Robert De Warren, "The National Ballet of Iran," *Dancing Times*, March 1968, 299.

38 Haideh Ahmadzadeh, *My Life as a Persian Ballerina* (self-published, 2008).
39 "Mahalli dancers of Iran," Tour of the United States of America, Opening at the Kennedy Center for Performing Arts, Washington, DC, 1–2 September, 1976, souvenir program.
40 Pari Safa, "Saz-ha-yi irani ba zaban-i jahani sukhan miguyand" [Iranian musical instruments speak global language], *Rudaki*, Isfand 1353/February 1975, 8.
41 "National Iranian Folklore Organization," souvenir program, season 1973–4.
42 "Antalya festivali yarin başliyor," *Takvim*, 31 May 1973; "Preserve folklore before it is lost," *Pakistan Times*, 14 April 1974; "Dirakhshish-i raqsandigan-i mahalli dar landan" [Mahalli dancers shine in London], *Ayandigan*, 21 Aban 1351/12 November 1972, 6.
43 The Annual Cultural Reports published by Muhammad Reza Pahlavi's Ministry of Culture and Arts proves the limitedness of the audiences of the performances given by the dance sectors dependent on that ministry. For instance, for all their performances in various governmental sites, including universities and garrisons as well as Rudaki Hall, the National Folklore Organization had 24,740 attendees in 1974 and 182,250 in 1976, while the Iranian National Ballet Company, which presumably performed mainly at the Rudaki Hall, had 27,490 attendees in 1976. See "Sazman-i milli-i fulklur" [National Folklore Organization], *Guzarish-i farhangi-i iran-1353* [Cultural reports of Iran, 1974] (Tehran: Shawra-yi 'Ali-i Farhang va Hunar, 1353/1974), 223–6; 223; "Istifadah kunandigan az barnamah'i raqs" [The audiences of the dance programs], *Guzarish-i fa'aliyat-ha-yi farhangi-i iran dar 2535* [Reports on cultural activities in Iran, 1975] (Tehran: Dafatar-i Mutali'at va Barnamahrizi-i Farhangi, n.d.), 481–3; 481.
44 Choreographic attitudes similar to those of *raqs-i milli* can be seen in the works of the Europe-based choreographers Nima Kiann and Shahrukh Mushkin-qalam as well as those staged by North American companies such as Vancouver Pars National Ballet and the Ballet Afsaneh.
45 Khan Malik Sasani, "Namayish dar ti'atr-i milli" [The play in the national theater], *Aftab*, 10 Ziqa'dah 1331/10 November 1913, 3; reprinted in *Guzidah'i asnad-i namayish dar iran, az inqilab-i mashrutiyat ta 1304*, vol.1, 29.
46 Murtiza Mushfiq Kazimi, "Ma'arif dar Iran: ti'atr va musiqi" [Culture and arts in Iran: Theater and music]," in *MajallehIranchahr*, ed. Husayn Kazimzadah Iranchahr (Tehran: Eqbal, 1363/1984), 326–34; 328; originally printed in *Iranchahr* 2, nos. 5–6, 1 Isfand 1292/15 February 1924.
47 Mir-Husayn Shabahang, "Firishtah'i umid" [The angel of hope], *Ittila'at*, no. 1158, 20 Mihr 1309/3 October 1930, 3.
48 According to Afsaneh Najmabadi, among what European travelers found unusual in Iranian public spaces was the homosocial behavior and appearances of some men, whom they perceived as homosexual. Trying to adjust to the European binary of man and woman, Iranians started heteronormalizing the public sphere by abandoning (or privatizing) some of these sexual behaviors and diminishing representations of them in visual arts. Najmabadi discusses the shifts in Qajar-era paintings of human bodies as well as the symbols of the sun and the lion. Other incidental changes include the banning of boys from dancing and the highlighting of the masculine signifier of the mustache; see Afsaneh Najmabadi, *Women with Mustaches and Men without Beards: Gender and Sexual Anxieties of Iranian Modernity* (Berkeley: University of California Press, 2005), 3.
49 As Najmabadi defines it, "young adolescent male" who acted as objects of desire for adult men were referred to as *amrad*, and *mukhannas* meant "an adult man desiring to be an object of desire for adult men"; see Najmabadi, *Women with Mustaches*, 3.
50 "Aqa-yi mudir-i muhtaram" [The respected manager], *Qanun*, 28 Qaws 1300/19 December 1921, 2; reprinted in *Guzidah'i asnad-i namayish dar iran, az inqilab-i mashrutiyat ta 1304*, vol. 2, 44–5.

46

51 Mohamad Tavakoli-Targhi, *Refashioning Iran: Orientalism, Occidentalism and Historiography* (New York: Palgrave, 2001), 54–5.

52 Firuzabadi, "Maqam-i mani'-i riyasat-i vizarat-i dam-ul iqbalah" [The great prime minister], 20 Tir 1305/12 July 1926, in *Guzidah'i 1snad-i namayish dar iran, az 1305 ta 1320*, 5; Mudarris, "Hazrat-i mubarak-i aqa-yi ra'is ul-vuzara" [The great prime minister!], 24 Zihajjah 1344/5 July 1926, in *Guzidah'i Asnad-i Namayish dar Iran, az 1305 ta 1320*, 8–9.

53 See Mas'ud Kouhestani-Nejad, ed., *Guzidah'i asnad-i namayish dar iran, az inqilab-i mashrutiyat ta 1304*, vol. 2, 300–305.

54 "Pasukh-i mujaddad-i nazmiyah bah darkhast-i hunarmand-i badkubah'i" [Nazmiyah's second response to the request of the Baku artist], 18 Isfand 1304/9 March 1926, in *Guzidah'i asnad-i namayish dar iran, az inqilab-i mashrutiyat ta 1304*, vol. 2, 304–5.

55 *Rawzah* here refers to gender-segregated religious mourning sessions; for the letter, see "Namah'i Qamar-al-Muluk" [Qamar-al-Muluk's letter], *Shafaq-i Surkh*, Dalv 1302/February 1924, reprinted in *Musiqi dar 'asr-i mashrutah* [Music in the Constitutional era], ed. Mas'ud Kouhestani-Nejad (Tehran: Mehrnamag, 1384/2005), 281–3.

56 "Shafaq-i surkh," *Shafaq-i Surkh* 207, 14 Dalv 1302/4 February 1924, reprinted in *Musiqi dar 'asr-i mashrutah*, 283.

57 'A Shaybani, "Ittila'iyah'i shirkat-i komidi-i iran dar mawrid-i fa'aliyiat-i in shirkat" [The announcement about activities of the company, Comédie Iran], *Ittila'at*, no. 567, 7 Shahrivar 1307/29 August 1928, 3, reprinted in *Guzidah'i asnad-i namayish dar iran, az 1305 ta 1320*, vol. 1, 25–6.

58 Schayegh discusses the ways in which the new forms of urban popular entertainment were blamed for the dissemination of the social maladies of corruption, venereal disease, and repression of the "healthy" sexual drives of men, thus leading to shrinkage of the average family size; see Cyrus Schayegh, *Who Is Knowledgeable Is Strong: Science, Class, and the Formation of Modern Iranian Society, 1900–1950* (Berkeley: University of California Press, 2009), 122.

59 Karim Dadgar, "Hizar va yik makr" [One thousand and one tricks], *Ittila'at*, no. 1025, 6 Urdibihisht 1309/27 April 1930, 2; Sidiqah Dawlatabadi, "Kanun-i bauvan-i tihran" [Tehran's women's association], 1317 Day 12/2 January 1939) in *Guzidah'i asnad-i namayish dar iran, az 1305 ta 1320*, vol. 2, 263.

60 Sidiqah Dawlatabadi, "Ahamiyat-i hifz ul-sihhah baray-i zanan" [The importance for women to keep healthy], *Iranchahr* 2, no. 1, 18 September 1923, reprinted in *MajallehIranchahr*, 18–23.

61 For examples of such articles, see "Chira khanum-ha bayad varzish kunand" [Why do women need to exercise?], *Iran-i Bastan*, Day 1313/January 1935, 8,10; 8; "Nimunah'i az varzish-ha va musabiqah-ha-yi baynulmilali-i ulampiya dar urupa kah hamah salah baray-i taqviyat-i ruh va jism-i nawjavanan va banuvan ma'mul va mutidavil ast" [Examples of European Olympic sports and competitions, beneficial for bodies and spirits of women and youth], *Iran-i Bastan*, 21 Aban 1313/12 November 1934, 8.

62 For an example, see "Luzum-i varzish baray-i zanan" [The importance of sports for women], *Mihrigan*, 23 Murdad 1316/14 August 1937, 4.

63 For example, see "Saz va raqs-ha-yi milli" [National instruments and dances of Iran], *Musik-i Iran*, Bahman 1337/January 1959, 9.

64 "Hunarpishah'i dah salah" [A ten-year-old artist], *Mihrigan*, 1 Farvardin 1319/21 March 1940, 13.

65 See Mansouri and Shirvani, *Fa'aliyat-ha-yi hunari*, 237; *Duvvumin jashn-i farhang va hunar dar sarasar-i kishvar, 4–18 Aban 1348* [The second festival of arts and culture throughout the country, 5–9 November 1969], n.d., 49.

66 The Pahlavi state had a dualistic attitude towards cultures of different ethnicities in Iran: even though some aspects of folk cultures such as folk dance and music were

promoted, the state had an oppressive approach to many aspects of ethnic identities, language in particular. For instance, although there were no restrictions on ethnic music or dance, in non-Persian regions of Iran, neither the students nor the teachers were allowed to speak in their mother tongue in school or to learn their mother tongue in the school system. I believe this difference in policy can be attributed to the lack of seriousness in accepting dance and music as modes of political communication, whereas a non-Persian language could have seemed directly harmful to the Pahlavi policy of "one nation/one language/one country." See Alireza Asgharzadeh, "The Development and Persistence of Racist Ideas in Iran: Politics of Assimilation and the Challenge of Diversity" (PhD diss., University of Toronto, 2005).

67 Nilla Cram Cook, "The Persian dance," *Iran and the U.S.A*, November 1946, 7–10; 10.
68 Mansouri and Shirvani, *Fa'aliyat-ha-yi hunari*, 33.
69 Kamal Shafi'i, "Guftigu-yi ba abdullah nazimi piramun-i raqs dar Iran" [A conversation with Abdullah Nazimi on dance in Iran], *Talash*, no. 6, Mihr 1346/ October 1967, 74–80; 77.
70 Jamal, quoted in Anthony Shay, "Choreographing Persia," *Nima Kiann's Forum of Persian and Middle Eastern Dance*, 2006, www.artira.com/danceforum/articles/sha y_choreopersia.html (accessed 29 April 2009).
71 Yahya Zoka', "Tarikh-i raqs dar iran" [The history of dance in Iran], *Hunar va Mardum*, no. 188, Khurdad 1357/June 1979, 2–12; nos. 189–90, Tir–Murdad 1357/ July–August 1978, 2–7; nos. 191–2, Shahrivar–Murdad 1357/September–October 1978, 38–41; and no. 193, Aban-Azar 1358/November–December 1979, 22–8; Yahya Zoka', "Raqs dar iran-i pish az bastan" [Dance in prehistoric Iran], *Musiqi* no. 86 (1964), 1–11; no. 87 (1964), 27–40; Yahya Zoka', "Raqs dar iran-i pish az bastan" [Dance in prehistoric Iran], *Naqsh va Nigar* no. 8 (1962), 44–5.
72 Cram Cook, "The Persian dance," 9.
73 Cram Cook, "The theater and ballet," 406.
74 Medjid Rezvani, *Le théâtre et la danse en Iran* (Paris: Maisonneuve et Larose, 1962); Ali-Akbar Baigi et al., eds., *Asnadi az musiqi, ti'atr va sinama dar iran, 1330–1357* [Documents on music, cinema, and theater in Iran, 1300–57], vols. 1–3 (Tehran: Sazman-i Chap va Intisharat-i Vizarat-i Farhang va Irshad-i Islami, 1379/ 2000), 1326.
75 Medjid Rezvani, "Paydayish-i namayish va raqs dar Iran" [The advent of theater and dance in Iran], in *Khastgah-i Ijtima'i-i Hunar-ha*, trans. Manizhah Araqizadah (Tehran: Farhangsaray-i Niavaran, 1357/1978).
76 Khan Malik Sasani, *Shahid-i Shiraz* [The witness of Shiraz] (Tehran: Firdawsi, 1341/1962), 80.
77 Ruhullah Khaleqi, *Sarguzasht-i musiqi-i iran* [History of music in Iran], 2nd edn (Tehran: Safi 'Alishah, 1378/1999), 471–86.
78 Ayoubi, *Zindigi va Asar-i Ali-Naqi Vaziri*, 12.
79 Hushang Irani, "Balah" [Ballet], *Khurus Jangi*, Day 1329/January 1951, reprinted in Sirus Tahbaz, ed., *Khurus-i Jangi-i Bimanand* (Tehran: Farzan-i Ruz, 1380/ 2001), 228–36.
80 Sarkis Djanbazian, "Raqs" [Dance], *Khurus-i Jangi* 2, 1329/1950, 25–8.
81 Ehsan Yarshater, "Jambazian ustad-i balih" [Jambazian, the ballet master], *Rushanfikr*, 20 Tir 1336/11 July 1957, 27.
82 "Balah dar Iran" [Ballet in Iran], *Pazhuhandah* 1, no. 1 (n.d.).
83 Jalal Sattari, *Dar bi-dawlati-i farhang* [The unfortunateness of culture] (Tehran: Nashr-i Markaz, 1379/2000), 51–2.
84 This section is based on my analysis of videos of some national-dance works in the last decade of the Pahlavi era, including *Haft-Paykar* and *Qajar* by the National Dance Company as well as *Ru-Nama* (1970) by the National Ballet of Iran. Due to the scarcity of such videos, I have also examined a number of images of dance

from the period for this analysis. As points of reference, I have used cabaret dance scenes of the genre *film-i farsi* as well as images of *zanpush* and *bachchah-raqqas*. While observing *bachchah-raqqas* as a point of reference—by virtue of their being the closest dancing persona in the traditional public setting to the *zanpush* explored in the context of the early twentieth-century modernist theatrical sphere—my main analysis relies on female dancing bodies.

85 In the later Qajar era, it was common for the traditional performance of *taqlid* to be staged at homes for ceremonial purposes.

86 Farrokh Safavi, "Raqs dar jam'iah'i ma" [Dance in our society], *Iran-i Abad*, Azar 1339/November 1960, 69–72.

87 Ja'far Shahri, *Tihran-i qadim* [The old Tehran], vol. 2 (Tehran: Mu'in, 1371/1992), 59–60.

88 Shahri, *Tihran-i qadim*, 50–65.

89 Shahri, *Tihran-i qadim*, 60.

90 Robyn C. Friend, "Status and preservation of Iranian dance: Cultural factors influencing the Iranian attitude concerning dance" (paper presented at the First International Conference on Middle Eastern Dance, Orange Coast College, Costa Mesa, California, 16–18 May 1997, http://home.earthlink.net/~rcfriend/Hojb–1997.htm (accessed 2 September 2015).

91 Anthony Shay, "Choreographing hypermasculinity in Egypt, Iran, and Uzbekistan," *Dance Chronicle* 31, no. 2 (2008): 211–38.

92 "Introduction: Inventing traditions," in *The Invention of Tradition*, Eric Hobsbawm and Terence Ranger, eds (Cambridge: Cambridge University Press, 1983), 1–14.

3 *Mutrib*s and their dancers
The counter-ideal performers of new Iran

This chapter explores the emergence of an interdisciplinary field of discursivity on performance in the first half of the twentieth century that marginalized the *mutribi* performers in the larger discourse of arts, dismissing them as ante-modern and "*mubtazal*" (degenerate). Understanding the formation of this discourse and the political dynamics shaping it is significant to this argument for it has largely shaped the social perceptions of cabaret dancers who had close ties to *mutrib*s. Arguably, these conceptualizations have also influenced Iranians' cultural categorization as well as their aesthetic taste (of performing arts) to this day.

As explored in Chapter 2, for those nationalists who sought to materialize ideas of modern Iran on stage, Iranian dance required a departure from its immediate past: it was in that process that on the national stage, the female national dancer with a controlled femininity emerged to replace the *bachah raqqas* of the *mutribi* scene, whose performance combined hyper-sexuality with homoeroticism. However, the multi-faceted *mutrib*s and the performers associated with them signified the unpleasant past not only for dance but also for music and theater, the two major spheres of performance in the first four decades of the twentieth century. As I will briefly explore, the nationalist discourse dismissed the *mutrib*s from the national stage for representing illiteracy, backwardness, and lewdness.

Moreover, a leftist discourse with an ideological view of the arts emerged in the 1930s had an unfavorable take on the *mutrib*s since they did not fit into its own distinct ideas for arts in Iran—that they be historically relevant, belong to the people, and help sublimate their taste while urging them to struggle for a better society.[1] In these propositions, the *mutrib*s came to represent the undesirable performers of the past. These ideas were further cultivated and disseminated in the Marxist-inspired writings and practices of the 1940s, when many prominent artistic and literary figures joined the Tudeh Party (founded in 1941), the major communist organization of Iran, which was active in the spheres of arts and culture. Among them was Abdulhusayn Nushin (1906–71), a pioneering theatrical figure of Iran, the height of whose artistic career coincided with that of the party's activism and massive publicity. His double role as artist and politician led to the formation of a myth surrounding him, and the cementation of ideas of committed (or *engagé*) and progressive arts in Iran: the height of his activity came to signify a "golden age" of theater in Iran (also discursively linked to the theatrical scene of Lalehzar Street), while his lamented departure demarcated its decline. Opposite Nushin's image were the *mutribs* and their dancers, who not only represented the counter-ideal performers of the past, but whose recruitment and predominance on the stage in the 1950s put them head to head with the mythic image of Nushin and all the sublime qualities he represented.

This chapter opens with *mutribs* and the earlier nationalists' othering of them as illiterate and ante-modern. It then moves to the emergence of the leftist discourse on arts (including theater and music) in the 1930s and their cultivation and practice in the 1940s. The rest of the chapter looks at the 1950s, when dancers and *mutribs* were recruited to the theatrical stage of Lalehzar, followed by a review of the historical narratives of theater which have been influenced by the earlier leftist notions and practices.

*Mutrib*s and the earlier nationalists' take on them

Genealogically traceable to the Safavid era, the twentieth-century multi-faceted *mutribi* troupes combined music, dance, acting, and comedy as they were hired to perform in various public and private ceremonies.[2] As described in Chapter 1, in the Qajar era, many of these performance troupes settled in larger cities and primarily in the capital, Tehran. Qajar kings were especially interested in *mutribi* performances and some of the most important musicians and actors resided in their courts. The urban transformations and the accessibility achieved through new transportation in the twentieth century enabled *mutribs* to reach wider audiences. Furthermore, with the opening of *shadimani* agencies after the 1920s, the *mutribi* scene became more commercialized. Mainly concentrated in the areas of "Sirus Intersection" (Sahrah-i-Sirus) and the Gumruk neighborhood, these agencies found their employees performance opportunities in various parts of the city and country.[3] Another transformation in the *mutribi* sphere was the recruitment of women to substitute the cross-dressing adolescent boy dancers (*bachchah-raqqas*), which according to historical interpretations happened after women's unveiling in 1936.[4]

Even though the *mutribi* and *taqlidchi* (imitators) performers embodied a long tradition of practicing performing arts in Iran, the bifurcation of culture in the twentieth century to "high" and "low" brows caused the *mutribi* troupes to be categorized as low. I propose that this situation was further prompted by the formation of the nationalist-modernist art scene of the early twentieth century (discussed in Chapter 2). Seeking to define a new meaning for performing arts and justify their own practice as "modern" and "educational," the newly emerged artistic sphere othered the vernacular *mutribs* in lieu of forming a distinct "modern" culture.

This stance is evident in the prominent music figure Ali Naqi Vaziri's lecture at the College of Music (Madrasah'i 'Ali-i Musiqi) in 1925, when he differentiated theater from *mutribi* performances, asserting:

> Tonight, I am speaking about theater! But be cautious! Theater, not *tiyart*; *tiyart* as it is regularly performed by *mutribi* groups is nothing but falsehood and trickery. But theater is a site for critiquing people's habits and a university for arts and ethics.[5]

While Vaziri's statement was about theater, a similar attitude can be observed in the commentary of the musical figure Arif-i Qazvini (1882–1934), who in describing the underprivileged status of music in Iran complained about the public's treatment of musical artists as *mutrib*s and *raqqas*.[6]

Reflecting back on the early decades of the twentieth century, many biographical narratives on individuals active in the early theater scene also reproduce this categorization, exemplified in an account on Mir-Sayfuldin Kirmanshahi (1876–1933) published in the journal *Hunar-ha-yi Milli*:

> Kirmanshahi, whose artistic personality largely transformed the world of theater in Iran, lived in an era when the arts in public opinion meant "clowning" (*dalqak-bazi*) and "imitating" (*muqallidi*).[7]

While clowning and *muqallidi* in the above text refers to the theatrical aspect of *mutrib*s, this trope of historically situating *mutrib*s as an unpleasant past for the "respected arts," and the new "respected artists" as their champion substitute is a common trend in historical narratives of theater.[8] This time-distancing attitude is discernable in Mansouri and Shirvani's account, *Artistic Activities in the Fifty Years of the Pahlavi Dynasty*, published by the Ministry of Culture in 1975. Valorizing the state's policies during the Reza Shah Pahlavi's era as "nationalization" and a "savior of the status of artists," the authors alienated *mutrib*s as performers of the past, the "labourers of joy" ('*amalah'i tarab*), and the "mercenaries" (*jirah-khar*) of the people in power, while ignoring the still active co-existent community of *mutrib*s.[9]

A similar assertion was made more recently in the historical account *Cross Over the History of Iranian Theater* (1999), authored by the leftist theater director Mustafa Oskoui, where he posited that the best imitators (*taqlidchi*s) and clowns had been "owned" by the courts and kings and were favored by them.[10] In his anti-Pahlavi stance, Oskoui went further in his accusation to identify the relative success of the *mutribi* troupes during the Reza Shah era—when *shadimani* agencies were created and a famous *mutribi* troupe succeeded in having a permanent theater—as part of a Pahlavi censorship disinformation scheme: by supporting these troupes in this period of severe censorship on theater, the state sought to promote a democratic image of itself. Labeling *mutrib*s as mainly "ill-reputed" and "illiterate" performers, Oskoui further identified the "promotion" of *mutrib*s as part of the state's conspiracy to disrespect the social position of "intellectual" (*rushanfikr*) actors.[11] In Oskoui's view, *mutrib*s further harmed Iranian theater in that period through their impolite and risqué acts, behaviors, and gestures in their *takhtah-hawzi* comedic performances.[12]

Indicating a critical stance of the author, the idea that *mutrib*s were owned by and served those in power are two common tropes of the leftist discourse that will be discussed later in this chapter. The labeling of *mutrib*s as illiterate was perhaps due to the fact that their art education had been orally transmitted. Relying greatly on their improvisational skills, most *mutrib* musicians were not able to read musical notes, and *taqlidchi* actors could not read a theatrical script. In the context of the early twentieth century, when Western-style art education became institutionalized in Iran, particularly through the establishment of the Acting College as well as Vaziri's Musical College, *mutrib*s were called out as illiterate. Such attitudes towards *mutribi* culture were in contrast to the nationalists' favoring of regional or "ethnic" folk performative genres, which were received as reminiscent of the Aryan culture and were used as inspirational sources for music and dance.[13]

Historically associated with social corruption, alcoholism, and addiction, *mutrib*s were further accused of immorality after recruiting female performers.[14] Unlike the female dancing body on the nationalist-modernist stage, which signified modernity, the dancer in the *mutribi* scene marked debauchery. It appears that the *mutrib*s' distinct communal lifestyle, which seemed "strange" in the newly emerging social setting of urban life, also added to their disreputation. As described by my interviewee the late Morteza Ahmadi (1924–2014), the *mutribi* arena was to some extent filially constituted—as an occupation it was inherited through lineage.[15] It was common for the wives and children of *mutrib*s, known as *mutrib-zadah*, to join the troupes in their early lives.[16] While it was usual for male performers to marry female performers, whom they would also promote in their career, *mutribi* troupes occasionally hired dancers from the café setting to perform with them.[17] Due to the sexual undertone of the comedic performances of *mutrib*s, the female performers in these troupes were subjected to sexually driven reactions and maltreatment by the audience members, who would interpret the performers' presence in a public performance setting as a sign of their sexual availability.[18] Nevertheless, *mutribi* troupe members, along with their dancers, were actively involved in performance spheres associated with the popular culture of the Pahlavi era.

The rise of Marxian practices and a systematic politically driven analysis of arts

This section shifts focus to the Marxist-inspired discourse on arts in the 1930s and 1940s that located the *mutrib*s in the past, though from an angle different from the abovementioned assertions. Treating arts with an interdisciplinary approach that included theater, music, painting, and poetry, this discourse sought to theorize and conceptualize arts for the new era, holding that they had to be relevant to their historical context, educate the (artistic) taste of the audience, and alleviate the society with its appropriate audience affect. Thus *mutrib*s, and all the practices attributed to them, including *taqlid* (imitation), *mazhakah* (buffoonery), *dalqk-bazi* (clowning), musical instruments such as the *tunbak* (or *tombak*), and the audience's emotional response to their art (including uncritical laughter), were discursively deemed *mubtazal*, and at the service of a particular class. In the active years of the Tudeh Party in the 1940s, these ideas came into practice and were solidified and disseminated through various periodicals of the party.

Arts for the new Iran, *Dunya* and Alavi's initial propositions

The urge for theorizing new arts in the leftist discourse seems to have emerged in their application of Marxist theory of historical and dialectical materialism to the Iranian context. A few articles with this inclination appeared in the important leftist periodical *Dunya*, published between 1933 and 1935 with the collaboration of the prominent Marxist figure Taqi Arani (1903–40) and other writers, some of whom became founding members of the Tudeh Party in 1941. An early instance was "Arts and Materialism," written by the literary figure Buzurg Alavi (under his pen name Firaydun Nakhuda). In the article he wrote:

> Art is a materialistic phenomenon, a manifestation of human spirit and humanistic social life, and it is shaped by and dependent on the economy and the "condition of production" (*vaz'iyat-i tawlid*) in the society of each era ... Art is the translation of emotions into material, and its social role is to "publicize individualistic emotions" (*'umumi kardan-i ihsasat-i fardi*). As such, it is mandatory to understand the conditions for the developments of the arts, and the ways the evolution of the society can lead to progress or the "decline" (*inhitat*) of the arts.[19]

Alavi then linked the evolution of arts to the progress of the materialistic and economic life of the society, deducing that the arts' impact on the society depended on its historical relevance and contemporaneity. Expanding the idea to the case of contemporary Iran and using the example of works of classical Persian poets, he then concluded that the consequence of relying on the old, long-standing arts in the contemporary world is nothing but a regression to the intellectual level of the past, and a deafness to "the horrifying and alarming sound of the European machines" and the then-current "intellectual revolution resulting from materialist thinking in the new civilized world."[20] In his plea for new arts for Iran, Alavi asserted that all art forms were directly and indirectly a byproduct of the economic conditions and technical means of (production) in society. To affirm his theory, he used the example of musical instruments as the technical means of music production, inferring that in a country where the public musical instruments are piano and organ, music is much stronger, effective, and progressive than in one where they are the *dayirah* and *tunbak*, the percussion instruments especially prevalent in *mutribi* music.[21]

The next step for Alavi appears to have been his essay entitled "New Art in Iran," in which he expanded on the ways new arts in Iran, including the European-style theater of his time, had the potential to improve the popular taste and in turn that taste would reciprocally force the artists to produce more profound arts.[22] Alavi then focused on analyzing a production on the classical poet Firdawsi, performed at the millennium celebration in 1934, a play directed by Nushin with music composition of the then-director of the Musical College, Ghulam-Husayn Minbashiyan.[23] Praising Nushin's directorship, he described the music as such:

> It was neither Iranian nor European but an international one which I greatly enjoyed. Perhaps the majority of people does not enjoy it but it is not Minbashiyan's fault, the taste and intellectual level of the people must be improved so that they would appreciate this music. Perhaps this work of Minbashiyan was the first step in enhancing people's "aesthetic taste" (*zawq*).[24]

The only section of the play that Alavi criticized was a dance piece, which to him appeared as Egyptian (belly dance) style, set to a music of an instrument that sounded like the *tunbak*, perhaps a hint to the newly emerging performances of the *mutrib*s and their dancers.

In a follow-up article entitled "Art in the New Iran," Alavi restated some of his earlier ideas of dialectical and historical materialism to advocate the notion of committed art, which he framed as art with a "purpose" (*manzur*) and "ideology"(*maram*), as the best alternative for the new Iran. In so doing, he described art (in general) as an aspect of civilization that created enjoyment and healed pain. He divided artists into two major groups:

> There are artists who promote and disseminate the ideas, emotions, and interests of the ruling class, the ones who think art is to console, comfort, and amuse the people, and instill in their audience the feelings of toleration, submission, and satisfaction with their pains and adversities. On the contrary, there are artists who, in addition to their personal pain, feel responsible for the suffering of society and "burn the midnight oil" (*dud-i chiragh mikhurand*); they dedicate themselves to uncovering the sources of people's miseries and to exposing them to those who suffer from them, thereby encouraging and empowering the people to eliminate the causes of their pain and to find themselves amusement and joy.[25]

Alavi linked the causes of the lag of Iranian arts, including music, painting, and literature, to the lack of "transformation" (*t'aghir*) of the means and tenets of production present in the preceding six centuries, identifying social and national movements as prerequisites of the arts. Alavi further recognized the post-World War I historical moment as a turning point for Iranians since their lives had been deeply transformed by a materialistic revolution in Europe. He then introduced potential candidates for the transformation of the situation of the arts in Iran. Among them were Minbashiyan and Nushin, whom he complimented for attempting to save music and theater from their previous (*mutribi*) state and their capability for refashioning the state of arts in Iran; he then commented on their work, linking their flaws to their lack of a "personal intellectual logic" (*fikr-i mantiqi-i shakhsi*) and "specified ideology" (*khatt-i mashy-i mushakhkhas*).[26]

Late in the Reza Shah era, with the crackdown on communist groups in Iran, in an unprecedented manner, Arani and Alavi, along with fifty-one of their comrades, known as group 53 (*53 nafar*), were arrested in 1937. Arani died (he was allegedly murdered) in prison, but with the Allies' abdication of Reza Shah, a new chapter was opened for arts in Iran—an era known for political freedom of expression, which in most historical narratives of Iranian theater marks its golden age.

1940s: The official era of activism of the Left

Muhammad Reza Pahlavi, the son of Reza Shah, replaced him in 1941, and for a decade the milieu was opened for political activities of different groups and the rivalry among the former Allied powers (Soviet Union, United States and Britain) in Iran in different realms, including culture and arts. During this interregnum, the Marxist doctrine in arts was practiced in two inter-connected groups: those belonging to the major communist party of Iran, the Tudeh Party, which was established in 1941 by a number of group 53 members including Alavi, and members of the Iran-Soviet Friendship Association, founded in 1940.

One of Tudeh's major platforms was arts and culture. Tracing their intel-lectual lineage to Arani and his periodical *Dunya*, many ideas initiated in the journal were realized by the party. A number of artists and literary figures of that era collaborated with the party, which in its heyday had several branches all around the country (including some for women and the youth), published several periodicals, and organized cultural events in the party's clubs as well as extravagant political meetings using various performative techniques. The party held social dancing events for fundraising purposes, as well as dance performances.[27] Theater and music were both considered a key part of the Tudeh's advocacy, and it sought to engage artists through meetings, commissioning, and performances held at the party's clubs.[28] Focusing on arts and culture, and with an organized mechanism of "publicity" (*tabliqat*), many ideas promoted by the Tudeh Party remain in the Iranian art discourse to this day.

The Iran-Soviet Friendship Association was another venue for artistic activities with leftist tendencies, especially due to its close association with

VOKS.[29] The association had several subcommittees related to the arts, including one for music and theater.[30] Recruiting theatrical and musical figures such as Nushin, Husayn Khayrkhah, Vaziri, and Ruhullah Khaliqi, this subcommittee's agenda included (1) introducing the state of arts in the USSR, (2) connecting the artists of the two countries; and (3) helping with the "progress" of music and theater in Iran through organizing lectures, the facilitation of visits by artists and scholars, and organizing performances and classes.[31] The journal *Payam-i Naw* (later renamed *Payam-i Nuvin*) was another outlet of the association to produce content in accordance with its objectives and to reflect on its activities. A number of artistic and literary figures, including Khayrkhah, Nushin, and Sarkis Janbazian, contributed to the journal.[32] While introducing the status of performing arts and key artistic figures and trends of the Soviet Union, the journal provided the groundwork for brainstorming ideas and ideals of arts in the new Iran through constant comparison with the paragon arts scene in the Soviet Union. Sharing similar ideologies and writers, the theater- and music-related content of the periodical echoed similar ideas as those of *Dunya* and the Tudeh Party.

This next section will provide a glimpse into the key tropes advocated and circulated in the discursive practices of the Tudeh Party and the Iran-Soviet Friendship Association in the 1940s. As will be seen in this introduction along with the appraisal of the ideal (committed) arts, a chain of equivalence was circulated around the *mutribs* (and their affects) which constantly sidelined them as counter-ideal figures of arts.

Committed arts and their affect

While the historian Muhammad Khusrawpanah recognizes Alavi's above-mentioned articles as the earliest instances of theorizing and configuring the concept of committed arts in Iran, theater as a political medium was used both during and after the Constitutional Revolution.[33] The idea of committed theater has usually been intertwined with an expectancy of a particular affect on its audience, evident in the following critique of the play *Arbab va Ra'iyat* (The peasant and the landowner) held by an early leftist group known as the Ijtima'iiun Party, in 1926: "In Iran most plays are *muzhik* and comedy, but this play made people cry over the impoverishment of the Iranian peasants who suffer from the tyranny of the landowners."[34] "*Muzhik* and comedy" refer to performances by the *mutribs*, and the statement indicates an urge for departure from the old *mutribi* performances to new committed forms with different theatrical affects, an attitude prevalent in the leftist writings on performing arts for the years to come. Arguably, this led to the formation of the nodal point "*ibtizal*" (degeneration).

It was with the establishment of the Tudeh Party and its wide investment in culture that for the first time theories of "committed arts" came to be practiced and assessed. While not all arts presented by the Party appeared as "committed," theater and music were upheld as important ideological mediums and used them for advocacy purposes.[35] One chapter of Tudeh concentrated specifically on musical activities, including its education, performance, and the selection of the party's march. According to the official newspaper of its central committee, *Namah'i Rahbar*, this chapter conducted a search for a composer to create a new march for the Tudeh in 1942, for which Parviz Mahmud's work was selected.[36]

In addition to ritualistic recitation of the march in routine Tudeh gatherings, the piece was also performed as part of symphonic concerts conducted by the musical figure Murtiza Hannanah (1923–89). A regular commentator on musical activities of the party, the critic Mansur Shakki, in his reviews of these concerts, echoed many of the ideas on art proposed earlier by Alavi in *Dunya*. Shakki held the symphonic orchestra of Tudeh as "a step towards a transformation (*tahavvul*)," which inflicted power, motion, and civilization on its audience, and was suitable for the joy, life, and freedom of the "Iran of tomorrow."[37] In configuring the ideals of today's music, he associated the Iranian arts (and music) of the past with feudalism, immorality, and economic and spiritual poverty and compared the affects on their audience with submission and servitude. Part of this assessment was based on the incapacity of Iranian instruments to satisfy the demands of contemporary times, reaffirming Alavi's position on music.[38]

The correlation between committed art and its specific affect on its audience was echoed in another piece by Shakki; reflecting on Mahmud's newly composed anthem for Tudeh, he praised the piece for embodying "a spirit of resistance and realism," and "filling the hearts with 'gratification' (*imtinan*)," concluding that the new march could facilitate a "decisive victory over 'social lethargy' (*khamud-i ijtima'i*) and 'backwardness' (*irtija'*)."[39]

Tudeh's committed theater at the time was very much fused with the name Nushin, given his multifaceted presence as a member of the party's central committee as well as his contributions as a theater director, educator, scholar, and writer for its periodical *Namah'i Rahbar*. One of Nushin's plays, which was of an obvious political nature, was *Ittihad-i Kargar va Rushanfikr* (The union of the worker and the intellectual, 1943), performed at the Tudeh's club. Centered on the laborer-employer relation, this piece had an enormous effect on its audience (comprised of workers and intellectuals), according to its reviewer Mihrigan (pen name). Analogizing the audience's reaction to a storm of screaming and clapping that shook the windows and the walls of the club, Mihrigan attested to the audience's deep sense of connection to the play and a harmony between the stage and the venue, the actors and the audience, and the play's content and their own spirit. Perhaps the combination of topic, cause, and the audience's response made this play the epitome of the notion of committed arts prefigured in *Dunya*.[40]

While not all of Nushin's plays were political, his artistry was generally viewed in light of him as a committed artist. Another interpretation of the high reception of Nushin and his artistry, and the promotion of theater in light of Alavi's earlier writings, could be the party's general attempts to improve the public's tastes. In addition to Nushin, Khayrkhah, Mustafa Oskoui, Mahin Dayhim, and others performed at the club, some of whom were also members of Nushin's theater companies, Firdawsi Theater (1947–48) and Sa'di Theater (1950–53), located at Lalehzar District.[41] Both companies were famous for production of the best plays of their time and for bringing a range of audiences including the political elite. According to my interviewees Anvar Khamah'i (b. 1903) and Muhammad Ali Amu'i (b. 1928), some of the rehearsals of Nushin's professional companies were held at Tudeh's club where their diverse members could watch them for free.[42]

As a successful theater director with a large spectatorship outside the party politics, Nushin's involvement with the party made him the defining figure of the new thriving status of theater as a committed art, one who single handedly saved Iranian theater from the degenerate performances of the *mutrib*s of the past. This attitude is best exemplified in the key Tudeh figure Ihsan Tabari's review on Nushin's rendition of J. B. Priestley's *Mustantiq* (An Inspector Calls) in 1947. The article was published in the monthly *Manhnamah'i Mardum*, an art and culture publication of the Tudeh Party. The script was translated by Alavi:

> In the Iran of our time, there is an obvious attempt to renew the face of life and reach towards a "new" (*nuvin*) civilization. In various social, scientific, philosophical, and artistic realms, such attempts have been happening on different levels. In each of these areas once in a while a champion emerges and leads the "transformation" (*tahavvul*) and movements. Dr. Arani led a social progressive movement and courageously initiated an intellectual resurrection. His bravery and nobleness were to a level that he could stand alone in the face of a decrepit society. His playground was history itself! Other comrades of his did this in more specific domains. An esteemed artist like Nushin has been making such honorable efforts in theater. He has been effective in establishing the true meaning of theater in our country, saving it from degeneration, tackiness, *muqallidi*, and clowning. Although he is not the only one who has made such an attempt, because the result of his struggle has been more stellar and precious, we can easily recognize him as the champion of upheaval of the art of theater in Iran.[43]

While a decade earlier Alavi had predicted Nushin's potential to save theater from its *mutribi* past, in the above quote he had already conquered the position of the champion of theater who had saved it from *ibtizal* with his commitment and discipline. In fact, Nushin actively distantiated his theater from *mutrib*s and the performers associated with them. For instance, according to his protégé Nusrat Karimi, Nushin did not allow a female actor—who also danced in a café—to join his company.[44] His impetus was to keep his stage "unpolluted."[45] Nushin's strict attitude and his tendency for high-quality art rather than solely considering its message is further conveyed in his rejection of the genre *pishpardahkhani*, a fusion of acting, dancing, and music, which he found to be "degrading to the literary and artistic environment of theater to the level of a cabaret."[46] Although this rejection put him in conflict with the party that sought to enforce political and ideological themes in his plays, he was nevertheless widely read as the epitome of a "committed artist," an attribute which to some extent was imposed on him.[47] It is within this context that Nushin's image dominated the 1940s theatrical scene and later represented the golden age of theater in Iran.

Sharing similar ideologies, members, and authors, many of the nodal points and signifiers of the discussed accounts were also replicated in the simultaneous realm of the Iran-Soviet Friendship Association, and their publication *Payam-i Naw*. Reporting on the state of theater, music, opera, and dance in various Soviet republics, comprehensive reports, essays, and travelogues in this journal recognized the Russian (October) Revolution of 1917 as the turning point that revolutionized the state of arts.[48]

Arts in the "contemporary" USSR at the time, referred to as "today" (*imruz*) were idealized as serving the people, while "yesterday" or the pre-revolution period, was perceived as the time when the arts were mere entertainment that catered to the interests of the ruling class and the aristocracy.[49] These descriptions of the Soviet utopia led to subconscious comparisons to the situation of arts in Iran and a blurring of boundaries of imagined ideals. It also resulted in the transmission of many concepts and assumptions frequently used for the Iranian art context, which found their way to the Soviet context.

One instance is a travelogue written by Ali-Asghar Garmsiri (1911–2000), a prominent theater artist, describing the status of theater in Soviet Azerbaijan.[50] Contrasting between pre- and post-October Revolution, he drew a dramatic picture of this difference of performances and their audiences of "yesterday" and "today": he described yesterday's performers as a group of arrant, disreputable men and women with overt sexuality, and recounted their performances as fake, inane, deceitful, degenerate (*mubtazal*), which inflicted moral corruption, indifference, and indolence on their audiences. He then contrasted the fakeness of "yesterday" performances with the truthfulness of the theater of his time. Describing the expansion of performing arts in Soviet Azerbaijan, he praised these art forms for incarnating modesty and in-depth social meaning. He reaffirmed his position by stating that "in the Azerbaijan of today, instead of just acting, the artists live on stage." While Garmsiri perhaps was referring to social realism promoted by the Soviet government at the time, such optimism towards this genre (social realism) was observable in other articles in *Payam-i Naw*.[51] His identification of the audiences of pre-revolution as "everyone but the real/actual people" and the post-revolution as "all people" resonated with the criticism of class-based theater spectatorship ciculated in *Dunya* and other Tudeh-affiliated sources. This attitude is evident in Khayrkhah's anecdote on the anniversary of the October Revolution in the same periodical, where he noted:

The October Revolution has transformed the history of human art and culture ... Arts and culture can only be useful if they are accessible to the people and serve them. Who can deny the fact that in a capitalist/bourgeois society art and culture also serve power and gold? In a capitalist society, not only can those who can afford them benefit from the arts, but also the artists give up their art and talent to serve capital interests and transform themselves into compulsive machines for the leisure and entertainment of a few aristocrats; in fact, instead of artists, they become clowns and buffoons.[52]

Such a connection between power and fortune and its transformative affect on artists (converting them to clowns and buffoons) was made quite often at the time. Arguably, this notion reinforces the idea of *mutrib*s as those who served the power, and their clowning and *mazhakah* as a consequence of serving the powerful, a connection clearly made by Oskoui and others. Another reference to buffoonery as belonging to the past is evident in Ihsan Tabari's lecture at the first congress of Iranian writers in 1947, held by Iran-Soviet Friendship Association, where he stated, "In medieval times, society required clowning and sycophancy from the artists, now it seeks leadership and struggle."[53]

Somewhere else Khayrkhah reiterated the ways in which in a socialist society art serves the people and is used as "an effective weapon to increase the level of culture and the public taste, a statement resembling the argument in Alavi's article, "New Art in Iran."[54] Also, a few articles published in *Payam-i Naw* reflected on the status of art in Iran, including one written by Nushin about the history of theater.[55]

With the beginning of the Cold War and the increase in tensions between Iran and the Soviet Union, the activities of the Tudeh Party and Nushin became more limited. After an attempted assassination of the Shah in 1948, Nushin was imprisoned. In 1950, he escaped to the USSR along with other core members of the party. During the coup d'état of 1953, Nushin's last company, the Sa'di Theater, was burned down, a dramatic event that only contributed to the mythic image of Nushin in the narratives of Iranian theater. Identified as the founder of "new" (*nuvin*) or "scientific" (*'ilmi*) theater in Iran, this image of Nushin in the discourse on Iranian theater is infused with his artistry, his political activism, and his imprisonment and exile to the Soviet Union. It is thus that his image came to represent the golden age of the Iranian theater scene (discursively located on Lalehzar Street), and his departure, which coincided with the coup, marked its decline.

*Mutrib*s and dancers as representatives of degeneration in the Lalehzar theaters

Concurrent with the departure of Nushin and the end of his theatrical activities, in the early 1950s, another incident is said to have occurred in Lalehzar:

the recruitment of *mutrib*s and their dancers onto the theater stage to perform in segments called *atraksiun* (attraction). This is said to have been to compensate for the loss of Lalehzar theaters' typical "elite or middle-class audience" as well as its status as a center for "high" cultural production. Historians link this situation to the following factors: (1) the expansion of Tehran, resulting in the repositioning of Lalehzar from a trendy area in the center of Tehran to an "outdated area" in "southern Tehran";[56] (2) the proliferation of competing media, including radio, television, and cinema;[57] (3) the lack of state support for private-sector theater;[58] (4) the mainstream, government-funded national-stage theater venues and schools moving to other areas in Tehran; and (5) the political pressure on theater after the coup.[59]

The anxiety over the loss of its audience and its consequent financial deficiency reverberated through the theater scene of Lalehzar's "golden era," discernable in the tone of the theater actor Hushang Sarang (1910–69), who in a 1952 article expressed sympathy for the managers of Tehran theater, wishing for "an invisible hand" (*dasti az ghayb*) to save the situation.[60] Finally, according to popular belief, the manager of the Tehran Theater, Nasrullah Vala (known as Dr. Vala) resolved the situation by hiring some "foreign" dancers to perform in his theater *atraksiun*s, thereby attracting new "popular" audiences.[61] It is important to note that the notion of a "popular" audience associated with post-1950 Lalehzar is discursively formed to contrast those "elite" audiences who were attracted to "real" theater as an "art."[62]

Highly condemning Vala's adoption of *atraksiun*, the press discourse as well as historical accounts diversely identified the background of "foreign dancers" in Lalehzar theaters as Turkish, German, Greek, or French.[63] Another key signifier in these accounts are the issues of morality that were raised due to the attire of the performers: some identified them as "nude" (*lukht*) while others described them as "half-naked" (*nimah-lukht*).[64]

Striving to survive the loss of their regular audiences and competing with Vala, other theater owners hired dancers and *mutrib*s, and *atraksiun* became prevalent and later took over Lalehzar. Consisting of dance, music, juggling, circus, and acrobatics, *atraksiun* took place before the show or in between curtains and was usually performed by outside performers and not the regular cast.[65] Furthermore, dance scenes in musical and comedy plays with a *mutribi* influence became prevalent in Lalehzar of this era, and *mutrib*s along with café and cabaret dancers from various artistic backgrounds were drawn to Lalehzar theaters. In addition to *ruhawzi*-style performances, many "exotic" types of dances—from invented and imaginary African dance to belly dance—were performed as part of *atraksiun*, and even as part of the plays themselves.[66] A number of cafés and cabarets as well as cinema theaters showing popular films were also added to the Lalehzar district in that era.

While dancers helped alleviate the financial shortcomings of the theaters, the idea of "naked" dancers in Lalehzar raised new moral issues and resentment from the arts community.[67] Some well-reputed actresses, for instance, left the Tehran scene to work in other cities.[68]

The art press, including *Sitarah'i Sinama*, frequently criticized the presence of dancers in Lalehzar for transforming the theater stage into that of a cabaret, upon which the "naked legs of foreign dancers" were displayed. The film director Samuel Khachikian, for instance, asserted: "The audience is so used to the white skin and the fine thighs of foreign beauties on the theater stage that any non-commercial production that does not feature dancers will go bankrupt."[69]

With the growing concern over foreign performers, the performance commissioner (*kumisiyun-i namayish*)—an entity under the ministry of state that was charged with regulating theaters, cinemas, and *attrakiuns*—banned the performance of foreign dancers on the theater stages in 1958, restricting them to venues (like hotels) mostly attended by foreign residents.[70]

Due to the government's restraint on the appearance of foreign dancers on theater stages, the Iranian dancers soon dominated the *atraksiun* scene of the theaters. As dancing paid better than acting, some Lalehzar actresses joined the *atraksiun*.[71] As Iran's entertainment district, Lalehzar was not just a place for theater artists and musicians, it also attracted non-artistic workers who sought employment. Coming from different cities, theater enthusiasts, women in need, and runaway kids were also hired to work backstage, either as extras or as performers-in-training.[72]

At first, many theater practitioners rejected hiring dancers. Among them was reportedly Isma'il Mihrtash, the musician and theater enthusiast who founded the Barbud Society. As one of the longest-running theater companies in Lalehzar, Mihrtash's company staged numerous nationalist operettas beginning in the 1920s (discussed in the previous chapter), training a number of the leading acting and musical figures of twentieth-century Iran.[73] It is reported that for years Mihrtash fought the idea of hiring (cabaret) dancers (*raqqas*) and advised other theater owners not to let the dancers into Iranian theaters, and thus not to allow people to get used to or deluded by naked bodies.[74] But in later years (after 1960), the Barbud Society could not survive financially without recruiting dancers.

The financial benefits of dancing in *atraksiun* also led some actors of the Barbud Society to dancing. This included my interviewee Rahilah, who, after several years of acting (which involved improvised acting, singing, and dancing), had to join the *atraksiun* scene as a dancer because the pay better covered her family's expenses. She expressed the discomfort among her theater colleagues:

> [The] first time that I performed as part of the *atraksiun* at the Barbud Society, my male co-actors sat in the last row of the house. They were ashamed of looking at me dancing naked. Later they asked the theater owner to raise my salary, so that I don't dance... but he was not able to do so ... my mom was sick and I did not have money to pay for her. I could not [did not want to] work as a prostitute, so I chose to dance.[75]

Compared to other actors, the *atraksiun* performers were treated differently and had to use separate changing rooms.[76] Getting paid much higher, dancing also led them to perform in other venues such as cafés and cabarets, as well as in the *mutribi* scene. Performing regularly on the respectable Barbud Society's stage, however, enhanced Rahilah's position in other arenas: the audience members who were interested in her work were able to hire her to perform at their private events through the *shadimani* agencies.[77]

Historical narratives of Lalehzar of the post-coup d'état

Though it attracted a popular spectatorship, Lalehzar after 1953 has been greatly neglected by theater scholars, as they dismiss its performance scene as cheap and worthless. The majority of historians stop their analysis right at 1953 and only offer a few general and often poetic sentences in reference to this Lalehzar scene, in which the cabaret dancer is ever present.[78] For instance, the committed-leftist theater historian Hiva Guran (pseudonym for Khosrow Shariari) asserted that after the coup dancers replaced the actors.[79] In these accounts, the presence of dancing bodies on theater stages signifies the "decline" (*uful*) of Lalehzar and its degeneration as a space for "actual theater" (*ti'atr bah mafhum-i vaqi'i*) as well as political art.[80] A chain of equivalence links the decline to the coup, the absence of the leading theater figure Nushin, and the introduction of dancers to the theater stage.[81] The association of Nushin's departure with the arrival of dancers to Lalehzar was best manifested in the commentary of the actor Zhaleh Muhtasham (a.k.a., 'Uluvv), who argued "when Nushin left, Lalehzar's [theater stage] was transformed to that of a cabaret."[82] Similar assertions are still made to this day.[83]

The political impetus behind some of these narratives and their influence by the pre-1950s leftist discourse is best summarized in the Marxist theater director Sa'id Sultanpur's critique of Pahlavi-era theater (and manifesto of political art), *A Way of Art, a Type of Thinking* (*Nu'i az hunar, nu'i az andishah*), in which he wrote:

> With the sudden [political] loss [referring to the coup], theater—as a part of this historical processes—broke down and was shut down, and the theatrical culture which was taking roots and growing lost its values. Concurrently, "unrestrained" (*biband va bar*) theaters grew with the direct support they received from the government. Theater became a venue for "recreation" (*tafrih*) and was filled with "dance and singing" (*raqs va avaz*), comedy, and acrobatics. The true meaning of theater faded under this "degeneration" (*ibtizal*), [a kind of] degeneration that was desired by the politics of the time. In this situation, theater became a constituent of colorful varieties that were surrounded by Turkish dancers ordered by the "high" (*vala*) policy makers. The audience not only did not receive any education but also lost their own remaining good manners.[84]

Not only did Sultanpur ascribe "degeneration" to theater post-coup, he also blamed the state for its "degeneration" of theater. Furthermore, the notion of degeneration in his narrative, as well as in Guran's, was signified by dance, music, fun, and recreation as performative elements that killed the spirit of resistance, a further expansion of the earlier leftist discourse that associated rejected *mutrib*s for their undesirable affects towards their audience.[85] A similar proclamation is evident in the account of Oskoui, who considered the insertion of "joy" (*tarab*) into theater (art) by *mutrib*s as a mistake and treachery to artistic and intellectual traditions, as well as an extrication of the creative aim and message of theater for future generations.[86] Parallel anti-*tarab* assertions are evident in the writing of Anvar Khamah'i, another Tudeh Party member.[87] Signifying "degeneration," in all abovementioned Marxist-influenced accounts, dancing and the comedic affects of clowning were seen as degrading to theater and as diverting the audience from actual reality.[88]

As a revolutionary theater practitioner, the "reality" for Sultanpur, who viewed theater as a medium for "class struggle" (*mubaraizah'i tabaqati*), had a political meaning. This applied not only to the Lalehzar of the post-coup era, but also to the official theatrical institutions and even the avant-garde theater scene of the 1960s and 1970s, which Sultanpur regarded as governmental, metaphysical, and apolitical. Instead, Sultanpur sought "an angry arts and literature, angry and even scary theater."[89]

Unlike the abovementioned leftist (revolutionary) theater accounts, the "nationalist" art press discourse did not interpret the presence of dancers as a conspiracy of the government or a marker of being apolitical. Still, the dancing body in the context of post-1950 Lalehzar signified degeneration in their discourse and was seen as having a potential contagious effect on the art environment.[90] This is evident in the film director Samuel Khachikian's resolution to the situation when in 1957 (only a few years after the recruitment of *mutrib*s and dancers to theater stage) he called for a "cultural reform" (*islahat-i farhangi*) to overcome the degeneration of theater and to bring about a return to the "golden past."[91]

Such attitudes led to the marginalization of *mutrib*s from the dominant arts discourse as they were considered to be ante-modern, illiterate, and degenerate. Although they were degraded in print and in official culture, with the expansion of urban sites of leisure, *mutribi* troupe members, along with their dancers, broadened their territory in the 1950s not only to the theater scene of Lalehzar, but also to all other realms of the urban popular culture of the Pahlavi era.[92] These included the cafés and cabaret scenes, which boomed after 1950, as well as the commercial cinema of the pre-revolutionary era that also re-emerged in 1950. Ever since, various new genres of popular music and dance, including Persian popular music, have developed with *mutribi* genealogies in style, rhythm, and affect, all of which have had a popular reception onstage but have also inherited some of the negative signifiers associated with the *mutrib*s, including degeneration. For their close ties to *mutribi* troupes, the cabaret dancers not only became heirs to these labels, but as will be discussed in the next two chapters, they brought new aspects to the social meanings and aesthetics of "degeneration."

Notes

1 The Maxist art discourse of pre-revolutionary Iran is by no means limited to the notions discussed in this chapter. Some important Marxist writings on the arts include Sirus Parham, *R'ialism va zidd-i ri'alism dar adabiyat* [Realism and anti-realism in literature] (Tehran: Nil, 1344/1965); Amir-Husayn Ariyanpur, *Jami'ah-shinasi-i hunar* [The sociology of art] (Tehran: Anjuman-i Kitab-i Danishkadah'i Hunarha-yi Ziba, 1354/1975); and Amir-Husayn Ariyanpur, "Zaminah'i ijtima'i-i shi'r-i farsi" [The societal foundations of Persian poetry], *Payam-i Nuvin* 7, no. 4, Farvardin 1344/March–April 1965.

2 See Sasan Fatemi, "Mutrib-ha az Safaviyah ta mashrutiyat" [*Mutribs* from the Safavid era to the constitutional movement], *Mahoor Music Quarterly* 12, no. 3 (Summer 2001); and Ardeshir Salehpour, *Taranah'i namayish-ha-yi pishpardah-khani dar iran, 1320–1332* [The lyrics of the *pishpardahkhani* in Iran, 1941–1953] (Tehran: Intisharat-i Namayish, 1389/2009), 120. As a result of the multiplicity of *mutribs'* performance mediums, including theater, music, and dance, those in musical studies, including the ethnomusicologist Sasan Fatemi, generally categor-ize these performances as *mutribi*, which accentuates the musical side of these troupes, while theater historians such as Bahram Bayza'i and Ardeshir Sahlepour highlight their *taqlid* ("imitation") theatrical aspects and *ruhawzi*. For the purpose of this study, I use the term *mutrib* which was also deployed by my interlocutors.

3 Naghmah, interview with the author, Tehran, 12 Shahrivar 1390/3 September 2011.

4 Bahram Bayza'i, *Namayish dar iran* [Theater in Iran] 5th ed. (Tehran: Intisharat-i Rawshangaran va Mutali'at-i Zanan, 1385/2006), 200; also see Ahmad, "Yadi-garan-i hunar-i qadim" [The remnants of the old art], *Sinama*, Mihr 1339/October 1960, 90–91; 91.

5 Ali-Naqi Vaziri, "Sukhanrani dar Madrasah'i 'ali-i Musiqi" [The lecture at the College of Music], Tir 1304/July 1925, reprinted in *Zindigi va asar-i Ali Naqi Vaziri* [Life and the works of Ali Naqi Vaziri], ed. Vahid Ayoubi (Tehran: Intisharat-i Kitabsary-i Nik, 1385/2006), 9.

6 Arif-i Qazvini, *Kulliyat-i divan-i shadravan Mirza Abulqasim Arif-i Qazvini* [Com-plete poetic works of Arif-i Qazvini], (Tehran: Amirkabir Publication, 1342/1963), 368.

7 Iraj Jannati Ata'i, "Mir-Sayfuldin Kirmanshahi," *Hunarha-yi Milli* 1, no.1, Murdad 1334/ July 1955, 23–34; 23.

8 Husayn Khayrkhah, *Tiknik-i Ti'atr* [Theater technique] (Tehran: Bungah-i Mat-bu'ati-i Naqus, 1330/1951); 4, 5.

9 Parviz Mansouri and Hasan Shirvani, *Fa'aliyat-ha-yi hunari dar panjah sal sha-hanshahi-i pahlavi* [Artistic activities in the fifty years of the Pahlavi dynasty: Theater, music, opera, and dance] (Tehran: Intisharat-i Vizarat-i Farhang va Hunar, 2535/1976), 17.

10 Mustafa Oskoui, *Sayri dar tarikh-i ti'atr-i iran* [Cross over the history of Iranian theater] (Tehran: Intisharat-i Anahita Oskoui Publication, 1378/1999), 287.

11 Oskoui, *Sayri dar*, 286.

12 Oskoui, *Sayri dar*, 289.

13 For instance, see "Saz va raqs-ha-yi milli," [National instruments and dances of Iran] *Musik-i Iran*, Bahman 1337/January 1959, 9.

14 Bayza'i, *Namayish*, 200.

15 Morteza Ahmadi, interview by the author, Tehran, 27 Murdad 1390/18 August 2011.

16 According to my interviewee Rahilah, some of the most famous pop singers of Iran were born to *mutrib* families; Rahilah, interview by the author, Tehran, 9 Shahrivar 1390/31 August 2011.

17 The foremost singer and dancer of the 1950s, Mahvash, was promoted by her husband who was a musician with a *mutribi* troupe; see Sasan Fatemi, *Jashn va*

musiqi dar farhang-ha-yi shahri-i iran [Festivity and music in the urban musical cultures] (Tehran: Mahoor Institute of Culture and Arts, 1393/2014), 207.

18 William O. Beeman, *Iranian Performance Traditions* (Costa Mesa, CA: Mazda, 2011), 231.

19 Firaydun Nakhuda, "Hunar va matiriyalism" [Art and materialism], *Dunya* 1, no.1, 1 Bahman 1312/ 21 January 1934, 20–25; 21–22.

20 Nakhuda, "Hunar va matiriyalism," 25.

21 Nakhuda, "Hunar va matiriyalism," 22.

22 Firaydun Nakhuda, "Hunar-i naw dar iran" [New art in Iran], *Dunya* 1, no.7, 1 Shahrivar 1313/23 August 1934, 221–22.

23 For more information on the modernist attitudes of Minbashiyan, see Keivan Aghamohseni, "Modernization of Iranian Music during the Reign of Reza Shah," in *Culture and Cultural Politics under Reza Shah: The Pahlavi State, New Bourgeoisie, and the Creation of a Modern Society in Iran*, ed. Bianca Davos and Christoph Werner (New York: Routledge, 2014), 73–94.

24 Firaydun Nakhuda, "Hunar-i naw," 22.

25 Firaydun Nakhuda, "Hunar dar Iran-i jadid" [Art in the new Iran], *Dunya* nos.10–12, Khurdad 1314/May 1935, 366–771; 369.

26 Alavi used "*dilhavasah*" (momentary pleasure) to describe the unpleasant state of music, and for that of theater he used "Amir-Arsalan." He rejected the idea of reform in Iranian music (*islah-i musiqi*), regardless of the choice of instruments (European or vernacular, such as the tar and tunbak), claiming that such attempts meant the degradation of European music to the level of Iranian music and that only meant regression. See Nakhuda, "Hunar dar iran-i jadid," 370–71.

27 "Rufaqa-yi hizbi!" [Party comrades!], *Namah'i Rahbar* 4, no. 797, 3 Shahrivar 1325/25 August 1946, 7.

28 "Bihtarin Namayishnamah'i risidah bah dabirkhanah'i tablighat-i kull" [The best plays/scripts received by the secretariat of the main office of advocacy], *Namah'i Rahbar* 4, no. 765, 21 Tir 1325/12 July 1946, 4; "Hunarpishigan-i 'uzv-i hizb-i tudah" [Actors of the Tudeh party], *Namah'i Rahbar* 4, no. 765, 21 Tir 1325/12 July 1946, 5; "Kunfirans-i duhaftigi-i sazman-i javanan-i tudah'i iran" [The bi-weekly conference of the youth organization of the Tudeh], *Namah'i Rahbar* 4, no. 766, 23 Tir 1325/14 July 1946, 3; Mihrigan, "Hunar-i bi-pirayah" [A low-key art], *Namah'i Rahbar* 1, no. 77, 3 Khurdad 1322/ 25 May 1943, 1–2.

29 Founded in 1925, VOKS was a Soviet governmental institution to foster cultural and artistic relations with other countries.

30 "Asasnamah'i anjuman-i ravabit-i farhagni-i iran ba ittihad-i jamahir-i shawravi," [The charter of Iran-Soviet Friendship Association], *Payam-i Naw* 1, no.1, 1 Murdad 1323/23 July 1944, 4, 63; 63.

31 "Barnamah'i karha-yi kumisiyun-i musiqi, t'iatr va sinama" [The agenda of the commission of the music, theater and cinema], *Payam-i Naw* 1, no. 1, 1 Murdad 1323/23 July 1944, 64. Sa'id Nafisi, "Tarikhchah'i anjuman-i ravabit-i farhagni-i iran ba ittihad-i jamahir-i shawravi," [The chronicle of Iran-Soviet Friendship Association], *Payam-i Naw* 1, no. 1, 1 Murdad 1323/23 July 1944, 58–64; 59. Husayn Khayrkhah held classes at the association; see "Guzarish-i hay'at-i mudirah'i anjuman-i ravabit-i farhangi-i iran ba ittihad-i jamahir-i shawravi" [Reports by the board of directors of the Iran-Soviet Friendship Association], *Payam-i Naw* 4, nos. 2–3, Urdibihisht-Khurdad 1327/April–May 1948, 112–141, 119.

32 Nafisi, "Tarikhchah," 61.

33 Muhammad Khusrawpanah, "Saraghaz-i ri'alizm-i susiyalisti dar iran" [The emergence of social realism in Iran]," *Faslnamah'i Zindahrud*, no. 52, Pa'iz-Zimistan 1389/Fall–Winter 2010, 199–228; 206.

34 The article was originally published in *Tufan* on 24 Azar 1305/16 December 1926. See Khusrawpanah, "Saraghaz," 204.

35 "Marsh-i tudah, shumarah'i yik" [Tudeh Party's first march], *Namah'i Rahbar* 1, no. 46, 12 Farvardin 1322/2 April 1943, 1.

36 "Agahi-i anjuman-i musiqi-i tudah" [Advertisement by the Musical Association of Tudeh], *Namah'i Rahbar* 4, no. 679, 8 Farvardin 1325/29 March 1946, 3; "Da'vat az kulliyah'i ahangsazan-i Iran bah manzur-i sakhtan-i yik ahang-i muhayij baray-i hizb-i tudah'i iran" [An invitation to all composers of Iran for the creation of an invigorating music (anthem) for the Tudeh Party of Iran], *Namah'i Rahbar* 4, no. 710, 16 Urdibihisht 1325/6 May 1946, 4.

37 Mansur Shakki, "Musiqi-i tudah baray-i hamah" [Tudeh's music for everyone], *Namah'i Rahbar* 4, no. 710, 16 Urdibihisht 1325/6 May 1946, 6.

38 Nakhuda, "Hunar va matiriyalism," 22.

39 Mansur Shakki," Duvvumin kunsirt-i sanfunik-i tudah" [Tudeh's second symphonic concert], *Namah'i Rahbar* 4, no. 740, 20 Khurdad 1325/10 June 1946, 1–2; 2.

40 Mihrigan, "Hunar-i bi-pirayah," 3. Nushin also wrote the play *Khurus-i Sahar*. The book was reviewed by an author of *Payam-i Naw*, who called it a unique masterpiece that bravely condemned the bourgeoisie and uncovered their hypocrisy. See Sa'id Nafisi,"Abdulhusayn-i nushin, khurus-i sahar" [Abdulhusayn Nushin, Chanticleer], *Payam-i Naw* 3, no. 7, Urdibihisht 1326/April 1947, 113. The script itself was also published in the journal.

41 "Kunfirans-i duhaftigi-i," 3.

42 Anvar Khamah'i, interview with the author, Tehran, 31 July 2014; Muhammad Ali Amu'i, interview with the author, Tehran, 9 Murdad 1393/14 July 2014.

43 Ihsan Tabari, "Nushin va namayish-i jadid-i u bah nam-i mustantiq" [Nushin and his new play entitled *The Inspector*], *Mahnamah'i Mardum* 2, no. 4, 1 Day 1326/23 December 1947, 98–101; 98.

44 As Nusrat Karimi reports, the woman was Tamara, an Azerbaijani actress with the Tehran Theater who received ballet training in Russia. Nusrat Karimi, "Khatirat-i Nusrat Karimi darbarah'i ustad Nushin" [Nusrat Karimi's memories about Master Nushin], in *Yadnamah'i Abdulhusayn-i Nushin, bunyanguzar-i ti'atr-i Nuvin* [Abdul-husayn Nushin, the father of the new theater], ed. Nusrat Karimi (Tehran: Nashr-i Namak, Badraqah'i Javidan, 1387/2008), 70.

45 As Karimi describes, Nushin also insisted his female company members get married so that people were assured that his theatrical environment was clean. Karimi, "Khatirat," *Yadnamah'i*, 70.

46 Karimi, "Muqaddamah" [introduction], *Yadnamah'i*, 13.

47 Karimi, "Khatirat," 68.

48 Sa'id Nafisi, "Hunarpishigan-i azarbijani dar tihran" [Azarbaijani artists in Tehran], *Payam-i Naw* 1, no. 1, 1 Murdad 1323/23 July 1944, 44–46; 46; "Bulbul muhmammaduf, hunarpishah'i milli-i azarbaijan" [Bulbul Muhammaduf, the national artist of Azarbaijan], *Payam-i Naw* 1, no. 5, 1 Azar 1323/22 November 1944, 53–4; 53; "Adabiyat-i milli dar ittihad-i jamahir-i shawravi" [The Soviet Union's national literature], *Payam-i Naw* 2, no.1, Azar 1324/December 1945, 1–18; 10.

49 "Si sal t'iatr-i shawravi" [Thirty years of Soviet theater], *Payam-i Naw* 4, no. 1, Farvardin 1327/March 1948, 120–23; 120.

50 Ali-Asghar Garmsiri, "T'iatr-i azarbaijan-i shawravi" [The theater of Soviet Azarbijan], *Payam-i Naw* 1, no. 5, Azar 1323/November 1944, 61–2; 53.

51 Ihsan Yarshater, "Astruvfski diram nivis-i mashhur-i rusiyah, 1823–1886" [Astrovsky, the famed playwright of Russia, 1823–1886], *Payam-i Naw* 4, no.2, Urdibihisht 1327/April 1948, 44–52; 51.

52 "Afkar va ihsasat-i rawshanfikran va mardan-i mutaraqqi-i iran darbarah'i inqilab-i uktubr va ittihad-i jamahir-i shawravi" [The ideas and emotions of Iran's intellectuals and progressive-minded men about the Soviet Union], *Payam-i Naw* 3, no. 11, Mihr-Aban 1326/October–November 1947, 4–8; 132–40; 133.

53 Ihsan Tabari, "Darbarah'i intiqad va mahiyati- hunar va ziba'i-i hunari" [On criticism and essence of art and aesthetics], published in the proceedings of Nukhustin kungirah'i nivisandigan-i iran [The first congress of the Iranian writers], Tir 1325/July 1946 (Tehran: 1325), 233–64, 256.

54 Hussyn Khayrkhah, "Jashn-i panjah salah'i ti'atr-i hunari-i akadimik-i muskaw bah nam-i gurki" [The celebration of the fiftieth anniversary of the artistic theater of the Academy of Moscow, Maxim Gorky], *Payam-i Naw* 4, nos. 6–7, Mihr-Bahman 1327/September 1948–January 1949, 101–16.

55 Abdulhusayn Nushin, "T'iatr dar iran" [Theater in Iran], *Payam-i Naw* 1, no. 6, Day 1323/December 1944, 30–34; Khayrkhah, "Jashn-i panjah," 101–16.

56 See Hiva Guran, *Kushish-ha-yi nafarjam: sayri dar sad sal ti'atr-i iran* [Futile endeavours: A journey across one hundred years of theater in Iran] (Tehran: Intishahrat-i Agah, 1360/1981), 185.

57 Salehpour, *Taranah'i namayish-ha-yi,* 520.

58 Mas'ud Dilkhah, "Jaygah va naqsh-i mardum, hunarmandan va dawlat dar shiklgiri va tusi'ah'i ti'atr-i khususi" [The role and place of people, artists, and government in the formation and development of private theater], in *Majmu'ah maqlat-i ti'atr-i khususi dar iran* [A selection of articles on private theater in Iran: On the occasion of the conference of private theater in Iran], ed. Mehrdad Rayani Makhsus (Tehran: Intisharat-i Namayish, 1388/2009), 224.

59 Salehpour, *Taranah'i namayish-ha-yi,* 518.

60 Hushang Sarang, "Ti'atr-i muhtazar ra daryabid" [Attend to the dying theater!], *Sitarah'i Sinama,* no. 1, 1953, 8.

61 Earlier cases of invited foreign dancers are Carmen and Kunchita (from Spanish and French backgrounds, respectively), who came to act in the film production *Buhlul* in 1945, both of whom were recruited by the director and film producer Muhammad Shabpareh, as well as the dance troupe which was brought as an *atraksiun* to the Tehran Theater, then under the direction of Dr. Vala. According to Habibullah Nasirifar, *atraksiun* first started in Lalehzar in 1958. See Habibullah Nasirifar, *Ustad Isma'il-i Mirtash va Jami'ah'i Barbud* [Master Isma'il Mitrash and the Barbud Society] (Tehran: Nashr-i Dunya-yi Naw: 1383/2004), 18.

62 My interviewee Rahilah described the "popular audiences" of Lalehzar as those who came to watch *atraksiun*. This included travelers who came to Tehran via the major bus terminal nearby, including soldiers. Guran identified these audiences as those who sought "recreation" (*sargarmi*) and "amusement" (*tafannun*). See Guran, *Kushish-ha-yi nafarjam,* 185.

63 For instance, see "Yik nishast ba yik dust" [A meeting with a friend], *Sitarah'i Sinama,* no. 104, 19 Isfand 1335/10 March 1957, 17; Samuel Khachikian, "In pardah'i jandar" [This living curtain], *Sitarah'i Sinama,* 18 Farvardin 1336/7 April 1957, 16; and Sa'id Sultanpur, *Nu'i az hunar, nu'i az andishah* [A kind of art, a kind of thought] (Tehran, 1349/1970), 33.

64 See, for instance, "Raqs-i lukht" [Naked dance], *Sitarah'i Sinama,* no. 103, 12 Isfand 1335/3 March 1957, 31; "Shahr-i farang" [Peep show], *Sitarah'i Sinama,* no. 105, Nawruz 1336/March 1957, 36; and Siamak Pourzand, "Kunkur-i hunari-i t'atr-i tihran va majara-yi an" [The art exam of Tehran's theater and its adventures], *Sitarah'i Sinama,* 1 Urdibihisht 1336/21 April 1957, 16.

65 Rahilah, interview with the author.

66 For instance, see "Shab, tihran va adam-ha" [The night, Tehran, and humans], *Sipid va Siyah,* 26 Isfand 1345/17 March 1967, 90–91; 90.

67 For example, see Khosrow Parvizi, "Didari az mahzun" [A meeting with Mahzun], *Sitarah'i Sinama,* no. 109, 8 Urdibisht 1336/28 April 1957, 8, 30; Khosrow Parvizi, "Didari az ziya', aktur-i baznishastah" [A meeting with Ziya', the retired actor], *Sitarah'i Sinama,* no. 112, 29 Urdibisht 1336/19 May 1957, 9.

68 "Falgush" [Eavesdropper], *Sitarah'i Sinama,* no.108, 1 Urdibihish 1336/21 April 1957, 3.

69 Khachikian, "In pardah'i jandar," 16.
70 For the state's restrictions on foreign dancers, see "Sanad-i shumarah'i 149" [Document number 149], 4 Tir 1337/25 June 1958, in *Asnadi az musiqi, ti'atr va sinama dar iran, 1300–1357* [Documents on music, cinema, and theater in Iran, 1300–57], 3 vols., ed. Ali-Akbari Baigi and I. Muhammadi (Tehran: Sazman-i Chap va Intisharat-i Vizarat-i Farhang va Irshad-i Islami, 1379/2000), 2: 700–706; 701 and 702.
71 Naghmah, interview with the author; Rahilah, interview with the author.
72 Naghmah, interview with the author.
73 This includes leading singers such as Mohammadreza Shajarian, Marziyah, and Muhammad Nuri, and the leading cinema actors of the 1950s, including Majid Muhsini, Hamid Qanbari, and Shahin.
74 "Shab, tihran," 90. See also Nasirifar, *Ustad Isma'il-i*, 18.
75 Rahilah, interview with the author.
76 Ibid.
77 Ibid.
78 Salehpour's book on *pishpardahkhani* is a recent example of such a manner; he describes Lalehzar after 1953 as such: "Lalehzar turned into a funhouse (*tarabkhanah*) where trick shows, acrobatics, circus, half-naked dancers, and stimulating fast-beat music entertained the audience. Theater became full of 'dance and singing' (*raqs va avaz*)." Salehpour then concludes that "this was the bitter end for the short golden era of Iran's theater." See Salehpour, *Taranah'i namayish-ha-yi*, 520.
79 Guran, *Kushish-ha-yi nafarjam*, 187.
80 The term "decline of Lalehzar" (*uful-i lalehzar*) was also used in the press. For instance, see "Dastan-i lalahzar zamani keh kartiyah latan-i tihran bud" [The story of Lalehzar when it was Tehran's Quartier Latin], *Ayandigan*, 19 Mihr 2536/11 October 1977, 8; "Actual theater" versus commercial productions with dance is brought up in several accounts; for instance, see Parvizi, "Didari az," 8.
81 For "chain of equivalence," see Louise Jane Phillips and Marianne W. Jorgenson, *Discourse Analysis as Theory and Method* (London: Sage, 2002), 43.
82 Khosrow Parvizi, "Didar-i haftah" [The meeting of the week], *Sitarah'i Sinama*, 16 Tir 1336/7 July 1957, 8–9; 9.
83 See Davud Rashidi, "Ba raftan-i nushin ti'atr-i 'ilmi ham az iran raft" [With Nushin's departure, the scientific theater also left Iran], in *Yadnamah'i*, 138–41; 140.
84 Sultanpur, *Nu'i az hunar*, 33.
85 Guran, *Kushish-ha-yi nafarjam*, 187.
86 Oskoui, *Sayri dar*, 291.
87 Anvar Kaham'i, "Khatirat va tafakkurat darbarah'i nushin" [Memories and thoughts about Nushin], in *Yadnamah'i*, 195–212; esp. 199, 201.
88 Khosrow Parvizi, "Vusuq, hunarmandi kah kamtar mishinasid" [Vusuq, the artist you know very little about], *Sitarah'i Sinama*, 18 Farvardin 1336/7 April 1957, 8; Khachikian, "In pardah'i jandar," 16.
89 Sultanpur, *Nu'i az hunar*, 50.
90 For instance, see Pourzand, "Kunkur-i hunari," 16.
91 Khachikian, "In pardah'i jandar," 16.
92 With all of the reforms in the twentieth century, the *mutribs*' genealogical relation to those of centuries prior had caused most of the performing arts associated with *mutribi* to be classified as "traditional."

4   The cabaret dancer in her quotidian life

The twentieth century was a period of rapid cultural transformations in Iran. Urban expansion, the proliferation of transportation and media technologies, and social and political reform of the country contributed to the creation of new modes of culture, cultural industries, categorizations, and artistic and moral evaluation. Among these new spheres, Tehran's nightlife, which expanded especially in 1950s, was both an economic and a cultural venture. Linked (discursively) to the entertainment and sex industries it became the signifier of urban "immorality" in the social, political, and cultural discourse of the twentieth century. The cabaret dancer, as the most visible representative of this sphere, was perceived as the "contentious commodity" of this newly emerged culture. While a metonym of the "failure" of modern urban life, the cabaret dancer attracted multitudes to the nightlife venues.

The multifaceted *raqqas*, or cabaret dancer, was in fact associated with and participated in various milieus (particularly in Tehran), constituting various aspects of popular culture in twentieth-century pre-revolutionary Iran. These included the cafés (*kafah*s) and cabarets; and the pre-revolutionary commercial cinema, *film-i farsi*; as well as the multi-faceted *mutribi* performance spheres and the post-1950 Lalehzar theatrical scene (discussed in Chapter 3).

The notion of "popular" was arguably not insinuated in these spheres, but was a by-product of a network of power-knowledge that throughout the twentieth century sought to define the "elite," the "modern," and the "national" and/or "committed" culture. In fact, these spheres of "popular," and the performances and performers associated with them, have acted as the "other" against whom the national and its artistic subjects have constructed themselves: at times they were labeled "old," "traditional," or "un-modern" to contrast and signify the "modern"; they were "marginalized" to highlight the mainstream; marked as "illiterate," "degenerate," and "low culture" to emphasize the "elite" and "high culture"; and measured as "vice" to mark the societal ideals of "virtue."

While this process of "othering" adds to the significance of studying these performance spheres and the cabaret dancer as their liaison, it imposes its own historiographical challenges. Part of the problem arises from the fact that the press, practitioners, educators, and even historians, or those who deemed cabaret "immoral" in contrast to the polite "national" cultures of twentieth-century Iran, were the main producers and audience of the written discourse on the subject; an issue which was explored with regard to the theatrical scene of Lalehzar post-1950 in Chapter 3. Thus, based on their own perceptions, they have regarded the cultures that they considered "other" in their daily practice to be "un-modern" and "immoral," unimportant, and even worthless to study. Meanwhile, the cabaret dancers—left with the dominant social position of the "other," and with a lack of literacy or access to the public written discourse—are almost mute in the dominant social discourse.

For this study, I consulted with several performers who were involved in the *mutribi* scene, Lalehzar theaters, café and cabaret scenes, and pre-revolutionary commercial cinema. While their insights tremendously guided me and helped me connect the documents and better understand the spheres of performances, at times I found them reacting according to or echoing the same stereotypes ascribed to these spheres; it was as if their reality has been shaped by these discourses. Apart from some such instances, however, this study largely benefited from the presence of their voices for counterbalancing the dominant discourse.

Focusing further on the female cabaret dancer as a multifaceted socio-historical character who emerged in twentieth-century Iran, this chapter continues the discussion of Chapter 3 by exploring the dancers in the *kafah* and cabaret scenes of Tehran's nightlife, which, with ties to the prostitution realm, were considered dissolute in the cultural discourse. It also examines the ways her commonly constructed "out-of-control" body and acts were subjected to a variety of disciplining mechanisms. Lastly, this chapter discusses the ways her dancing body was commodified along with her image and myth, upon which her male audiences' fantasies were projected. While exploring the rhetoric surrounding her and the cabaret sphere, I also explore a chain of equivalence surrounding the dancer that included "nakedness" (*lukhti*), "eroticism" (*shahvat*), "prostitution" (*fahsha*), "degeneration" (*ibtizal*), as well as identification of her audience as "popular," all of which formed her social narrative.

Dancers in the *kafah* (café) and cabaret settings

In addition to the theater and *mutribi* scenes (discussed in Chapter 3), the *kafah*s and cabarets were the main spheres of the *raqqas*'s performance, where they often danced to the music of *mutrib*s. Employing female dancers in café settings seems to have begun in the 1940s. While Hotel Palas is said to have had recruited foreign dancers for the first time in Iran, by 1947 both Café Pars and Café Palas (perhaps located at the abovementioned hotel) held dance performances by Iranian and Egyptian dancers, discernable from the religiously oriented press that disavowed them.[1] The audiences of these cafés, in which people of different classes intermingled, were generally interpreted as "modernized" (*mutajaddid*).[2]

In the mid-1950s, with the increase in nightlife activity, the café culture appears to have been bifurcated to "upper-" and "lower-"class venues.[3] Later, the cabarets replaced the upper-class cafés.[4] The "class" of these venues was to a large degree based on their location and facilities, type of *atraksiun* (attraction), and the price range, as well as the stereotypes associated with their "monde."

Depending on their status and salaries, some dancers worked in the "upper-class" cabarets while others worked for the cafés known as *saz-va-zarbi/saz-zan-zarbi*, referring to their performances by the *mutribi* troupes. *Saz-va-zarbi kafah*s, which I will herein refer to as *kafah*, seemingly grew in the 1950s. This was concurrent with the *mutribi* troupes' increasing presence in Lalehzar theaters. These *kafah*s, with performances by the troupe members, boomed in some areas of Tehran including the Lalehzar district and nearby streets as well as close to the prostitution district of Shahr-i Naw.[5] In addition to music, the *kafah*s hosted a wide range of dances ranging from vernacular Iranian dances to exotic dance styles, including belly dance. One of my interviewees, Naghmah, noted that each *kafah* had about fifteen to twenty performers, and the majority of *kafah* performances featured dancers.[6] To view performances, the audience members had to purchase food and drink. My other interviewee, the late Morteza Ahmadi, described the food and drink in these cafés as being affordable and consisting of vernacular vodka (*'araq*) and beer, and a variety of foods, ranging from *jigote* and *ragoute*, to vernacular *sirabi-va-shirdun*, *chulukabab*, and *dil-va-jigar*.[7]

As revealed by my conversations with my interviewees Rahilah and Naghmah, who worked in this environment, these *kafah*s were dominated by male audiences.[8] An important signifier within the *kafah* discourse was the audience members of these venues. As regularly depicted in the fictitious *film-i farsi* genre, some of the prominent stereotypical figures identified as *kafah* audience included groups of *jahil*s and *kulah-makhmali*s. *Jahil* was a masculine social character-type of the Pahlavi era, with a range of characteristics ranging from chivalry and fairness to hooliganism. He was often portrayed as wearing a black suit, a white shirt, and a black velvet brim hat—making the character also known as *kulah-makhmali* (literally velvet-hatted).

According to Sasan Fatemi, this group particularly found greater presence in this society after the abdication of Reza Shah.[9] Occupations discursively ascribed to the audience members of these venues included wholesale dealers of fruits, vegetables, and meat (*bar-furush* or *mayduni*); soldiers; and construction workers (*'amalah*).[10] Accordingly, the *kafah* dancers were stereotyped as "favored by wholesalers" (*mayduni-pasand*) and "having large hips, big breasts, and fat calves," as the *kafah* audience was stereotyped as being interested in women with corpulent characteristics.[11] Further Marxist-driven political ascription to the members of the *kafah* audience was to associate them with the culture of *lumpenproletariat*: being a fan of dance, including *babakaram*, for their own practice, and enjoying Indian and Arabic café dancing, the audience of *kafah*s was recognized as those who were not productive forces, were not class conscious, and thus did not participate in the class struggle.[12]

In the (mainstream) social imagination and in the common cultural classifications, the *kafahs* often were associated with the culture of "southern Tehran." In this discursive ascription, *jahils* were the representative of the cultural consumers of "southern Tehran"—who also influenced cultural production.[13] Another implication of the *kafahs* of "southern Tehran" or "the lower city" (*pa'in shahr*) were the venues close to or inside the prostitution district of Shahr-i Naw (which was located in southwest Tehran). This was not to indicate the actual geographical area of southern Tehran, but rather, to implicitly denote venues affected by "prostitution." As articulated by Naghmah, the *kafahs* identified with the second interpretation were not attended by women as customers, as their presence in those venues could have been construed as their sexual availability or "looseness." While there are no statistical reports on the location and the number of *kafahs* in Tehran, an article in *Ittila'at-i Haftigi* estimated about 50,000–70,000 *kafah* visitors in Tehran in 1974.[14] This lack of precise statistics is due to the fact that there was no particular standardization for holding performances at food-related business, such as restaurants, cafés, or hotels, where owners could add a stage and hold "shows" and *atraksiun*.[15]

With the premise of a "family-friendly" ambience and a high-quality *atraksiun*, cabarets (*karabat*), conversely, attracted female as well as male attendants.[16] Constructed as "classy" venues—and as an alternative to the *kafahs*—cabarets, which came about from the 1940s and especially after 1960, arguably replaced the earlier "upper-class" musical cafés. Cabarets often promoted a cosmopolitan image, signified by their regular "non-Iranian" performers (see Figures 4.1–4.2).[17] The "class" of cabarets, as well as the type and the quality of their *atraksiun*, depended on several factors, including the location of the venue, the tastes of the monde that attended them, and the type and price range of the food and drink.[18] Serving a variety of expensive and high-quality drinks and dishes, the cabarets were able to select their participants from those who could afford the price. The menu of a cabaret would include foreign alcohols, like whiskey and gin, as well as steak, fish, and *jigote*, along with Iranian rice and kebab (*chulu-kabab*) and rice and stew (*chulu-khurisht*) (see Figure 4.3).[19] The price range was evaluated by the government, according to a number of variables, including the décor, the quality of the performances, and the food and drink served.[20] According to a book compiled by a government institution dependent on the Ministry of Culture and Arts in 1977, Tehran had eleven cabarets, which were concentrated in three areas of Tehran, including the Lalehzar area in central Tehran, the outskirts of the red-light district of Shar-i Naw, Sirus Intersection, and along Pahlavi Avenue (municipal districts 2, 4, and 9).[21] Another report estimated that seven cabarets existed in the Lalehzar district in 1977.[22] Periodicals and some other accounts, however, do not agree on the number of cabarets in Tehran in the 1970s, as it was sometimes hard to distinguish between cafés and cabarets as a number of cafés and restaurants with better decoration and *atraksiun*s also called themselves cabarets.

Figure 4.1 A foreign group performing at Shecufeh Now, 1970s
Ida Meftahi's personal archive.

Regardless of class and types of food and drink, the key commonality of both types of venues was the *atraksiun*, symbolized by the female dancers who joined this scene from various parts of the country and the world. While some of these women, including those from *mutribi* troupes and theater actresses, had performance experience, the majority of the early cabaret dancers had no expertise other than their home-based familial dances. Daring to climb onto the stage to perform in the locus of everyone's attention, they had to train themselves in a variety of trendy "foreign" and "exotic" genres and dance styles, including Indian, Arabic, Spanish, and even American, by watching films as well as each other.[23] As the dancers' age, beauty, onstage behavior and outfits contributed to their reception, they were subjugated by their employers to a certain disciplinary corporeal regime, including the wearing of obligatory "scant" clothing.

The emerging nightlife of Tehran not only generated new jobs for performers, but also provided opportunities for those with business ideas to create large establishments and to find enormous power within the entertainment industry. This is exemplified by the cabaret tycoons Sayyid-Baba Hijazi (the owner of Shecufeh Now) and Muhammad-Karim Arbab (the owner of Bakara-Mulan Ruzh), both of whom rose to prominence, from humble beginnings, through their success in the entertainment industry.

Figure 4.2 The dancer Katayoun
Ida Meftahi's personal archive.

According to Fatemi, Hijazi, a low-income government employee, started with a traditional *qahvah-khanah*, inviting performances by the indigenous-style *lutis*, animal entertainers, folk musicians, and low-ranking *mutrib*s, turning it later into Kafah Shecufeh, with performances by major *mutribi* troupes. Making arrangements with hotels that brought foreign performers to Iran in the early 1950s, he then transformed his *kafah* into the largest cabaret of Iran in 1957, where famed Iranian pop singers and internationally known

Figure 4.3 Performance at the *cabaret Lidu*
Ida Meftahi's personal archive.

foreign troupes performed, attracting diverse audiences.[24] Similarly, Arbab,
the famed cabaret and cinema owner and later film producer, rose from a job
as a publishing laborer to a concert organizer for the then-emerging performer Mahvash.[25] He then bought an amphitheater in Lalehzar to convert it
into a venue for the Mulan Ruzh cabaret dancing (*kabarah-dansing-i mulan
ruzh*), in which famed singers such as Vigen, Dilkash, and Susan performed.

Perhaps due to cases similar to the aforementioned, the powerful cabaret owner became a symbol of the "nouveau riche," one who emerged in the class shuffling enhanced by the expansion of the entertainment industry of the Pahlavi era. Construed as a negative character, the cabaret owner was a recurring figure in the commercial cinema of pre-revolutionary Iran (which will be discussed in Chapter 5). In the last decade of the Pahlavi era, a number of famous singers who regularly performed at cabarets opened their own cabaret institutions.[26]

Regulating the nightlife

The venues associated with nightlife, as well as their performers and audiences/participants, were regulated by the ministry of state as well as the municipal police (*shahrbani*) and local police stations (*kalantari*). The laws for public spaces enforced on *kafah*s and cabarets obliged the owners to obtain licenses for the operation of their businesses. These venues were assigned to particular ranks based on their *atraksiun*; type and quality of food and drink, decoration, building facilities, and hygiene levels. The owners of these cafés and restaurants were responsible for only allowing the entrance of customers over eighteen years and policing them against rude utterances and lewd manners.[27] Such policing also extended to the genres of dance the customers could publicly practice in these venues, as exemplified by the banning of playing rock 'n' roll as well as the practicing of rock 'n' roll or hula hoop in the late 1950s.[28]

The *atraksiun* performances were also supervised and previewed by the performance commissioner of the ministry of state.[29] Both the performance commissioner and the venues themselves were responsible for making sure that the dancers did not appear onstage "semi-naked" (*nimah 'uryan*) or donning outrageous clothing.[30] In one case, when the venue did not require its Turkish dancers to wear more covered clothing upon the performance commissioner's earlier notice, the performance was cut short and the performers were deported back to Turkey.[31]

Atraksiun performers were also regulated offstage: while various sectors of the government and the police were in charge of validating the passport, travel documents, and duration of stay of foreign performers, a 1966 law (passed specifically for them) allowed them to perform only in the venue which sponsored their travel.[32] Iranian cabaret dancers were also monitored offstage through their work permits, which obliged them to take compulsory medical exams every few months.[33] This was to make sure that the performers were not transmitting venereal diseases in case they engaged in sexual acts with their audience members.

While the law strictly prohibited the public venues from facilitating or providing any means for immoral or unchaste (sexual) activities, and from hiring or giving wages to people for this purpose, it was common that some venues furthered their profit by selling their male customers the right to drink with the dancers.[34] This off-the-record practice, which was called *fishkhuri* or *jiton-khuri*, also meant that a dancer was agreeing to an unofficial contract that required her to meet with the male customer afterwards. As described by Rahilah, to conceal the illegal act of *fishkhuri* from the authorities, the guard at the front door had to turn on an alarm lamp when the police were approaching.[35] Since each dancer drank with several customers every night, handling these customers—either by engaging in an intimate encounter with them, or avoiding them by inventing reasons to leave—outside of the *kafah* was a risky business, often resulting in dangerous situations for the dancers, including fights between them and the audience members. The police kept watch in order to stop such incidents, but did not always succeed in preventing them. To lower the hazards of *fishkhuri* for the dancers, and to prevent their intoxication in the process, the waiters often poured water for them while serving alcohol for the customer.[36]

Fishkhuri linked the cabaret stage to the prostitution realm, and its dancer's body became a loose symbol of prostitution, not only in the popular imagination, but also for the state that treated these performers as potential prostitutes.[37] The required health document for the renewal of their work permits enabled the authorities to trace the dancers offstage, as was also the case with prostitutes of the red light district Shahr-i Naw who had to take similar exams regularly.[38] The paradoxical attitude of government towards *kafah*s and cabarets and their (female) performers is further revealed in the report *About Prostitution in the City of Tehran*. Conducted by order of the ministry of state, the report sheds light on the official classification of prostitution that categorized cabaret dancers as prostitutes associated with the nightlife's recreational venues (*tafrihgah-ha-yi shabanah*).[39] Such a classification, and therefore recognition, of prostitution, on behalf of the police—the same entity in charge of controlling the venues as well as the work permits—placed the *kafah* and cabarets in a liminal position between performance spaces and covert prostitution sites (with the systematic management of *fishkhuri* as an off-the-record business item).

The cabaret dancer and her multiple dancing selves

All cabaret dancers donned stage names. This was done to disguise their identities from the public and to protect their families and their (families') reputations. Using aliases was a way for the dancers to disown their bodies or mediate their selves through another person's body. Some chose Iranian names like Shahrzad, Mahin, Surur, Mahvash, and Niku, while others chose fancy foreign names like Piransis ("princess"). But the majority of stage names ended with "ah," to imply an Arabic origin or influence. Azizah, Jamileh, Nadiyah, Samiyah, and Rahilah are only a few instances of the Arabic-inspired cabaret stage names, chosen due to the trendiness of the genre (Figure 4.4). The prevalent admiration for the famed Egyptian belly dancer, Samia Gamal (1924–94), is especially evident, with an Iranian cabaret-style dancer having adopted "Samiyah" as a stage name, and also using the titles "Gamal" or "the famed foreign dancer" in order to further her associations with the Egyptian performer.[40]

The impersonation of foreign identities appears to have been common in the 1950s among some of the less famous local dancers; this was due to the trending of performers from various countries who traveled to perform in *atraksiun*s. The media often ridiculed the popular fascination with "foreign" dancers: some comic accounts scorned Iranian men who fantasized about the blonde hair and white skin of the German dancers, while others ridiculed the Iranian dancers who forged foreign identities.[41] This is exemplified in the caption of an illustration of two Iranian-looking women posing in Hawaiian costumes, which reads:

> Perhaps like us, you don't know these two gals … we wanted to provide their profile, but we did not find it wise to do so! Apparently, they are foreign dancers who empty Iranian youths' pockets on the corners of the city under the guise of being "foreign."[42]

Traveling among various scenes, the dancers not only offered different acts, but also presented themselves as different personalities. The *raqqas*'s

Figure 4.4 The famous dancer of 1950s performing Hawaiian dance, Azizah Ida Meftahi's personal archive.

situational subjectivity resembles Erving Goffman's notion of the presentation of self in everyday life.[43] Using the metaphor of theater for everyday social interaction, Goffman argues that social actors present themselves differently, according to their situations, through their act and appearance.

While working with *mutribi* troupes hired by *shadimani* agencies in weddings and private ceremonies, they performed "traditional" dances such as the "statue" (*mujassamah*) or "stunned" (*mat*), among others (referred to by my interviewees as sahrah-i sirus dances).[44] These styles were also favored in *saz-va–zarbi kafah*s, where the audience was also interested in new stylized versions of vernacular dance and music, developed by the *mutribi* troupes. In Lalehzar theaters, the dancers often performed the "feast of khayyam" (*bazm-i khayyam*), "oriental dance" (*raqs-i sharqi*), and a variety of Iranian folk dances, as well as belly dance. Within the *mutribi* acts and also as part of Lalehzari plays (mainly those that were categorized as historical), a regular segment was to entertain the king or the sultan onstage.[45] This segment began with an actor uttering the command "Musicians! Play! Dancers! Dance!" (*Navazandigan binavazand! Raqqasan biraqsand!*).[46]

In *kafah*s and cabarets, the dancers did not dance for kings, but rather for the audience who came to be entertained. Such amusements catered to the trends of the day: dances from different cultures—Arabic, Spanish, Indian, Hawaiian, African, and American—as well as, of course, trendy vernacular Iranian dances.[47] The Iranian cabaret dancers presented multiple "exotic" and "oriental" dancing bodies onstage, namely *raqs-i sharqi*, "Arabic dance" (*raqs-i 'arabi*), and "Indian dance" (*raqs-i hindi*). While this "orientalism within the orient" was linked to a globalized interest in spectatorship of the exotic, it is important to note that each of these genres had its own historical points of connection with the Iranian performance scene.

Presumably, the utmost enthusiasm for Arabic dance in Iran was due to the appeal of belly dancers who were either seen on Iranian cabaret stages or on the cinema screens in Egyptian and Hollywood harem films.[48] There are uncertainties as to who was the first dancer to perform belly dance in Iranian *kafah*s. A *Tihran-i Musavvar* article recognizes Tamara, the Azerbaijani dancer-actor, as the first, while my interlocutor, Naghmah, identifies Surur-Siyah as the pioneering figure in daring to perform belly dancing.[49] As its costuming was considered "revealing," performing belly dance was considered provocative in the 1950s and even later.

Two of my interviewees, Naghmah and Firishtah, attest that back in the early 1950s in theater *atraksiun*s and *kafah*s they often wore more "covered" clothing, which included harem-like pants—*chaqchur* (or *shakhtur*)—underneath their skirts.[50] Only a few years later, however, the dancers changed the material of their *chaqchur* to see-through lace, as the *kafah* audiences' expectations turned towards watching scantily clad dancers. Subsequently, in the late 1960s and the 1970s, miniskirts were widely worn, and the Arabic dance attire became less controversial. As Naghmah stated:

There came a time in Lalehzar when you were expected to be almost naked, showing off your legs (*par va pachah*). The audience did not accept you if you were covered. The *kafah* owner himself did not allow you to do that.

My interlocutors also assert that, in comparison to the *kafah*s, the dancers wore more conservative outfits on the cabaret stage; this was perhaps due to the continued premise of a family-friendly environment. Arguably, the constant use of the term "familial" in regard to cabarets was meant to denote a safe environment for women as audience members—perhaps "safety" in that context meant that women were not to be exposed to evocative or overt sexuality on behalf of "half-naked" or "naked" dancing bodies.

Significantly, in order to understand the temporal nature of such terms as "naked" and "half-naked"—which were overtly repeated in the multiple discourses surrounding the cabaret dancer and have been mentioned several times in this chapter—it is important to place them within their particular socio-historical context. For instance, perhaps both a dancing body in *chaqchur* in the 1950s and one in Arabic dance in a far more revealing costume in the 1970s were seen as provocative and labeled as "naked" by their respective audiences. The label of dancing "naked" (*lukht*) or "half-naked"(*nimah lukht*) in all the contexts of pre-revolutionary Iran, however, never meant a nude body on stage, but rather one that appeared underdressed in relation to the costuming norms of the time.[51]

Depending on the context, the dancer's onstage self, act, and "feeling technology" encompassed comedy and sexual evocation for her male audiences.[52] By means of costuming that varied from the more covered traditional-style period clothing to the revealing belly dance attire, music that ranged from upbeat and romantic to that of Arabic belly dance, and lip-synching to often romantic or suggestive lyrics, the dancer enhanced the sensory appeal of her performance. Her act also affected responses in the spectators, ranging from the humorous gestures chosen from jerky movements as well as free-flow rotations of hands, hips, and the neck in vernacular *ruhawzi* and *mutribi* dances, to the more provocative shimmies and exaggerated *qir*.[53] *Qir,* the free-flow rotation of hips, is at once informed by enticing and comedic affects: a culturally familiar movement, *qir* arguably not only has a sexual affect for its accentuated hips, but its free-flow rotation creates elation in its audience, who most often had their own embodied experience of *qir*.

If the dancers were forced to extend their performance to include the practice of *fishkhuri*, part of their onstage act was to make eye-contact with audience members and later to travel (*charkh zadan* or *gashtan*) through the audiences in order to receive drink invitations from patrons. The more famous dancers who performed in the classy cabarets were exempt from this practice and maintained their distance from the audience by remaining strictly onstage. For the dangers inflicted on dancers because of *fishkhuri*, some dancers carried cold weapons (such as a knife) for their personal safety after leaving the performance venue in case they needed to defend themselves and had to be prepared to transition from their onstage femininity to an offstage brand of vigilantism.[54]

The dancer traveled through multiple arenas, aided by a mutable stage persona. From one venue to another, she presented a new dancing self, one that matched the desire and fantasy of her audience while adhering to the regulations of specific venues. Becoming a "traditional" dancer in the *mutribi* setting or in the historical plays of Lalehzar, she wore a costume in the style of previous centuries and enacted a harem woman, entertaining the sultan who gazed at her along with her quotidian audience. In *kafah*s and *atraksiun*s, she regularly became an "exotic" dancer performing foreign movements or a more sexualized and exaggerated version of vernacular dances. Picking from a range of identities—moving from Western to Eastern ethnicities—the dancer adopted the image of the "exotic other" for her audiences. Some dancers went even further, adopting these new foreign identities not only onstage but offstage as well.

Working at some *kafah*s and cabarets in which they were obliged to engage in *fishkhuri*, some dancers were deemed offstage prostitutes. Whether they met with and engaged in intimate relations with their spectator-clients outside those venues, or succeeded in escaping the situation, the act of *fishkhuri* marked the dancer as a prostitute. The cabaret dancer was widely regarded as "out of control," despite the strict regulations that monitored her performance in the cabaret venue and her subjugation to both these regulations and the specific expectations and fantasies of her audiences. Nevertheless, her image was greatly constituted and overshadowed by the dominant prostitute-dancer myth—an all-encompassing narrative that tied her to the "suspicious" nightlife of Tehran.

The cabaret dancer and her myth: an aspiration in the arts

During the last three decades of the Pahlavi era, Tehran's growing nightlife was not only a big business venture—where numerous cafés and cabarets were competing to attract more spectators and creating employment opportunities for people of diverse backgrounds—but it also became a source for cultural production. Tehran's nightlife and its controversial dancing subject inspired numerous periodical accounts, fictions, novels, stories, films, and plays; she was also, in turn, questioned, condemned, ridiculed, pitied, or admired by them. Examples include Ali Muhammad Afghani's novel *Shawhar-i Ahu Khanum* (Ahu Khanum's husband, 1961) and Sadiq Hidayat's short story *Dash Akul* (1932), Simin Danishvar's short story "An Shab-i 'Arusi" (That wedding night, 1947) and that of Simin Behbahani, "Sang ra aramtar biguzarid" (Place the gravestone more gently, 1996).[55]

Phrases from the famous sound track of the 1953 film, *Tehran's Nights* (*Shabha-yi Tihran*), are an early instance of such a response that touches on cabaret, crime, and the other social maladies of urbanism, all linked to Tehran's mysterious nightlife: "Tehran's nightlife hides many scenes ... Every night this land is full of accidents, one side pleasure and joy (*'aysh va tarab*), the other pain and 'prejudice' (*ta'assub*)."

Tehran's "suspicious" nightlife and its underworld sex industry were often symbolized by *kafah* and cabaret dancers. Arguably, Tehran's nightlife and its interconnected industries built themselves on the dancing body as well as its related image and social narrative. The past, present, or future of a dancer's life story, however, was often bound to prostitution. In various forms of writing, including reports and fiction, male journalists sold papers, as well as the desired image of the prostitute-*raqqas*, while simultaneously condemning or ridiculing her. An example of this attitude is found in a pseudo-autobiographical fictive, "Chigunah hunarmandam kardand?" (How I was made an artist?), published in the monthly *Sitarigan-i Sinama*. The narrator, who asks readers to identify her as Parvin (and whose fictional bikini-clad picture is also provided), states: "I am not from Tehran, but I won't reveal my origin as I do not wish to upset my parents."[56] She then narrates her "dark past": deceived by a lover, she left behind her family and her small city for Tehran, where she was sold to a prostitution house (presumably in Shahr-i Naw) by a new lover.[57] Then, after many years, with the help of a sympathetic client, she escaped that house and found a job in a *kafah* as a server. About six months later, on a night when the dancer who regularly performed at their *kafah* did not show up, Parvin climbed the stage to fill her place. She then became a popular star.[58]

As exemplified in Parvin's narrative above, the mythlike narratives around these performers, which permeated the media, included the central speculations on the dancer's origins, and her relationship to the man she loved—who in turn often played the role of the dancer's savior.[59] Linking the dancer to the nightlife of Tehran, another example of this mythologizing is a report entitled "The Night, Tehran, and Humans":

> The women of *kafah* all share the same past with a slight difference. They have either failed in (film) studios or theaters and have sought refuge here; or have escaped from smaller cities to Tehran and found this job after being unemployed for a while; or were misled to do this by other *kafah* women ... These women each love a man or have been in love with one or will love a man. His name is "private friend" (*rafiq-i shakhsi*) ... *Kafah* women sacrifice for their personal friends.[60]

As mentioned in the above passage, in addition to the dancer having origins in a rural or small town, another prevalent part of this narrative is the *rafiq-i shakhsi*, a man who supported and protected the dancer, echoing Parvin's rescuer in the previous example. Similar figures were prevalent among narratives surrounding prostitutes, but for them "private friends" were not only friends but also financial beneficiaries.[61] This reductionist attitude is also observable in *About Prostitution in the City of Tehran*, which provides an all-encompassing narrative of the cabaret dancer, who, compared to other servants of nightlife entertainment, appeared to be a better-paid prostitute:

These dancers and performers appear on stage with a half-naked body and sing, dance, or perform acrobatics ... they often perform at several venues every night; and in their last venue, they drink with the clients ... They normally have sex with the client either at a place that he provides or somewhere that the woman presents.[62]

This stereotypical prostitute-dancer narrative which dominated the media and the film industries (discussed more thoroughly in the next chapter) certainly was not an accurate depiction of the real situations of all who danced in such settings. It excluded those who were born and grew up in the *mutribi* families and were brought up as *mutribi* artists, like Jamileh (b. 1946) and Shahnaz Tehrani (b. 1954). Moreover, the all-inclusive conflation of prostitution and cabaret dancers does not match the alternative stories introduced by my interlocutors, all of whom testify that *fishkhuri* was not prevalent among all dancers or in all spheres of the cabaret dancer, including the theaters. For instance, an actor with the Barbud Society claimed that the managers of the company only hired "proper" women to perform in their *atraksiun*. My interviewee Firishtah speaks of a married woman who used to perform for their theater's *atraksiun*:

Entering the theater wearing full hijab (*chadur*), she used to get changed [in]to her dance costumes, and right after the show, she used to leave the theater wearing her *chadur* once again.[63]

Rahilah also asserted that many women who worked in bars and *kafah*s were "pure" (*pak*) and were often married; even those who were engaged in *fishkhuri* did not necessarily sleep with their customers, and such refusal to engage in intimate relations with these men was one of the main reasons for the prevalent *kafah* fights.

Instead these interlocutors identify *fishkhuri* as a practice occurring in some *kafah*s that they articulate as "southern Tehran" or "lower" *kafah*s (*kafah-ha-yi pa'in*). Again such a stereotypical ascription to "southern Tehran" was not meant to denote the geographical area, but rather the area close to the prostitution district of Shahr-i Naw around which several of these venues existed.[64]

Given that dancers received a higher salary performing in theater *atraksiun*s or as part of the *mutribi* performances arranged by the *shadimani* agencies (as compared to the lower salary for acting in a play), the all-encompassing prostitution narrative was a myth attached to the dancing body of this type. In the growing nightlife of Tehran, cabaret dancing was an occupation and a financial opportunity for many women, likely those women living on the margins.

Presentation of real personas in the press

While these myths have probably been inspired by the lives of some individuals, they nonetheless fed the news with nothing more than sellable gossips, to the extent that it becomes extremely difficult to separate the myth from "reality." This phenomenon is most evident with regard to the famed artist Mahvash (Ma'sumah Azizi Burujidi, 1920–60), who rose to prominence from the *mutribi* scene in the 1940s and was one of Iran's most popular singer-dancers of the 1950s (see Figure 4.5). Aside from her artistry (largely categorized as *'ammah*, or *kuchah-bazari*), as well as her courageous and independent character, another important factor to her success was her crossover to the radio and film industries.

According to an interview with her second husband, Bahram Hasanzadah, entitled "The secrets of the life and death of Mahvash," published in *Tihran-i Musavvar* after her death in 1961, Mahvash, who was native to the city Bur-ujird in the western province of Lurestan, migrated to Tehran at age seven with her single mother.[65] Her talent in mimicry and dance was soon discovered by two women acquaintances who worked in the *kafah* setting; with their encouragement, she became an *atraksiun* performer with *kafahs* at the age of eight. At fifteen, her career took her to perform at a theater in Abadan (a southern city with an active nightlife), where she married an army officer. Pregnant from her husband, she divorced him only two months after and returned to Tehran. There, she met Hasanzadah after a show at a Lalehzar theater and joined his singing classes. The couple soon married (when she was eighteen) and began their artistic collaboration together while she gave birth to a son. According to Hasanzadah, her breakthrough came when she started performing his compositions of "*tudah pasand*" popular songs on Tehran Radio, and later the Radio of the Air Force (*niru-yi hava'i*). Concurrently she began performing at cafés and cabarets (including Kafah Astara and Kafah Kuntinatal) and later in the film industry. He claimed that her song "Ki migah kajah?" (Who Says it is Slanted?) (composed by him) was the pinnacle of her popular attention. After five years of partnership, the couple separated: he took the custody of their son while her daughter lived at a boarding house. As inferred from Hasanzadah, he gave her a hard time after their divorce: for example, for some time he would not allow her name to be added to their son's birth certificate as he did not find her to be a deserving mother.

Already some of the elements of the above narrative, told by a close relative of hers, replicates that of the seemingly fictive life of Parvin, including her small town origin, accidental discovery of her talent as a peformer, and her supporting children as a single mother. But the social myths surrounding Mahvash included another stage in her life, similar to Parvin's: they claimed that Mahvash was a prostitute at some point in her past. Some even speculated that she worked at Shahr-i Naw, perhaps because it was the first spatial correlation that came to mind for most regarding a prostitute. One instance is Behbahani's fictional story in which she narrated Mah-vash's life story in her grave and recounted her old days in this red-light district.[66]

What greatly contributed to this rumor was the ascription to her of the short book *The Secret of Sexual Fulfillment* (*Raz-i Kamyabi-i Jinsi*),

Figure 4.5 Lady Mahvash in the 1950s
Ida Meftahi's personal archive.

published multiple times in the late 1950s. A fictive autobiographical narrative with references to the narrator's life story and experiences (for the purpose of the sexual education of the reader), the book describes several erotic and sadist scenes with her "self" (body) vividly present. The author introduced herself as Mahvash, a sexually experienced, fallen woman ("to the level of a prostitute") with a dark past. While the last name and the birthplace provided in the book do not match that of the performer, the book includes several pictures of Mahvash.[67] Even though there were serious doubts about the authorship or the permission of the book by the celebrity, or indeed the authenticity of the provided life story, her "prostitute" myth and the imagery of her tormented body combined with the implicit sexual sadism of the narrative were widely consumed.

This was not the only account on her with fictive and stimulating elements. Due to her utmost popular reception, stories and rumors about Mahvash were circulated in the press which often depicted her in strange and even dangerous adventures. This included detailing her bravery in a physical fight with armed thieves who left her naked in the middle of a desert, and her being accosted by her lover who threatened to pour acid on her face.[68] The rumor of her engagement with an Arab businessman and the question of whether she would leave her job after marriage were other topics of discussion in periodicals. Her death in a car accident and her well-attended funeral (estimated at between one hundred thousand and two hundred thousand people) prompted a widespread press coverage as well as debates about the reasons behind her popularity.

Other famous cabaret dancers' personal lives, especially those with active cinematic careers, were also subjected to gossip and often ridiculing. For instance, the divorce of Nadiya from her husband, the singer Kayvan, elicited the media's attention, some even reporting her audience's angry reactions in the cabaret environment.[69] Shahrzad, (Kubra Sa'idi, b. 1946) was another dancer-actor who received heavy media attention. As she described, she was born in Tehran in 1946 and was forced to dance to earn money in her teens by her father and step-mother, both of whom also consequently made her marry three times for money. She worked as a dancer and an actress in several *kafah*s and theaters, including the Barbud Society. She later broke the mold through her interest in education, which led her to pursue her studies. Shahrzad acted in several films, garnering fame for herself, specifically through such films as *Qaysar* (1969) and *Dash Akul* (1971), wherein she played the role of a dancer-prostitute. While some parts of her early life fit into the usual *raqqas* narrative of the "marginalized" urban woman, Shahrzad became a poet and later a filmmaker in 1978.

When she was featured in the periodicals, however, she was regularly framed as a "former dancer with a dark past" who now had found the light of intellect as a poet.[70] The apologetic tone used by both the interviewer and Shahrzad when referring to her dancing past exemplified the continued illegitimacy of a dancer, even after having achieved relative success in more "legitimate arts," such as poetry and cinema acting.[71] She was often cast in films as a fallen woman (which will be further discussed in Chapter 5).

The media treatment and press coverage of one cabaret dancer was an exception: Jamileh (Fatimah Sadiqi) the dancing legend of the 1960s and 1970s (see Figure 4.6).[72] Born to a *mutribi* family in 1946 (her uncle was a musician and her father was a *siyah-bazi* actor), she started performing from a young age in her father's *mutribi* troupes.[73] She first married a *mutribi* musician who also worked as her agent and then joined the *kafah* and theater scenes, mostly performing self-trained Bollywood-style Indian dance.[74] Her life as a "low-status" café dancer is said to have drastically changed when she remarried to the cabaret tycoon, Muhammad-Karim Arbab. While Jamileh continued her career by dancing in Arbab's Bakara-Mulan Ruzh and her own cabaret, Lidu, she also acted in a number of films. It was then that she became recognized for her specific style of belly dance, as well as a variety of Iranian dances such as *jahili*.

Jamileh's image, as promoted in the media, was definitely not that of the stereotypical cabaret dancer, but rather one of "a valuable artist," most probably improved through the help of her powerful husband's network.[75] *Ittila'at-i Salanah* published an interview with her with the self-explanatory title, "Jamileh, the Manifestation of Art in Dance," wherein she draws a comparison between herself and the famed Egyptian dancer Samia Gamal.[76] Her role as a "moral" cabaret dancer who maintains her manners even in the dirty entertainment industry—as seen in the film *Khushgiltarin Zan-i 'Alam* (The most beautiful woman on earth, 1971) produced by her husband's Firdawsi Film—confirms the couple's efforts to construct a different image for the dancer than the common one. Jamileh sought to keep that image after her husband's death in 1973, stating in an interview, "I only want to live for my children as after Arbab's died, everything is finished for me."[77] Jamileh continues her dancing career in the diasporic Iranian community in Los Angeles.[78]

Cabaret and its discourse

As reported by an article on cabarets published in 1974, Jamileh was still the highest paying cabaret dancer of Iranian origin, something that came with her power and image.[79] Her representation in the press and on screen as a respected artist was also part of the pro-cabaret discourse largely established by the two cabaret tycoons, Hijazi and Arbab (Jamileh's husband).

These two competing rivals largely used the print media to promote a "cosmopolitan" and "modern" image for cabaret to convey it as a recreational means required in the modern world.[80] An example of such an attempt is found in the following passage selected from a paid article that was written about Shecufeh Now in 1970:

Figure 4.6 Jamileh in the late Pahlavi era
Ida Meftahi's personal archive.

In today's civilized and developed world in which machined life and the endless disturbance of society distresses the body and soul of human beings, recreational means are essential to rejuvenate their souls and nerves and enable them to start off their work the next day. In this situation, cabaret has a major and crucial role, as people can also get to know the latest developments and artistic phenomena in Iran and the world. It is often heard that when enthusiasts and families discuss recreation and a place to view artistic performances, they first choose to discuss Shecufeh Now: this beautiful and luxurious cabaret with years of bringing brilliant activities and exciting and rare presentations which mostly are being staged concurrently with the important cities of the world such as Paris, London, and New York, is now ranked as one of the top four large and famous cabarets in the world.[81]

These accounts are obvious attempts at countering the more dominant discourses in the press and society that blamed these sites for social corruption. Such notions were evident in several parliamentary debates in which members attributed the economic and social corruptions in society to spaces such as cabarets.[82] Another example of such a popular attack on the cabarets is found in an article published in the social section of the weekly *Khandaniha* by Husayn Shahzaydi, entitled "Muravvijin-i fisad" (Disseminators of immorality).[83] Posing the question (perhaps to the government) "Wasn't it supposed to forbid foreign dancers from coming to Iran?," the article continued:

Why, in the few famous cabarets of Tehran, are these [foreign dancers] thieves of money and chastity, these plunderers of society, these instructors of vice, these nurturers of crime who strip women of their sacred rank of motherhood, stealing purity, faith, and virtue from our people, have a bustling market in the heart of the nights? Then, after their stimulating performances, they perform in another cabaret, and afterwards they end up boosting the bars from late night to morning and opening their arms for mixed dances.[84]

Calling the dancers "shameless prostitutes," the author condemned them for corrupting society, loosening family ties, and increasing crime, as men of all ages are willing to do anything to earn money to pay to see these dancers' attractive and fanciful naked bodies. The author also asserted that cabarets and dancers and their disgraceful programs were against the sacred attempts of the Shah to improve social conditions—this referred to the Shah's reforms, which began after 1963 under the title of the White Revolution. In contrast to the latter assertion, another article in *Ittla'at-i Salanah* on Bakara-Mulan Ruzh cabarets linked the ways such cabarets are in line with the Shah's reforms, as they enhance the nation's quality of life and respond to the needs of the society.[85]

In addition to associations with prostitution and immorality mentioned in Shahzaydi's article, the negative response to cabaret dancers had other sources as well. Their connection to the *mutribi* scene led them to inherent *"ibtizal,"* while their rise in the 1950s not only brought them to the center of this discourse but escalated and complicated the application of the term "degenerate." This was then intensified with their further advancement to the cinema screen, especially in 1960s (this will be discussed in Chapter 5). Furthermore, their connection to the *mutribi* stage put them in the category of "unmodern;" while their underclad body and their association with the nightlife were imbued with certain signifiers of "modernity," albeit an unpleasant one for most social critiques. Not only did the dancers' ties with *mutribs* place them in the category of "popular" (*'avam pasand*, or *kuchah-baghi*), but also it put them in conflict with Lalehzar's golden age and artistic past as well as the concurrent national dancers, and further solidified the view of their being un-artistic.

A great point to explore the cabaret dancers' discourse in the press is in 1960, when, with the death of Mahvash and her epically well-attended funeral and its press coverage, these signifiers were all crystalized in the intense discussion of writers who attempted to analyze the reasons behind her unusual popularity. For that I will be focusing on three articles published in *Tihran-i Musavvar* which reflected the opposing positions of their authors. The exchange started when a male author with the pen name Sipidah (who was a regular contributor to the magazine) in an unprecedented manner praised Mahvash for her honesty to her audience.[86]

Writing in an emotional tone, Sipidah claimed that his impetus was to recognize Mahvash and her audience, who had been greatly neglected by the intellectuals and the press. Pointing to the existing binaries of artistic and high versus popular and low in Iranian culture, Sipidah identified Mahvash's fans and funeral participants as *jahil*s and *kulah-makhmali*s as well as masons, laborers, tailors, wholesalers, and women holding their children; those who contributed to the workforce and were residents of Tehran who showed their respect to Mahvash by attending her funeral. He vindicated her popularity as attributed to her integrity, her authenticity (depicting the vernacular culture) and faithfulness to her humble origins, and to her evoking joy and happiness in her audiences. Concurrently, he criticized the dominance of an Iranian "intellectual" culture that dismissed and ridiculed Mahvash with labels such as prostitute, degenerate actor, and dancer of the degraded *kafah*s. He further condemned the press for favoring those (women) with illegitimate "literary" and "artistic" entitlements, who imitate foreign culture, have a loose moral standing, and use the media for their advancement.

In the next issues of the same magazine, Sipidah was attacked by his colleague Shiftah, not just on the basis of his unusual positive tone on Mahvash but also on his promotion of *"mahvashism"* (a term coined by Shiftah to refer to the culture she represented and disseminated), which had a potential transformative effect on young women in the society.[87] Shiftah's take on Mahvash was very similar to Shahzaydi's discussed above: he saw her as a representative of a culture that took advantage of the sexual complexities of society by presenting them her "certain" body parts and thus disseminated immorality and crime in the society. Furthermore, using the example of Harriet Beecher Stowe's *Uncle Tom's Cabin* (1852), he expressed his preference for tears shed after reading such a book, which provoked its readers to change the world, over the laughter of a bunch of "drunks and *kulah-makhmalis*" in the audiences of Mahvash's performances. He concluded, "I would prefer an intelligent cry to a drunken laughter," a statement resembling the Marxist discourse of committed arts explored in Chapter 3, in terms of articulation of the hierarchies of emotive responses and affects in the audience.[88]

A week later, Sipidah defended his initial position, reporting on the unusually positive reception of his first article by readers who identified as "bare-feet people" (perhaps stereotyping them as impoverished or non-elite).[89] Criticizing Shiftah's intellectualist attitude, he asserted in the title "*Mahvashism* is not cholera, illiteracy and imitation is the calamity of our generation."[90] He re-emphasized his respect for Mahvash's faithfulness to vernacular ways of behavior and attire that appealed to the "Iranian taste." He further related the source of social problems brought up by Shiftah to the ignorant imitations of foreign cultural practices that had become prevalent in Iranian society (including European social dancing), and the tendency of the press to receive them as "artistic."

These communications after the death of Mahvash are indicative of the established cultural categories of high "artistic" versus low "popular."[91] It also indicates the complexity of the term *ibtizal*: with its application to dancers, it did not only connote comedy but carried a somewhat sexual connotation as well. Similarly the audiences who favored these genres of work were later framed as *lumpan*, a reference to *lumpenproletariat*. In the decades to come, with the domination of dancers on the cinema screen, both of these terms were widely deployed as tools of criticism for the popular genres.

Nocturnal economy: a bio-economy of amnesia

> This is the tale of night, a tale of the nightlife of those who seek forgetfulness … The people of the night are of two kinds: the performers and the spectators, and both seek to forget the day and themselves, some through gazing (at performers) and some with their act.[92]

As illustrated in the above passage, Tehran's nightlife is regarded as a space which offers the forgetting of the day-to-day, and such a desire was widely echoed as the aspiration of its male customers who, by watching "enticing" dancing bodies, delved into their own fantasies. Mixed with the dominant dancer-prostitute narrative, the projecting of fantasy onto the dancing body constructed its mythic image as naked and exotic, as well as aligning its function with that of a prostitute. Cabaret dancers became the alluring "commodity" of Tehran's nightlife, to be consumed along with cabaret culture's other products: alcohol, food, and music. To some, the dancing body was sold cheaply every night: "We are playing drums as these "naked" slaves go under the hammer every night; every night there is an auction and every night the drums are beating."[93] To others, the dancing performer was a disseminator of social corruption. While widely condemned, she inspired many cinematic productions and became a prevalent character type in Iranian films, especially post-1960. Popular media condemned her and sold her image along with her myth. The private sector theater of Lalehzar saved itself economically through marketing the illusory naked dancing body, but historians of theater condemned her as the signifier of the demise of independent theater. *Kafah* and cabaret owners also regulated and marketed the dancer's performing body, while illegally selling the right to drink with her. In its contradictory tactic towards *kafah*s and cabarets, the state also used these covert sites of prostitution to regulate the sexual drive of those who gathered there. While the cabaret dancer's initial dancing arena, that of the *mutribi* scene, was othered and rejected by the modernist-nationalist perspective as an "antemodern" point of reference, the dancing body which emerged in this first space immensely contributed to the construction of the "ideal" national dancing body onstage. The cabaret dancing body in turn became the attractive staged representative of the "other" or "enticing" woman, one whose dancing act showcased those marginalized (subaltern) groups that failed in the new order of Iran's modern, urbanized society.

Notes

1 "Yik ripurtazh-i khandani az kabarh-ha" [An interesting report on cabarets], *Film va Hunar*, no. 470, 1353/1974 12–15; 14. Café Pars was referred to in Sayyad Murtiza Khalkhali and Abdulhusayn Mu'tazidi, "Namah'i sargushadah" [The open letter], *A'in-i Islam*, 23 Bahman 1326/13 February 1948, 14–15; see also H. Karbasi, "Tihran dar atash-i fisad misuzad" [Tehran is burning in the fires of corruption], *Parcham-i Islam*, 12 Azar 1326/4 December 1947, 1, 2; 2.
2 Bahram Bayza'i, *Namayish dar Iran* [Theater in Iran] 5th edn (Tehran: Intisharat-i Rawshangaran va Mutali'at-i Zanan, 1385/2006), 199. The association of café culture with (imitated) "modernity" (*tajaddud*) permeated Islamic discourse.
3 Early instances of café culture in the first two decades of the twentieth century are Café Boulevard and Café Lalehzar, both situated on Lalehzar Street, where people watched films while enjoying ice cream and tea. The Municipality Café (*kafah'i shahrdari*) was another early café of that nature which also had musical performances by classy musicians. See Abbas Baharloo, *Ruz-shumar-i sinamay-i iran, az aghaz ta Inqiraz-i Qajariyah* [The chronicle of Iran's cinema from the beginning to the end of the Qajar era] (Tehran: Farhangistan-i Hunar, 1389/2010), 43–4, 113. As reported in this book, film screening was also prevalent in the Casino Salon venue (*salun-i cazinu*), where such dishes as ragoute, jigot, cotelet, and chulukabab were served (ibid., 61); see also "Shabnishini dar kafah'i shahrdari" [The Soirée in the City Hall café], 8 Tir 1323/29 June 1944, reprinted in *Hashtad sal huzur-i mustamarr* [Eighty years of continuous presence], ed. Jalal Rafi', vol. 1 (Tehran: Mu'assesah'i Ittila'at), 75.

4 Café Pars was also identified as Cabaret Pars, see "Jashn-i gul-ha dar kabarat pars" [Festival of Flowers in Cabaret Pars], *Kasra* 4, no. 506, 25 Isfand 1326/16 March 1948, 3.
5 Sasan Fatemi, *Jashn va musiqi dar farhang-ha-yi shahri-i iran* [Festivity and music in the urban musical cultures], (Tehran: Mahoor Institute of Culture and Arts, 1393/2014), 205.
6 Naghmah, interview with the author; also see "Tihrani-ha dar sal-i 1353 shab-ha ra chigunah miguzaranand?" [How do the people of Tehran spend their nights in?], *Ittila'at-i Haftigi*, no. 1723, Day 1353/December1974 or January 1975.
7 Ahmadi, interview with the author.
8 Rahilah, interview with the author; Naghmah, interview with the author.
9 Fatemi, *Jashn*, 204.
10 Naghmah, interview with the author; Sattareh Farmanfarma'ian also associated *jahil*s and *kulah-makhmali*s with occupations such as truck drivers, and wholesale meat and produce dealers (*bar-furush*); see, Sattareh Farmanfarma'ian, *Piramun-i ruspigari dar shahr-i tihran* [About prostitution in the city of Tehran], 2nd edn (Tehran: Amuzishgah-i 'Ali-i Khadamat-i Ijtma'i, 1349/1970), 23.
11 See "Shab, tihran va adam-ha" [The night, Tehran, and humans], *Sipid va Siyah*, 26 Isfand 1345/17 March 1967, 90; also, this came up in my interview with Ahmadi.
12 Ali-Akbar Akbari, "Darbarah'i sinama-yi farsi" [About the Farsi cinema], *Arash*, no. 20, Bahman 1349/February 1971, 41–59.
13 See, for instance, Parviz Khatibi, *Khaterati az hunarmandan* [Memoirs of artists] (Los Angeles, CA: Intisharat-i Bunyad-i Farhangi-i Parviz Khatibi, 1994), 423.
14 See "Tihrani-ha dar."
15 "Parviz hijazi: dayir kardan-i kabarah kar-i har kasi nist" [Parviz Hijazi: Opening cabarets is not for everyone], *Film va Hunar*, no. 464, 11 Bahman 1352/31 January 1974, 10–11; 11.
16 For an example of writing on this aspect of cabaret attendance, see "Shukufah'i naw bihtarin kabarah'i khavar-miyanah shinakhtah shud" [Shecufeh Now recognised as the best cabaret of the Middle East], *Film va Hunar*, no. 38, 9 Day 1344/30 December 1965, 13.
17 "Cabaret" is mentioned in *A'in-Namah'i amakin-i 'umumi* [The regulations of public spaces], 1328/1949, www.dastour.ir/brows/?lid=%20%20%20%20%2041893 (accessed 13 Azar 1391/3 December 2012).
18 "Parviz hijazi: dayir kardan," 10.
19 Ahmadi, interview with the author.
20 For instance, see Nizam Panahi of Luculus Dancing Cabaret to Dr. Bihnam of the Ministry of Trade, 4 Sharivar 1354/26 August 1975, 340–208, the National Archives of Iran, 1586; Tahmasib Kalantari of Kulah Farangi Cabaret to Mahdavi the Minister of Trade, 16 Azar 1354/7 December 1975, 340–208, the National Archives of Iran, 1583; Girami of Mulan Ruzh Cabaret to Dr. Bihnam of the Ministry of Trade, 21 Murdad 1354/12 August 1975, 340–208, the National Archives of Iran, 1589–1590.
21 Zabiullah Budaghi, "Kabarah-ha" [The cabarets] in *Atlas-i farhangi-i shahr-i tihran* [The cultural atlas of Tehran] (Tehran: Markaz-i Mutali'at va Hamahangi-i Farhangi-i, Shawra-yi 'Ali-i Farhang va Hunar, 2535/1976), 150. According to this account, the first cabaret in Tehran was established between the years 1941 and 1945. My interviewee Naghmah believes that the first cabaret was Cabaret Bastani, while other sources indicate that Cabaret Jamshid was the first in Tehran. The cabarets Bakara, Qasr-i Shirin, and Kulah Farangi were located on Pahlavi Avenue.
22 See "Dastan-i lalahzar zamani keh kartiyah latan-i' tihran bud" [The story of Lalehzar when it was Tehran's Quartier Latin], *Ayandigan*, 19 Mihr 2536/11 October 1977, 8.

23 This situation is drastically different from that in Egypt, where public dancing for women as *ghawazi* had been an occupation, according to some, at least from the eighteenth century; see Karin van Nieuwkerk, *A Trade Like Any Other: Female Singers and Dancers in Egypt* (Austin: University of Texas Press, 1995).

24 Fatemi, *Jashn*, 209.

25 Fatemi, *Jashn*, 207.

26 "Parviz hijazi: dayir kardan," 10.

27 "A'in-namah'i amakin-i 'umumi, musavvab-i 1328 ba islahat-i ba'di" [Laws of public space, passed on 1949 with later revisions] in *Qavanin-i maliyat-ha bah tur-i kulli* [General laws of taxation] (Chap-i Ittihad, n.d.), 224–47; 230.

28 Amir Khalil Yahyavi, "Sanad-i shumarah'i 153" [Document number 153], 15 Day 1337/5 January 1959, in *Asnadi az musiqi*, 2: 730–34; and Nasir Zulfaqari, "Sanad-i shumarah'i 149" [Document number 149], 4 Tir 1337/25 June 1958, in *Asnadi az musiqi*, 2: 700–706; 704.

29 "A'in-namah'i amakin-i 'umumi," 228.

30 "Sanad-i shumarah'i 149," 704.

31 "Mukatibah'i vizarat-i kishvar dar khusus-i tashkil-i kumisiun-i asli-i namayish bara-yi risidagi bah umur-i vurud va khuruj-i hunarpishigan-i khariji" [The correspondence of ministry of state regarding regulation of foreign performers], Aban 1336/November 1957, in *Asnadi az Musiqi*, 2: 658–61.

32 Fathullah Jalali, "Sanad-i shumarah'i 139" [Document number 139], 15 Aban 1336/6 November 1957, in *Asnadi az musiqi*, 2: 658; "Sanad-i shumarah'i 139/1" [Document number 139/1], 18 Aban 1336/9 November 1957, in *Asnadi az musiqi*, 2: 659–61; *A'in-namah'i hunarpishah'i khariji* [The regulations on foreign performers], 1345/1966, www.dastour.ir/brows/?lid=61561 (accessed 13 Aban 1391/3 November 2013).

33 See *A'in-namah'i bimari-ha-yi amizishi, maddah'i 7* [Regulations on sexually transmitted diseases, item 7], 1325/1946, www.dastour.ir/brows/?lid=38386 (accessed 13 Aban 1391/3 November 2013). My interviewees Naghmah and Rahilah confirmed this. In the written regulations of venereal disease, there is no direct mention of *atraksiun* performers, but it states "prostitutes and similar to those" are obliged to take such exams.

34 "A'in-namah'i amakin-i 'umumi," 230. Purchasing tokens (*jeton*) was also a system used in the prostitution houses of Shahr-i Naw. See Farmanfarma'ian, *Piramun-i*, 14. Also, the term *Fishkhuri* was prevalent in some bars and restaurants where female waiters were paid to drink with the customers—under the false label of "whisky"—and received a percentage from the bar owner; Farmanfarma'ian, *Piramun-i*, 20.

35 Rahilah, interview with the author. A similar practice was common in Egyptian nightclubs, called *fath*; and a similar method was used for its concealment from the police. See van Nieuwkerk, *A Trade Like Any Other*, 43, 49.

36 Rahilah recounts an incident where a drunken dancer insulted a gang member at a *kafah* and then was chased by the gang after leaving her work; Rahilah, interview with the author.

37 Following *shahrbani*'s classification, Farmanfarma'ian provides the all-encompassing narrative of the cabaret dancer who, compared to other servants of nightlife entertainment, appeared as a better-paid prostitute; see Farmanfarma'ian, *Piramun-i*, 20–21.

38 Jamshid Behnam, Conversation, Toronto, 7 June 2012; *A'in-namah'i bimari-ha-yi amizishi, maddah'i 7*; as well as Farmanfarma'ian, *Piramun-i*, 224.

39 Led by Farmanfarma'ian, this report was conducted by the government's social services academy (Amuzishgah-i khadamat-i ijtima'i). The inclusion of these women in the report (for having an influential role in the business of prostitution) is linked to their being more generally classified by the police office (*Idarah'i shahrbani*) as "servants" (*khidmatguzaran*) of nightlife recreational centers, a

category which also includes women who worked at the bars and restaurants attended by *jahil*s, meat and produce wholesalers, truck drivers, and *kulah-makhmalis*. See Farmanfarma'ian, *Piramun-i*, 20–23; see also 227 on *shahrbani*'s control of these spaces.

40 In credentials of the Iranian film *Payman-i dusti* (The pact of friendship, 1960), the dancer was introduced as "Samia the foreign dancer."

41 Husayn Madani, "Majara-yi shab-i zafaf" [The story of the first night], *Sitarah'i Sinama*, no.105, Nawruz 1336/March 1957, 105; "Raqqasan-i ispaniyuli, sar-qufli-i hutil-ha-yi tihran" [Spanish dancers, the key source of revenue for Tehran's hotels], *Rushanfikr*, no. 164, Pa'iz 1335/Fall 1956, 36.

42 "2-in du nafar ra hatman shuma ham misl-i ma nimishnasid" [2-Like us, you probably do not know these two], *Dunya-yi Jadid*, no. 16, 16 Tir 1335/7 July 1956, 28.

43 See Erving Goffman, *The Presentation of Self in Everyday Life* (Garden City, NY: Doubleday, 1959), 208–37.

44 For more stylistic details on these dances, see Azardokht Ameri, "Raqs–e 'amianeh–ye shahri va raqs–e mowsum be klasik: Bar–rasi–ye tatbiqi dar howze–ye Tehran" [Urban popular dance and the so-called classical dance, a comparative study in the Tehran region], *Mahour Music Quarterly* 20 (Summer 2003), 51–74.

45 For a description of such scenes in *mutribi* settings, see William O. Beeman, *Iranian Performance Traditions* (Costa Mesa, CA: Mazda, 2011), 230–31.

46 Similar segments were also prevalent in the modernist theatrical arena of the 1920s. An example of this is Pari Aqabayov's "Dance of the Seven Veils" in Oscar Wilde's *Salomé*.

47 For instance, my informant Rahilah believed that *raqs-i sharqi* was considered outdated in 1970, while *bandari*, a dance ascribed to southern Iran, remained trendy. American dance was mentioned in "Dastani az raqs va dastani az hifz-i abiru" [A story about dance and a story about safeguarding honor], *Rushanfikr* 200, 30 Tir 1336/21 July 1957, 7.

48 Examples include *Thief of Damascus* directed by the American Will Jason (1952) and *Son of Sindbad* directed by the American Ted Tetzlaff (1955).

49 Naghmah, interview with the author; M. Mihr, "Biraqs, bipich, bitab, biraqs" [Dance, swirl, swing, dance!], *Tihran-i Musavvar*, no. 23, Nawruz 1352/Spring 1973, 19.

50 Naghmah, interview with the author; Firishtah, phone interview with the author, winter 2012.

51 For instance, wearing belly dance attire is described as "getting naked" (*lukht shudan*) in Mihr, "Biraqs," 20.

52 I am using Erin Hurley's definition of "feeling technology" as "a theatrical mechanism that does something with feeling—directs sense perception, increases or dampens emotional response in the audience, creates moods, and so on." See Erin Hurley, *Theatre and Feeling* (London: Palgrave McMillan, 2010), 40.

53 Two of my interviewees, Naghmah and Rahilah, also employed the term *qir* to describe rotation of other body parts, including the neck (*qir-i gardan*).

54 In an interview, the famous singer Afat explained that she was a victim of an attack with a cold weapon in a café setting, orchestrated by an audience member who constantly disturbed her. See "Afat miguyad ay mardum" [Afat says hey people], *Filmha va Pardah-ha*, no.5, 1337/1958, 19, 24; 24.

55 Ali Muhammad Afghani, *Shawhar-i Ahu Khanum* [Ahu Khanum's husband] (Tehran, 1340/1961); Sadiq Hidayat, "Dash Akul," in *Sah Qatarah'i Khun* [Three drops of blood], 1311/1932; Simin Danishvar, "An Shab-i 'Arusi" [That wedding night], *Iran va Amrika*, Mihr va Aban 1326/October–November 1947, 45–7; and Simin Behbahani, "Sang ra aramtar biguzarid" [Place the gravestone more gently], *Arash*, no. 58 (October–November 1996). The latter was referred to in Houshang Chehabi, "Voices Unveiled: Women Singers in Iran," in *Iran and Beyond, Essays in*

Middle Eastern History in Honor of Nikki R. Keddie, ed. Rudi Matthee and Beth Baron (Costa Mesa, CA: Mazda, 2000), 151–66.

56 Parvin [pseud.], "Chigunah hunarmandam kardand" [How I was made an artist?], *Sitarigan-i Sinama*, no.3, Tir 1338/June–July 1959, 38–9; 38.

57 This part of Parvin's fictive narrative resembles the prevalent rumors still associated with the famous performer, Mahvash; see Gisu Shakiri, "Mahvash, sida'i az a'maq" [Mahvash, a voice from the abyss], *Persian Deutsche Welle*, radio broadcast, 27 January 2013, www.dw.de/مهوش-صدایی-از-اعماق/a-16553825.

58 Parvin, "Chigunah," 39.

59 "Tihrani-ha dar sal-i 1353."

60 "Shab, tihran," 90.

61 Farmanfarma'ian, *Piramun-i*, 23–4.

62 Farmanfarma'ian, *Piramun-i*, 20, 23.

63 Firishtah, interview with the author.

64 For instance, see "Shab, tihran," 12, 14. "*Pa'in*" and "south" in this article refers to Hafiz-i Naw Theater and the cabaret club Shecufeh Now, both of which were inside the prostitution district.

65 "Asrar-i zindigi va marg-i mahvash" [The secrets of the life and death of Mahvash], *Tihran-i Musavvar*, no. 908, 7 Bahman 1339/27 January 1961, 55.

66 As narrated in Chehabi, "Voices," 161.

67 In the third edition of the book, the author introduces herself as Mahvash Riza'i Fard, who was born in Paris, while the performer's actual name was Ma'sumah Azizi Burujidi, and she was born in Burujid, Iran. See Mahvash, *Raz-i kamyabi-i jinsi* [The secret of sexual fulfillment], 3rd ed. (Bungah-i Matbu'ati-i Afshin, 1336/1957), 68.

68 "Vaqti duzd-ha ba aslahah bah mahvash hamlah kardand" [When armed thieves attacked Mahvash], *Film-ha va Pardah-ha*, no. 4, Isfand 1337/February 1958, 22–3; and "Ma bah surat-i mahvash asid pashidim" [We have poured acid on Mahvash's face], *Film-ha va Pardah-ha*, no. 6, Isfand 1337/March 1958, 12.

69 "Nadiya tard shudah ast" [Nadiya has been boycotted] *Film va Hunar*, no. 473, Urdibihisht 1353/April 1974, 6.

70 For an example, see Alireza Nourizadeh, "Zani kah az zulamat miayad" [The woman who comes from the darkness], *Firdawsi*, no. 1033, 12 Mihr 1350/4 October 1971, 12–14.

71 Since the 1979 Revolution, Shahrzad has been living in poverty in Iran. See Shahab Mirza'i, "Qissah'i shahrzad" [The story of Shahrzad], *Jadid Online*, 29 August 2008, www.jadidonline.com/story/29082008/frnk/shahrzad_tale. For more on the life and work of Shahrzad, see Kamran Talattof, *Modernity, Sexuality, and Ideology in Iran: The Life and Legacy of a Popular Female Artist* (Syracuse, NY: Syracuse University Press, 2011).

72 Hamid Shu'a'i, *Frahang-i sinama-yi Iran* [Iran's cinematic culture] (Tehran: Shirkat-i Hirminko, 1354/1975), 220.

73 Khosrow Shariari, *Afsanah'i shabzindah-daran* [The tale of night birds] (Tehran: Intisharat-i Kavushgar, 1377/1998), 63.

74 Rahilah, interview with the author.

75 "Jamilah, hunarmand-i ba isti'dad va muvaffaq" [Jamileh, the successful and talented artist], *Ittila'at-i Salanah* 12 (Tehran: Mu'assisah'i Ittila'at, 1350/1971), 644.

76 "Guftigu'i ba jamilah, tajali-i hunar dar raqs" [A conversation with Jamileh, the manifestation of art in dance], *Ittila'at-i Salanah* 12 (Tehran: Mu'assisah'i Ittila'at, 1350/1971), 680–81, 680; allegedly these articles were publicity advertisements and were paid for by Arbab.

77 Mihr, "Biraqs," 22.

78 She has been acknowledged as "the goddess of Persian dance" by the American dance scholar Robyn C. Friend; see, Robyn C. Friend, "Jamileh, the Goddess of

Persian Dance," *Habibi* 16, no. 1 (Winter 1997), available at home.earthlink.net/ ~rcfriend/jamileh.htm (accessed May 2012).

79 "Yik ripurtazh," 13.

80 "Bakara-mulan ruzh, du kabarah'i mumtaz-i paytakht, dar sath-i buzurgtarin kabarah-ha-yi jahan" [Bakara-Mulan Ruzh: The two superior cabarets of the capital in the same tier as the best cabarets of the world], *Ittila'at-i Salanah* 12 (Tehran: Mu'assisah'i Ittila'at, 1350/1971), 654–56; 654.

81 "Kabareah shukufah'i naw, pishraw-yi kabarah-ha-yi ma'ruf-i jahan" [Cabaret Shecufeh Now, the pioneer amongst the most famous cabarets of the world], in *Ittila'at-i Salanah* 12, 650–52; 650.

82 National Consultative Assembly, *Iran Official Gazette*, Parliamentary proceedings, Majlis 21, Session 87, page 19; National Consultative Assembly, *Iran Official Gazette*, Parliamentary proceedings, Majlis 23, Session 146; and Parliamentary Proceedings, page 20; retrieved from *Lawh-i Mashruh* (*Parliamentary Proceedings* DVD), 2nd ed., published by Kitabkhanah, Muzah va Markaz-i Asnad-i Majlis-i Shawra-yi Islami [Library, museum, and document center of Majlis].

83 Husayn Shahzaydi, "Muravvijin-i fisad" [Disseminators of immorality], *Khandaniha* 27, no. 65, 13.

84 Shahzaydi, "Muravvijin-i," 13.

85 "Bakara-mulan ruzh," 654.

86 Sipidah, "Ki migah kajah, mahvash rast miguf" [Who says it is slanted? Mahvash was telling the truth], *tehran-i Musavvar*, no. 909, 14 Bahman 1339/3 February 1961, 5, 56.

87 Shiftah, "Mahvashizm va filurism ..." [Mahvash-ism and Flore-ism ...], *Tihran-i Musavvar*, no. 910, 21 Bahman 1339/10 February 1961, 7, 55.

88 Shiftah, "Mahvashizm," 7.

89 Sipidah, "Mahvashizm vaba nist, bisavadi bala-yi nasl-i mast" [*Mahvashism* is not cholera, illiteracy and imitation is the calamity of our generation], *Tihran-i Musavvar*, no. 911, 28 Bahman 1339/17 February 1961, 7, 55.

90 Sipidah, "Mahvashizm vaba," 7.

91 For Behbahani's deployment of this binary, see Shaker, "Mahvash, sida'i az a'maq."

92 "Shab, tihran," 12.

93 "Shab, tihran," 90.

5   Dancing bodies in pre-revolutionary films and the "enticing" reel cabaret dancer

From the early years of cinematic production in Iran, dancing bodies were featured in films. Along with other "amusing" bodies—such as acrobats, cross-dressers, horse riders, and small people—the dancing bodies contributed to the visual attraction and hence to the financial success of the independent film industry of pre-revolutionary Iran. The choices of style and the look of the dancing bodies featured in films were contingent upon the social and historical context of the film narratives. Dancing bodies further provided means for projecting a sexual gaze onto female bodies. The Pahlavi-era Iranian cinema presented a diverse variety of dances and dancing bodies, ranging from European social dances to Iranian folk dances and art dances of different origins. The cabaret dancer, however, was arguably the most dominant dancing body in Iranian films.

This chapter seeks to employ film as a venue to trace the dancing cultures of pre-revolutionary Iran, rather than looking at Iranian cinema purely through a cinema-studies lens. Providing an overview of various dance genres presented in films within their larger socio-cultural context, this chapter then focuses on the cabaret dancer as a multi-layered character type who dominated the commercial genre of pre-revolutionary Iran, often known as *film-i farsi*.[1] While the cinematic constructions of the onscreen cabaret dancer, her space of performance, and the intradiegetic audience are juxtaposed with larger socio-political and historical discourses, the bulk of this chapter investigates the transformation of the cabaret dancer as a character type developed in the three decades prior to the revolution, one that largely contributed to the bio-economy of the private-sector film industry of Iran.

Screening performing artists

In discussing dance and performing bodies in pre-revolutionary cinema, especially in its early decades, it is very important to consider Iranian cinema's discursive interconnectedness to the pre-existing (live) performing arts scene, mainly the theater. Ideas, themes, genres, and even movement styles prevalent in the Iranian nationalist-modernist theater scene passed into Iranian cinema especially through the actors and directors who became involved in both.[2] Traces of the nationalist operettas and musicals, as well as the historical plays of the post-1920 era that remained in Lalehzar theaters of the pre-revolution period, were also manifested in the Iranian cinema.[3]

The nationalist notions prevalent in the performing arts sphere were also shared by some early cinema directors, including Abdulhusayn Sepanta (1907–69), the director of the first Persian talkie—*Dukhtar-i Lur* (The Lur girl).[4] Like others who endeavored to create a national performing arts industry in early twentieth-century Iran, Sepanta considered Iran's literary treasures, its authentic historical and social subjects, and its rituals, habits, and ceremonies as great sources of inspiration for the creation of culturally and intellectually rich movies. Such cinema, he believed, could showcase the "national soul" of the country and compensate for the technological shortcomings of the Iranian cinema industry.[5]

A number of performing arts and literary personalities were drawn to cinema in the years between 1930 and 1960. These included proponents of national music and operettas, including Ali-Naqi Vaziri, Isma'il Mihrtash of the Barbud Society, and Ruhullah Khaliqi, who composed scores for several feature films of his time.[6] Given the small size of the film industry and film productions in that period, the presence of these cross-over artists could have been influential.[7]

More important for this discussion were the corporeal transmissions of performing styles from stage to screen, via several theater actors who crossed over to the filmic productions after 1945.[8] Among them were the disciples of Mihrtash who were involved in the musical theater productions of the Barbud Society and often appeared in the musical segments of 1950s films, in which the actors moved and performed gestures while lip-synching.[9] This musical interaction often happened between two actors—namely two lovers who sang to each other—or one actor's correspondence with a group that had obvious links to operettas of Lalehzar as well as the *pishpardahkhani* genre.[10]

The graduates of Nasr's Foundation for Acting College (Bunyad-i Hunaristan-i Hunarpishigi) were also drawn to the film industry.[11] While a reason for the relocation of theater actors to cinema after 1950 was the "decaying" situation of private sector theaters in Lalehzar, the exaggerated acting and literary tone of speech in the early films were often linked to the acting style of the Moral theater of the school of Nasr. Furthermore, the cinema of the 1950s also inherited the notions of moral education and themes concerning family and modern lifestyle from the Moral theater.[12]

Dancers involved in the nationalist theater and operetta scenes also crossed over to cinema. These include Asiya Qustaniyan, who acted and danced in the silent film *Haji Aqa Aktur-i sinama* (Haji Aqa, the cinema actor, 1933), and Madame Escampie, who appeared in *Tufan-i Zindigi* (The turmoil of life, 1948) as well as *Variyti-i Bahari* (Spring's variation, 1949). Nilla Cram Cook's company dancers were also involved in cinema as actors, dancers, and dubbers.[13]

Screening the dancing practices of contemporary social life

Informed by off-screen discursive constructions of the dancing body, its space of performance, and spectatorial culture, the dancing body in cinema was often deployed as a signifying medium for identity. A social dance scene, or even a segment focused on an (uncustomary) bodily practice like women's swimming in bathing suits, was often meant to reflect the social life of a group. This is especially evident in films of the 1950s, which in the tradition of their theatrical predecessor—the moral plays of the first Pahlavi era—exposed their contemporaneous life style through a moral lens. The result was a binary representation of the upper-class versus lower-class, urban versus rural, (nouveau riche) cosmopolitan versus pure and simple, and immoral versus moral. The former in these binaries practiced European social dances and a corporal signifier of the latter was (Iranian) folk dancing. While interacting, these binary groups often went head to head with one another.

The recurrence of European and American social dances in films from the 1950s onward aimed to display the life of "upper-class" Tehranis. Having gained popularity in the social nightlife of large cities (mainly in Tehran), practicing European social dances was also viewed as the corporeal behavior of "modernized" (*mutajaddid*) urbanites in the periodicals of the era. In films, while the main actors could also participate in this activity in various venues, as simplified imitation of these dances did not require much bodily technique, these scenes also reflected the trends of the nightclubs.[14]

Among the European social dances, Rock 'n' Roll had an especially negative undertone, as reflected in the 1957 film *Shabnishini dar Jahannam* (Soirée in hell), where a satirized version of this dance was featured in a scene that takes place in hell.[15] This negative representation echoes the social responses towards this dance, which were also reflected in the periodicals of the era, to the extent that Rock 'n' Roll was identified as a dance in which the female participant loses her virginity.[16] Other urban corporeal practices, which were screened in relation to the cosmopolitan Tehranis, were skiing and swimming.[17] Bathing suits in earlier eras provided the opportunity to showcase underdressed bodies, exemplified by the actress Irin's bikini body in *Qasid-i Bihisht* (Heaven's messenger, 1958), which for some critics marked the beginning of a new era in the presentation of female bodies in Iranian cinema.[18]

In contrast to the aforementioned practices of the "modern" and "upper-class" urban life, regional folk dances showcased rural life, especially in celebratory ceremonies like weddings. While occasionally professional groups appeared in such scenes, most filmic performances were performed by local people who danced to folk instruments in regional costumes of the area.[19] In such segments, the dancers are normally surrounded by an audience; nonetheless, the camera does not emphasize said audience's gaze.[20]

Screening "staged" dancing bodies and their intradiegetic audience

In addition to films that featured social dance practices in rural and urban settings, as I explore in this chapter, most dance segments in films also had an immediate intradiegetic aim: to entertain the spectators within the plot whose identity was constructed as the dance's audience. In these films, the audience watched the dancing bodies simultaneously with the intradiegetic spectators, whose "third" gaze at the dance was also intended to be viewed by the film audience.[21] In correlation to the genre and the period of the film, these intradiegetic spectators and their type of spectatorship varied.[22]

On a rare occasion, in the 1954 *Dukhtari az Shiraz* (A girl from Shiraz), the film's leads attended the performance of Sarkis Djanbzaian's Tehran Ballet Academy, where they watched dance performances of the "national dance" genre.[23] The intradiegetic audience members attending the amphitheater were of both sexes, and their spectatorship was constructed to be only the viewing of dance as an artistic medium. The camera mostly focused on the dancing bodies on stage but also showed the film characters in the audience.[24] While the dance segments were deployed as attractive elements, displaying the recreational activities of the "upper-class" urban life was another purpose behind them.

Dancing for the intradiegetic spectators was a common characteristic of most historical films, where "exotic" dancers were featured to entertain kings or sultans in their courts and harems.[25] Such dance segments, often called "*raqs-i sharqi*" (oriental dance), permeated the historical films of the 1950s, exemplified by the 1957 *Buhlul Divanah'i 'Aqil* (Buhlul, the wise lunatic), written and produced by Muhammad Shabparah.[26] A screen adaptation of a play staged in Lalehzar, the film was one of the most extravagant films of its era, which garnered media attention. *Buhlul* was specifically advertised for its dance scenes described as "large ballets" (*balah-i buzurg*) performed by "oriental" (*sharqi*) dancers, highlighted by the two leading dancers of Spanish and French backgrounds, Carmen and Kunchita.[27] Despite their oriental attire and the Persian-Arabic-inspired music, these performers executed ballet-based dances in harem-like settings which very much resembled Hollywood renderings of oriental dances (see Figure 5.1).

Referring to the excessive number of screenings of Indian and Egyptian films in pre-revolutionary Iran, most film scholars relate the prevalence of dance sequences in the Iranian films to the influence of cinema from these countries, both of which had a large popular reception in Iran.[28] Aesthetic-wise, however, the dances in harem scenes in Iranian films resembled scenes found in orientalist Arab Hollywood movies, largely shown in the 1950s in Iran.[29] *Thief of Damascus* (1952), inspired by *Arabian Nights*, is one example of dozens of films of this genre that were shown in Iran in 1954.[30] The film was introduced in the weekly *Sitarah'i Sinama* as the first *sharqi* film to present the characters Scheherazade, Ali Baba, Sinbad, and Aladdin with the usual *sharqi* dances and harem scenes of this genre of Hollywood films.[31] The

Figure 5.1 Dancer in a historical film of the 1950s
Ida Meftahi's personal archive.

film *Son of Sindbad* (1955) was also reviewed in the same magazine as "a film full of harem scenes with seditious beauties and adorable bodies in such hilarious scenes that the audience would not notice the time passing."[32] Using similar terminology, costuming, and style as *raqs-i sharqi*, the harem scenes in many Iranian films of the historical genre were rather influenced by orientalist Hollywood films.[33]

The most dominant venues for dance featured in Iranian films after 1950 were cabarets and cafés. In this context, the films not only highlighted female dancing bodies but simultaneously showcased the voyeuristic gaze of their intradiegetic male audiences.[34] *Kafahs* and cabarets were commonly featured in these films, when one or a few of the main (male) characters of the film visited such venues to drink and be entertained.

Performers with different backgrounds appeared as cabaret dancers in films. According to published documents on cinema, in some of the earlier cabaret-related films, professional dancers with ballet training acted and danced in café settings.[35] The majority of those who participated in the early *kafah* scenes in films, however, appeared to be "untrained" dancers, and their lack of experience and training manifested in their movements. The dancers Linda and Zina, as they were introduced in the movie credits, performing two pieces to a live jazz orchestra on the café stage in the film *Ghiflat* (Negligence, 1953) belong to this group.[36]

Another genre often performed in the onscreen *kafah* setting (as in the off-screen *kafah* settings) was belly dance. The execution of the style in earlier films varied among the performers, and perhaps depended on their movement abilities.[37] For instance, a dancer who performed belly dance both on a *kafah* stage as well as in a home gathering in *Ghiflat* is relatively stationary, and amateur-looking, and only changed levels while moving her torso and shoulders.[38] *Raqs-i 'arabi* segments featured in films after 1968 were executed in a more professional style by famous cabaret dancers including Jamileh and Nadiya, who also acted in the films.

As with off-screen *kafah*, Indian dance (*raqs-i hindi*) was also featured in the onscreen *kafah* and cabaret settings. Examples of this can be seen in *Payman-i Dusti* (The pact of friendship, 1960), performed by Nadiyah (as introduced in the movie credits). The dancer wore a sari and emphasized some presumably Indian gestures, including quick side-to-side neck isolation movements, raised eyebrows and eyes, and finger pointing to the chin, to semiotically transform her Iranian dance into an Indian one.

Iranian solo-improvised dance was popularly featured in the onscreen *kafah*s and cabarets. The films of the 1950s often featured home-based dances, in (relatively covering) quotidian Western-style attire, which appeared to be performed by members of the *mutribi* troupes or the film cast members. One example involves the dancer in *Lat-i Javanmard* (The manly *jahil*, 1958), one of the earliest "tough-guy" (*jahili*) films, in which the dancer moves to the tune of *babakaram*, which became the signifier of the *jahili* milieu (see Figure 5.2 for an example of jahili depiction).[39] Moving in an amateur manner, her dance includes some jerky movements of the *mutribi* style, as well as humorous gestures (like throwing kisses to her audiences).

Another intradiegetic spectatorship for dance was that of the male lover. In this context, the dancer used dance as a mode of bodily communication, that is, the female character expressed love and flirtatiousness to her lover.[40] This is exemplified by the actress Furuzan's (a.k.a. Parvin

Figure 5.2 Mard-ha va Namard-ha (Manly men and unmanly men), movie poster, 1973
Ida Meftahi's personal archive.

Khayrbakhsh, b. 1937) famous dance segments in *Ganj-i Qarun* (Qarun's treasure, 1965): dancing in a garden for her lover's view, she lip-synched to an affectionate song.[41] The flirtatious dance of the lover also appeared as the mindscreen segments, when the central male figure recalled her in his day-dreams.[42] Unexpected and out-of-place dance segments were also featured in some films, especially when the actress playing the key character was also a capable dancer.[43] For instance, in *Dalahu* (1967), Furuzan did a flirtatious dance in a car and later in nature.[44] Because of the popularity of dance segments, such scenes were sometimes shown in color.[45] Relying on these unexpected dance and song scenes, and referring to them as key elements of fantasy, the film scholar Muhammad Tahaminejad identifies the pre-revolutionary Iranian cinema as *raw'ya-pardaz*, or, the "escapist" who is out of touch with the reality of the society of the time.[46]

The cabaret dancer on the cinematic screen

Starting with the film *Sharmsar* (1950), the *kafah* and cabaret served as spaces for the transgression of corporeal norms; as well, their (predominantly) female performers and male audiences were regularly depicted in films which were arguably in accordance with their negative discursive and social associations. The café and cabaret were regularly shown in films to be places for partaking in dissolute activities, such as committing fraud, planning a robbery, engaging in a physical fight, or having a rendezvous with an indecent woman.

The earlier films made in the 1950s featured cafés attended by a range of audiences, which were perhaps closer to those termed by Sasan Fatemi as "modern" café chantants.[47] Among audiences of both sexes in these *kafahs*, some men were depicted as wearing ties—a type that the film scholar Hamid Naficy labels as dandy, while some women were outfitted in European-style trendy dresses.[48] In the later films, and parallel to the off-screen setting, these types of audiences were moved to the upper-class cabarets and their wealthier monde.

The other type of café that gradually emerged in films was *saz-va-zarbi kafahs*, which showcased a male-dominated audience. This was concurrent with the emergence of the "tough guy" (*jahil*) character, complete with gangster hat, as a central figure of pre-revolutionary commercial cinema, especially in the films *Junub-i Shahr* (South of the city, 1958) and *Lat-i Javanmard*. As discussed in Chapter 4, this character was discursively associated with the subculture of southern Tehran. While celebrating certain manly values that represented the "traditional" sector of society, this character mingled in *kafahs* and cabarets to drink alcohol and watch dance.

When the films focused on the female employees who worked in such settings, including the dancers and singers and even food servers, the narratives often constructed them with morally dubious reputations—an attribute that was attached to them through their work space.[49] Featuring moral messages while showcasing *kafahs* and cabarets as pleasurable sites of immorality, the films often framed cabaret dancers as women who were deceived and thus took refuge in that dissolute environment. Such narrative constructions first began with the successful *Sharmsar* and permeated the films produced shortly thereafter. These films often depicted a cabaret performer of rural origin, who was deceived by an urban man to leave the village for an exciting urban experience. In Tehran, she first found a job as a singer in a low-key *kafah*, and later she became a famous performer.[50]

By 1954, such a theme was already exhausted to the point that film critic Tughrul Afshar complained that most films produced after *Sharmsar* portrayed a "deceived woman" (*farib khurdah*) or a "misled" (*gumrah*) one, or as he termed her, an "oppressed prostitute" (*fahishah'i sitamdidah*) who took refuge in a cabaret and ended up a successful singer or a dancer. Afshar further noted that in such films, even a "chaste woman" could ordain to become a performer.[51]

Concurrently, others, like Hasan Shirvani and the director Samuel Khachikian, expressed similar criticism about the prevalence of cabaret themes in Iranian film.[52] Both Afshar and Khachikian also attested that the improper insertions of dance and song segments damaged the plot, as it had to be paused while the intradiegetic *kafah* spectators and the cinema audiences all gazed at the dancing bodies.[53] Aligning dance segments with the rise of box office sales, critics vastly disputed the intentions behind their insertion into the films' plots.

In the eyes of these "dance and song" critics, the situation worsened when Mahvash (introduced in Chapter 4), from the *mutribi* scene, was introduced to the screen. With her off-screen fame, as well as her grace, her serendipitous voluptuousness, and her vernacular feminine "flirtatious" gestures (*'ishvah*), Mahvash's dance and song segments guaranteed box office sales, even for the European and American-cowboy films into which her song and dance segments were inserted (see Figure 5.3).[54] In the years to follow, other celebrated dancers also joined the screen to increasingly act as film characters. The films did not only feature dancers of Iranian background; indeed, non-Iranian dancers also danced and/or acted on the screen. This even included the appearance of Nadia Gamal, the famed Egyptian belly dancer, who acted in the Iranian films *Bazi-i Shans* (The game of luck, 1968) and *Bazi-i 'Ishq* (The game of love, 1968).

While in the late 1960s the cabaret dancer became a recurring character type in films, she accrued a more central role in general movie plots, especially after the 1970 film *Raqqasah'i Shahr* (The city's dancer). Thereafter came films such as *Mutrib* (1972), *Duktur va Raqqasah* (The doctor and the dancer, 1974), *Jahil va Raqqasah* (The *Jahil* and the dancer, 1976), *Ashk-i Raqqasah* (The tear of the dancer, 1977), and *Ramishgar* (The performer, 1976), featuring dancer-actors like Shahrzad, Jamileh, and Shahnaz Tehrani, and actors such as Furuzan and Shourangiz Tabata'i enacting the dancer roles (see Figures 5.4–5.7). With this new shift, the appearance and characterization of dancers in the films also changed. In what follows, I analyze

Figure 5.3 On Mahvash's popularity
"I am sure you all know Ms. Mahvash, she used to take part in all *film-i farsi*s; and her dance was so popular among the third-rate class that in some cities her dance would be inserted into cinematic programs, even if the film is a foreign one."

Figure 5.4 Raqqasah'i Shahr (City's dancer, 1970), movie poster
Ida Meftahi's personal archive.

Figure 5.5 Harja'i (The mobile harlot, 1974), movie poster
Ida Meftahi's personal archive.

Figure 5.6 Usta Karim, Nawkaritim! (Lord I am at your service, 1974), movie poster
Ida Meftahi's personal archive.

Figure 5.7 Dushmani-i Zan (Women's enemy, 1958), movie poster
Ida Meftahi's personal archive.

the gradual reconfiguration and transformation of the dancers' characters, as well as their corporeal presentation and depiction in the three decades of their presence in Iranian cinema (1949–79).

The transformation of the onscreen cabaret dancer

With the growth of Tehran's nightlife, the filmic productions focusing on cabaret personalities increased. The earlier films mostly focused on singers, usually cast with a few famous performers of the time, including Puran (Farrukh-dukht Abbasi Taliqani, 1933–90) and Dilkash (Ismat Baqirpur Babuli, 1925–2004); dancers only appeared in films in minor roles. While the *raqqas*'s character gradually became more dominant after 1970, the dancer-prostitute narrative surrounding her quotidian life had persistently repeated in the movies. This resulted in the creation of a character type for *raqqas*, who had recurring personas (both positive and negative) in her private and public cabaret life (onscreen). Turning to these melodramatic films with the dancer as a character type, below I explore some of these commonalities.

As with the off-screen narratives, the dancers and most women associated with *kafah*s and cabarets shared similar origins and life stories in the films. Some of them were depicted as "capricious" (*havasbaz*) women who appeared to be enjoying their jobs.[55] The majority of onscreen dancers, however, were depicted as independent women who had no men to support them financially, and maybe morally; thus, they needed to work, and so their job in the "dissolute" environment of the café was somehow justified. Since they were not considered "licentious" women by nature, they could be saved from the cabaret and converted to chaste women. In their private lives on film, the dancers were even self-sacrificing single mothers—who often did not expose their child to others—or were supporting their needy/ill mother.[56]

While the earlier films with the cabaret theme portrayed the cabaret performers as runaway girls from small towns or villages, most of the onscreen dancer-characters of later decades came from poor or broken urban families.[57] Intradiegetic "decent" married women from wealthy families, who were deceived and as a result lost their families, could also end up on the cabaret stage.[58] Even being popular stars in their private lives, the onscreen dancers could appear to feel lonely and abandoned, in a few instances to the extent that some committed suicide.[59]

Cabaret was often depicted as an indecent space, where cabaret dancers and other *kafah* women were exploited. A regular antagonist in cabaret-related films, the cabaret owner was often depicted as an oppressive and malicious "nouveau riche" who used his impoverished laborers in various illegitimate ways; this is similar to the discursive characterization of cabaret owners offscreen. His hegemonic power not only governed *kafah* and cabaret employees in their professional careers, but also factored into their private lives.[60]

One of the work conditions of *kafah*s and cabarets, depicted onscreen, was the "promissory notes" (*saftah*)—a large amount of money that the performer had to pay at the time of contract, making her commit to that venue for the duration of the contract. Many cabaret-related films evolved around the struggling condition of a dancer who is forced to bear the despotism of a racketeer cabaret owner for fear of imprisonment due to her inability to pay the heavy fine.[61] The onscreen cabaret owner also forced the dancers to drink with the customers and even to sleep with them. While this was a reference to the common *fishkhuri* practice discussed in Chapter 4, in films it was referred to as "sitting with the customers" or "working at the bar."[62]

Even when the performer got married and left the cabaret, the cabaret owner was capable of blackmailing her by exposing her "dark secrets" to her new family.[63] To do so, he forced the dancer's former co-workers to help deceive her. Forced to collaborate with the cabaret owner, the co-workers were sometimes depicted as jealous women, though occasionally they were more sympathetic.[64] In some films, the cabaret owner was able to drag the former cabaret dancer's daughter down "immoral" paths, including prostitution and other crimes.[65]

As a regular part of the cabaret mise-en-scène, the intradiegetic audience often responded to dancers with enthusiastic gazes and comments.[66] While some intradiegetic spectators desired only to have drinks with the dancers in the performance venue, in some films they expected a continued relationship and reacted harshly when the dancer did not respond positively.[67] The female intradiegetic cabaret audiences were normally portrayed as jealous and negating, especially when in a relationship with a key male character in the film.[68]

In cabaret-related films, as in social narratives, the legitimacy of the cabaret dancer as an artist was repeatedly questioned; she would progress in her job merely for being sexually involved with the cabaret owner.[69] Films also depicted aging as an issue for a dancer's career: she was only able work for a short period of her youth; when she aged, she lost her attractiveness to male audiences. With the exception of a well-to-do dancer in *Ashk-i Raqqasah* (1977) who looked back fondly on the successful days of her career when she was admired by her fans, older dancer characters were often impoverished and abandoned. This is exemplified by the characterization of Guli in *Payman-i Dusti* (1960) as a bankrupt older dancer who begged for money and vodka ('*araq*) in *kafahs*. In a scene when advising a young dancer on stage of a café, she lamented:

> Do you know me? My real name is Ma'sumah [literally, "innocent"], and I am truly innocent. But these people have hurt me so much. Don't let them deceive you. Value your youth and art. Once, I also used to dance on this stage. The audience would have killed to watch me and the *kafah* owner adored me. But when I aged, and lost my success, they kicked me out like a wandering dog. Now I have to beg for a glass of '*araq*.

As leading characters or in minor roles, the dancers were often depicted in a relationship with the leading hero of the films; the length and strength of their connections, however, varied from one-night stands to passionate love affairs and, often, marriage. Echoing the off-screen dancer-prostitute narrative and without direct references to *fishkhuri*, in some films the dancers were portrayed as offstage prostitutes after participating in their onstage acts; such transformation in film narrative was not overseen in the plot, but was assumed and thus unfolded organically.[70] Moreover, the prostitute characters were often capable dancers.[71]

When partaking in seductive plots in films, the dancer character was normally depicted as a "licentious" woman, rather than a needy, oppressed dancer type.[72] She was often rejected by the leading man in the film. Another type of relationship was when the dancer fell for the male character, but had no hope of uniting with or marrying him due to her occupation; subsequently, she admitted the man's superiority to her, encouraging him to find a better woman.[73]

The marriage plot was common in the *raqqas*-centred movies, when a mutual romance between a dancer and the leading man—often an audience member—led to their marriage.[74] A prerequisite for such a marriage was for the dancer to withdraw from her career and become a housewife. Although the dancer was the one who left her job, the male-centric treatment of the topic in films was manifested in the common use of specific expressions in this regard, which made the male lover the subject and the agent in the action, reducing the dancer to a mere object with no agency.[75] In some films, "pouring the redemption water" (*ab-i tawbah rikhtan*), that is, the man pouring purifying water onto the woman, was enacted as a symbolic purification ritual in domed religious places, such as a holy figure's shrine (*imamazadah*), where the woman swore to give up her job and forget her past.[76]

Such "celebrated" re-treatment of the dancer from the public stage to home was the happy ending of some plots.[77] In many productions, however, the marriage was just the beginning of the challenges of keeping a steady relationship with a former *raqqas*, especially due to the interventions of the cabaret owner, who usually created trouble for the now-married dancer.[78] Threatening her with the promissory note, or with revealing her dark past to her new extended family, the cabaret owner sought to drag the dancer back to the "dissolute" environment of *kafah*—from the confines of her husband's home to the public stage. Emphasizing the enduring mistrust of the dancer's husband towards his wife, the cabaret owner often easily succeeded in ruining the new life of the dancer.

The virtuous husband, who constantly was told "a *kafah* woman is always a *kafah* woman," finally lost his trust.[79] He slapped his wife, called her a "mobile harlot" (*harja'i*) and expelled her from his private home back to the public sphere.[80] The rest of the narratives in this vein unfolded with the dancer's struggle with her new life. She went back to dancing, or found a "proper" job working in a factory.[81] The second climax of such narratives occurred when the husband recognized his misjudgment and rushed decision; he then asked her back into his life, taking her yet again from the public sphere to the safe environment of her home.

The onscreen *raqqas* as a character

Besides her physical desirability, the onscreen *raqqas* character type was normally portrayed as an attractive femme fatale with a variety of characteristics. She was often a smart, witty, young, and independent (to some extent) woman who exhibited good manners of a *jahil*. The ultimate "virtuous" act for a dancer in the film was when she stopped dancing and was transformed to an angel-like housewife; momentarily, she lost some of her attractive characteristics, including her wit and tough-guy tone.

When the cabaret dancer became a leading role in film plots, her act and costuming changed. Her 1950s-style mid-length dress was replaced with a low-cut mini-dress.[82] Her solo-improvised dance became increasingly sexualized and more professionalized, with an overstressed increase in the radius of her *qir*.[83] This style of solo-improvised dance was repeatedly executed in films after 1968 by the *raqqasah* character, wherein she often lip-synched and mimed to the flirtatious and often humorous diegetic songs.[84] Gazing back happily at her audience, the cinematic *raqqas* was portrayed as an over-confident performer.

As an onscreen persona, the dancer was often self-reflexive: the confessionary lines of her speech or the diegetic music lyrics—those that she lip-synched during their act—revealed or highlighted some "unknown" aspects of her character or life. In those diegetic songs, she often spoke of herself as an attractive "commodity" for men's gaze. For instance, in *Gulpari Jun*, the dancer (enacted by Jamileh) tried to portray herself negatively by singing:

> (You know) who I am? I am the one who craves from head to toe! Don't go away, come close, hug me until you are alive, the white glass of my body is for everyone, my warm breast is for everybody, I give away my body to anyone who wants it, I have a gadabout heart, I want to spend tonight with this guy and the next night with the other, I am an erratic woman, I am flirtatious, and *harja'i*, the fire of my body is hot, I am coy from head to toe.

The sad-clown narrative was also common for dancers to express in such situations, perhaps handed down to them from their *mutribi* backgrounds. This is exemplified in *Mitris*, where the cabaret-*raqqas* (enacted by Jamileh) sang: "my body is filled with sorrow, but I dance; my life is upsetting, but I laugh instead of crying." Reinforcing the power relations within the larger social discourse, such confessionary narratives of self were also expressed in the dancer's conversations with her lover, when she commonly condemned herself for her bad reputation.[85] For instance, in *Bihijab*, Kulthum is a dancer/prostitute who is in love with the leading male character, who in turn falls for a Christian girl. Kulthum tells her lover, "I live in the ignominious area of the city; I am a *harja'i*."

The act of self-condemnation for having an association with the nightlife industry was visibly performed in *Junub-i Shahr*, in which 'Iffat, a chaste woman and a single mother, found a job as a server in a *kafah*. Persuaded and threatened by another *kafah* customer, she asked her lover to leave her, stating, "I am a woman of *kafah*, you can find a better person." Then, to force him to leave her, she got drunk, climbed the stage and started dancing hysterically with a tambourine in hand.[86] From there she yelled at her lover, "leave me, I belong to everyone," equating performing on the *kafah* stage to being owned by everyone. As his response, her "virtuous" lover slapped her onstage. Later, he succeeded in getting her hand in marriage.

The striking action of slapping a dancer onstage was not unique to the abovementioned film; the *raqqas* in *Raqqasah'i Shahr* was also dragged from stage and slapped by her *jahil* lover who commanded her: "leave the *kafah* before I break your neck!" The intradiegetic dancers were also slapped off-stage in various situations in the plots for their disobedience by different male characters. The slappers included a dissatisfied cabaret owner, an angry audience member, a disappointed lover, and a revengeful husband.[87] Slapping the dancer, the male character also uttered demeaning words that reflected the common stereotypes associated with the job off-screen. This included terms such as "mobile harlot" (*harja'i*), prostitute (*bad-karah* or *ruspi*), as well as "*kafah* woman" (*zan-i kafah'i*).[88] Most of these demeaning terms were based on the negative associations of *kafah*s as their performance space: the *kafah/*cabaret stage constituted a public space that made its performer a public woman (*harja'i*); dancing on that stage was the equivalent of an intimate relationship with each audience member.

These terms were also deployed as controversial titles of some films featuring a *kafah* entertainer as a central character. For instance, the leading characters of the films *Ruspi* (The prostitute, 1969) and *Harja'i* (1974) were both cabaret performers. Unlike their controversial titles, their characters were talented performers with no evidence of "loose" behavior or engaging in sexual activity for payment. It is important to note that such an uncritical attitude was not only common in the films but also in secondary literature on Iranian cinema, where imprecise terms such as "entertainers," "notorious woman" (*zan-i ma'rufah*), or "prostitute" (*fahishah*) are interchangeably used to refer to cabaret performers.[89]

Real "reel" dancers, off-screen power and onscreen roles

As some of the key dancer roles were enacted by renowned off-screen dancers, including Mahvash, Jamileh, and Shahrzad (whose biographies were explored in the previous chapter), as well as Furuzan, I turn here to the ways these real personas were portrayed as film characters. As I will demonstrate, there is an interrelation between the off-screen discursive construction and power relations and the performer's casting and characterization in films.

Mahvash appeared in about twenty-eight films, all at the height of her off-screen career in the 1950s: her screen presence was often not in the capacity of an actor, but rather of a performer whose dance and music segments were inserted into the films. Her off-screen fame and the popularity of her dance and music segments made her a representative of the dance and song film genre at the time. In response, some cinema owners and directors resisted this situation by boycotting the films featuring Mahvash, or by ridiculing her.[90] Yet, even this anti-Mahvash movement in the cinema community did not stop the producers from forcing her segments onto committed anti-dance and song directors such as Hushang Kavusi, the Iranian pre-revolutionary cinema's foremost critic.[91] After Mahvash's death in a car accident, once again, her fans proved their appreciation for her dance and song segments by casting votes to view her recordings in the film *Gul-i Gumshudah* (The lost flower, 1961), in a referendum held in the press by the company 'Asr-i Tala'i.[92] Mahvash's role in *Birahnah'i Khushhal* (1957) as herself (see n. 72), where she unexpectedly appeared in her underwear to seduce Murad, was seemingly quite similar to the stereotypes associated with her off-screen.

Like her off-screen roles were depicted in the press, Jamileh's roles in films were often not stereotypical. With an athletic body and a fast-pace dance style (up to double-time of the music), her onscreen character was a strong and successful dancer who engaged in physical fights with men in the manner of a martial artist—a rare activity for women in Iranian cinema.[93] As specified in her interviews, Jamileh aimed to have a distinct position as a dancer-actor in Iranian cinema, similar to that of Samia Gamal in Egyptian cinema.[94] She certainly achieved her desired role as an independent woman in several films, especially those produced by her powerful husband, Muhammad Arbab.[95] Her onscreen character, like her off-screen self, never sacrificed her dancing career for the love of a man.

Her "decent" dancer character was glorified in Jamileh's central role in *Khushgiltarin Zan-i 'Alam* (The most beautiful woman on earth, 1972): acting as Sitarah ("star"), an independent and good-looking artist, she resisted the unjust conditions of cabaret where women were subjected to sexual exploitation.[96] Again enacting Sitarah, another leading role for Jamileh was in *Kaj Kulah Khan* (1973) as a successful and prestigious dancer who used her irresistible sexual appeal to assist the police in arresting the criminal cabaret owner.[97] In *Mitris* (1973), she was the leading female character again: here she was a *raqqas* who escaped the dirty environment of the cabaret and its despotic cabaret owner/manager to become a nurse. While depicting the common stereotypes associated with cabaret dancing, Jamileh's role embodied agency, power, and purity.[98]

Shahrzad (Kubra Sa'idi) also danced and acted in dozens of films, but unlike Jamileh, she never appeared in leading roles and certainly never in the role of a privileged woman. When acting as a *raqqas*, her roles often came close to the quotidian dancer-prostitute narrative as exemplified in *Qaisar* (1969) and *Dash Akul* (1971). In *Tangna* (Impasse, 1973), Shahrzad acted as Ashraf, an older *kafah* woman who sought to save her beloved, the male hero of the film, Ali; yet, she was forced to sleep with the antagonist. Although there were no hints to her character's earlier involvement in dancing, some film scholars interpreted her to be an old dancer, connecting her quotidian life to her onscreen role.[99]

Contrasting Jamileh and Shahrzad, it appears that power relations could have influenced the ways the performers were represented in films. Jamileh, on the one hand, as a wealthier woman empowered by the socio-economic status of her husband, Arbab, was able to secure better roles onscreen. Her desire to control her onscreen role is reflected in her interviews where she declared her unwillingness to dance onscreen unless her character required it.[100] Shahrzad, on the other hand, with all her literary achievement, was not able to escape the shadow of her "dark past" onscreen as well as off-screen.[101] Yet, becoming one of the earliest female directors of Iranian cinema, she later challenged the male-dominated cinema industry of Iran.

With the advent of women as central characters in cinema, and their subsequent gaining of power, some female actresses expressed their desire to negotiate their roles or challenge the established "hierarchy of feeling" in the Iranian cinema.[102] Furuzan, one of the highest-paid actresses of the Pahlavi era and the lead character of *Raqqasah'i Shahr*, for instance, in an interview expressed her dissatisfaction with her recurring weeping scenes in films, declaring "I won't cry again."[103] Later on, however, she appeared to have lost hope in controlling her onscreen depiction when she stated: "I am not willing to act in films anymore; I can't stand being in front of the camera when the director asks me to be more sexy and flirtatious, to pull my skirt higher or move seductively."[104]

As Furuzan attested, similar to off-screen cabaret owners, the film directors disciplined the dancers and actors. This included regulating the dancers' movements, clothing, and behavior to appear "unrestrained" onscreen.[105] Directing the extras that acted as the intradiegetic audience—as cabaret films' usual mise-en-scène—the directors also controlled the ways they looked at, interacted with, and responded to the dancer. The directors also guided the gaze of the cinema audience by framing certain bodily sections of the dancers.

In the final years of the Pahlavi era, there was a backlash from the cinema community towards representation of women onscreen and their mistreatment off-screen, exemplified by controversial coverage of the sexual exploitation of young female acting enthusiasts by film studios in *Film va Hunar* in 1974.[106] Questioning and condemning the actresses who "got naked" in front of the camera became another recurring theme in this weekly.[107] At the same time some powerful female casts who resented the ways their bodies had been treated left their jobs forever as they could not tolerate the pressures imposed on their bodies in performance.[108] Others announced that they would not act in erotic films anymore.[109] Nevertheless, new faces were replacing them to keep the private-sector entertainment industry of the Pahlavi era running—an industry which, in the absence of governmental support, was highly dependent on the bio-economy of its dancers and actresses.

The concerns expressed by these actresses were interconnected to the larger discourse on "nudity" (*birahnigi*) in the performing arts that had started earlier, especially with the recruitment of dancers into the Lalehzar theater and cinema. This was reflected in numerous accounts produced between 1950 and 1979 in the national(ist) cinema discourse. One example is a *Sitarah'i Sinama* article written by M. Alkhass which ridiculed cinema for showing "seductive" (*tahrik amiz*) dancers, with their naked waving bellies.[110] Such explicit reference to nudity in relation to belly dance permeated the cinema discourse of the 1950s, exemplified in Siamak Pourzand's account that interpreted the insertion of "seductive" belly dance (*raqs-i shikam*) performed by "naked dancers" into films as an abuse of the audience's sexual complexes.[111] Arguably, the belly dancing body in the Iranian films of the era compensated for the lack of sex scenes in the films. This is similar to the role of oriental dancing bodies in harem scenes of Hollywood Arab films in the years between 1930 and 1950, which, as described by Ella Shohat, provided a "legitimate" means for the directors to show eroticized "othered" female bodies, while bypassing the codes of moral censorship.[112]

The popularity of belly dance and its irrelevance to the plot structure was testified to in earlier accounts such as Afshar's, which questioned the performance of belly dance in a small home gathering in the film *Ghiflat* for which the actress got naked (*lukht shud*).[113] The sensitivities towards belly dance were to the extent that, up until the early 1960s, a film actress who took part in this genre was perceived as contentious and was classified as a loose actress who was willing to engage in sexual relations with the film directors offstage to be able to progress in her film career.[114] Moreover, the dancers who played roles only in the dance segments of the films were largely interpreted as being prostitutes, exemplified in a *Sitarah'i Sinama* article that labeled these performers "the prostitutes of southern Tehran," whose display would disseminate "prostitution" (*fahsha*) in society.[115]

The dancing body was largely associated with "eroticism" (*shavat*), a selling factor in films.[116] Most critics aligned featuring dancers with bringing in more audiences to cinema. For instance, the director Aziz Rafi'i related the financial failure of his film *Mahtab-i Khunin* (The bloody moonlight, 1955) to the lack of dance scenes.[117] Others, like the famous actor and director Majid Moshini, who first criticized such common filmic presentations of dance in Iranian cinema, later employed dance scenes in his productions.[118]

However, my close examination of the dancing body in Iranian pre-revolutionary films indicates that, except for belly dance, which due to its attire marked "nakedness" (*lukhti*) in the cinema of the 1950s, the dancing body and perceptions of "nakedness" changed over time. For instance, the attire of cabaret dancers who were perceived as "semi naked" were, in fact, more covered than those of the late 1960s.[119] Similarly, the attire of post-1968 onscreen cabaret dancers—who wore mini-skirts to pave the way for cameras to zoom in at their legs—was more revealing than the midi skirts of early 1960s.

This change of attitude in the depiction of the dancing bodies runs parallel to the clear inclination of the media to depict nudity and sex. Within the last three decades of Iranian film production prior to the 1979 Revolution, the female actress of Iranian cinema drastically transformed. While early on female actresses often appeared as chaste performers with a covered body—whose faces and eyes were framed by the camera—in the late 1950s and early 1960s, a new type of woman emerged: typecast as a "vamp" (as termed by one journalistic account), her portrayer's calves and neck were the subject of the camera's gaze.[120] By the late 1960s, it seems "sex was trendy" in the Iranian cinema—as indicated by the title of an article in the cinema journal *Film va Hunar*. While the explicit discussion of "sexiness" and "sex idols" in regard to Iranian performers permeated in the cinema-related press, the camera emphasized the sexualized bodies of underdressed actresses onscreen to the extent that in some films the actresses appeared topless.[121]

This transformation presumably corresponded with the state's regulation of films. The government's performance commissioner looked after the cinema from early on, banning or censoring films that were considered to be against public morals and national policy, including those films with overt exposure of sex, nudity, and violence.[122] But in 1965, to minimize the cutting out of segments of the films due to censorship, the state imposed a limitation on the entrance of children and youth under the age of eighteen for films containing nudity and explicit scenes of sex, sadism, and violence.[123] Nevertheless the label "restricted for under 18" itself only increased the box office for these films.[124] While, as reported by the film directors, the state imposed more bodily restrictions on Iranian films, the prevalent scenes of sexuality and those exposing women's scantily clad bodies in the last decade testify to a more relaxed attitude in the previewing stage.[125] With all the controversies surrounding the dancer's character, the dancing body corresponded with the moral codes of Iranian cinema, and the transformation of onscreen actresses. Moreover the refashioning of the dancing body in films, especially in terms of attire, corresponded with the transformation of the quotidian female body on a larger scale.

The dancing body, a signifier of degeneration in commercial cinema

In cinema discourse, the dancing scenes were regarded as "commercial" (*bazari*) and degrading to cinema as an art form.[126] The early film critic, Tughrul Afshar, with clear influence from the Tudeh Party, seems to be one of the first to apply the term "degenerate" to commercial cinema, in his book published in 1954.[127] Considering his activism an "artistic struggle" (*mubarizah'i hunari*) for the purpose of intellectual and cultural progress of the masses (*tudah*), he rejected commercial cinema in favor of admirable and educational cinema.[128] Later on, however, without having that initial political connotation, degeneration became a prevalent trope in the cinema discourse and one which was often correlated with "dance and song scenes" (*raqs va avaz*) in the 1960s. This theme was explored in a series of articles published in *Film va Hunar*, which focused on resolving the issues of "Persian cinema" (*sinama-yi farsi*).[129] Similar to such discussions on Lalehzar theater, other signifiers of *ibtizal* were *mutribi* performances, comedy scenes as well as "romanticism."[130]

The discussion of "degeneration" in Iranian cinema persisted in *Film va Hunar* to the extent that in 1973 its editors created a section entitled "What is Degeneration and Who Is Degenerate?" to publish the responses of their readers to this question. The published feedback indicates that in comparison to a decade earlier and due to the prevalence of sex scenes and the sexual depictions of the characters, "sex" had become a more dominant manifestation of degeneration.[131]

Along with the *mutribs*, post-1950 Lalehzar, and the *kafah* culture, *film-i farsi* has been categorized as "popular" (*'avam-pasand*) for its dancing and singing scenes and degenerate sexual depictions. Similarly, the audience of *film-i farsi* was often stereotypically cast as being from southern Tehran.[132] To some critics, the films themselves were also seen as propagating the subculture of "southern Tehran." One well-known and prevalent example of such analysis was by the writer Ali-Akbar Akbari, who deployed the term *lumpanizm* (a combination of *lumpenproleterait* and -*ism*) in regards to *film-i farsi* to dismiss the genre's tough-guy characters, behaviors, and culture, as well as its *kafah* dancers.[133] His main criticism was that this social group was not one of the productive forces, was not class conscious, would not participate in the revolution, and therefore their recurring depiction in films would cultivate a culture that harms the revolutionary spirit in society. Akbari's take on *film-i farsi* certainly resembles the initial expectations of new arts proposed by the Tudeh Party, as discussed in Chapter 3. While for the Tudeh Party in the 1940s, *mutribi* culture represented "degeneration", three decades later, *film-i farsi* with ties to the *mutribi* scene, was perceived as anti-revolutionary due to its specific affect on the audience.

Raqqas: a sensual body or a popular character?

Struggling from its early days with various economic issues, including taxation and censorship, the private-sector Iranian cinema found the insertion of dance segments a solution to its economic crisis.[134] The dancer's so-called sensual body onscreen provided an opportunity and a pretext for collective gazing at the female bodies of the "othered," "dissolute" *kafah* woman, while compensating for the lack of sex scenes in the films. The dancing scenes not only showcased the "naked bodies"—as they were imagined at the time—but also teased the imagination of the audience, leading it to thoughts of sexual acts not shown on the screen.[135] While featuring dancing bodies, especially those of belly dancers, marked the commercial cinema as "unworthy" of state support, presumably it had contributed to the marketability of Iranian films locally and possibly in neighboring countries.[136]

The *raqqas*'s corporeal characteristics, including her movements and mimicry, were elating and humorous, while her supposedly out-of-control body, attire, and movements were striking and recognizable. The types of feelings associated with her—sensual, seductive, and passionate—also seemed to fit well with the "hierarchy of feelings" in male-centric Iranian cinema. Often a sidekick or a foil to the male hero of the film, *raqqas* complemented and provided the opportunity for him to be highlighted. This becomes evident in light of the statement made by Siamak Yasimi, a key director of the genre, who described the male heroes of his films as having large souls and chaste characters, and thus hesitant of approaching and expressing their feelings to women.[137] Therefore, the dancer by his side enabled the male hero to exercise his intradiegetic physical power and gender "supremacy," which were demonstrated by his constant slapping of the dancer-character in pre-revolutionary productions.

An heir to the moral theater of the Reza Shah era, Iranian cinema deployed the pleasure of watching the dissolute, while condemning them as immoral. Thus, the framing of the dancer in *kafah* and cabaret settings, the attractive venues of vice—combined with popular tales and comedy—all added to the appeal of these films.[138] Moreover, as a powerful medium for heightened emotionality and the direct addressing of sensibility, melodrama effectively provided a platform to frame the male hero and his sidekick *raqqas*.[139]

The way the cabaret dancer was imagined, presented, and glorified in cinematic productions largely echoed the social narrative of the dancer-prostitute. In these Iranian movies, the dancer's life story unfolded in different ways but always reproduced the dominant narratives of her offstage life and bound her past, present, and future to prostitution. In light of Ann Ubersfeld's notion of "pleasure of understanding" as a subcategory of pleasures associated with spectatorship, the *raqqas* as a familiar character type provided the platform for the audience's pleasure of recognition, while being blamed at the same time.[140]

Adding to Muhammad Tahaminejad's analysis of the escapist nature of the pre-revolutionary Iranian cinema by means of its unexpected dance scenes, I argue that films also became a medium for unfolding the imaginations surrounding the *raqqas*'s character and cultivating the audience's fantasies.[141] If "cinema was the cabaret for the impoverished who could not afford watching it live," as maintained by some film directors, then in the fantasy of films, the male audience could identify with the intradiegetic cabaret audience and the movie hero, the one who rescued this femme fatale by possessing and disciplining her.[142]

In a liminal position between a prostitute and a desirable woman, the *raqqas* was a character depictable on the screen.[143] Moreover, in the late Pahlavi era, when exploitation of the workforce and unjust work conditions were considered Marxist-inspired themes and were banned from being reflected in the media, the financial and sexual exploitation of the cabaret dancers were reflected onscreen, circumnavigating around codes of censorship.

Iranian film scholars often relate the prevalence of dance sequences in films to influences of Indian and Egyptian cinema that were widely seen in Iran.[144]

Perhaps this argument is justified in the case of early films; however, it ignores the influence of the harem dances of Hollywood films on the Iranian historical-films genre and undermines the vital relationship between the cabaret life of Tehran, the onscreen cabaret, and the fact that the cabaret scene and its dancer's character and body were manufactured locally.[145] The Iranian cabaret dancer was often portrayed differently than her Egyptian and Indian counterparts as, in those countries, public dancing for women as an occupation had longer precedence.[146]

Concurrent with the expansion of cities and the monetization of entertainment, some women stepped out to take up these occupations: some came from *mutrib* families who accepted entertainment as a job, but many had to leave their families to join the industry.[147] But the general stigma of the female public performer as the runaway girl or a loose woman whose body belonged to the public's gaze and scrutiny, remained in the social discourse, forcing even the famed female actresses to leave public performance after marriage.[148]

Embarking on the nationalist notions that pervaded performing arts in the early twentieth century, Iranian cinema, which relied on the private-sector economy—and not government funding—soon found dancing bodies a means for its survival. While raising moral concerns and negative responses for its depiction of female dancing bodies, the popular pre-revolutionary cinema conformed to many stereotypes prevailing in society. In Iranian movies, the *raqqasah*'s body acted as a palimpsest upon which traces of myths of her quotidian life, and the fantasies of a male-dominated society, were projected.

Notes

1 Coined by the film critic Hushang Kavusi, *film-i farsi* is a derogatory term used to denigrate the artistic and cultural value of an era (or a genre) of Iranian film production, one roughly covering most films produced beween 1950 and 1979; see Parviz Jahid, "Filmfarsi va guftiman-i intiqad-yi film dar iran" [*Filmfarsi* and the critical discourse on film in Iran], *Radio Zamaneh*, 7 Shahrivar 1391/28 August 2012, www.radiozamaneh.com/47989#.UdIT_T772XQ.
2 For an overview of some of the theater directors who tried the medium of cinema both in the roles of director and actor in the earlier years, see "Bazar-i ashuftah'i sinama-yi iran" [The confused state of the Iranian cinema], *Sitarah'i Sinama*, no. 2, Day Bahman 1332/January or February 1954, 56.
3 Examples of historical/period films include *Rustam va Suhrab* (1957) and *Aqa Muhammad Khan-i Qajar* (1954).
4 Sepanta was involved with the Zoroastrian Theater (*Ti'atr-i Jami'ah'i Zartushtiyan*) before migrating to India, where he directed five films.
5 Abdulhusayn Sepanta, quoted in Hamid Shu'a'i, *Sinama-yi Iran* [Iranian cinema] (Chap-kahnah'i Gilan, 1973), 37; this was a letter written by Sepanta to Shu'a'i in 1959.
6 Examples of such collaborations include Vaziri's composition for Sepanta's *Layli va Majnun* (1935) and Mihrtash's music for *Zindani-i Amir* (Amir's prisoner, 1948). See Ghulam Haydari, *Filmshinakht-i Iran: Filmshinasi-i Sinama-yi Iran,*

1309–1340 [Iranian cinema: A filmography, 1930–61] (Tehran: Cultural Research Bureau, 1994), 45–7.

7   For instance, Ali-Naqi Vaziri, the composer and director of the Musical Club (*kulup-i musiqi*) who produced many nationalist operettas, and Pari Aqabyov, the major star of 1920s operettas, both sought to open cinemas for women.

8   See Haydari, *Filmshinakht*, 23.

9   See Habibullah Nasiri, *Ustad Ismai'l Mihrtash va Jami'ah'i Barbud* [Master Isma'il Mirtash and the Barbud Society] (Tehran: Nahsr-i Dunya-yi Naw, 2004).

10 Examples of such interactions include Majid Mohsini's act in *Bulbul-i Mazra'ah* (The nightingale of the farm, 1957) and Ali Tabish in *Payman-i Dusti* (The pact of friendship, 1960). Some of my interviewees, the actresses Shahin and Fakhri Muradi, both of whom acted in a number of 1950s films, as well as Rahilah and Naghmah, who acted and danced in films of the 1960s, all started their careers in the Barbud Society in their early teen years. My other informant, Firishtah, started her career at age six in the theater of Isphahan (Ti'atr-i' Sipahan). Morteza Ahmadi, the famed theater actor/singer of the genre *pishpardahkhani* whom I also interviewed for this research, acted in films of the 1950s and onward. Shahin, interview with the author, Toronto, 10 October 2011; Fakhri Muradi, interview with the author, Toronto, 25 February 2012. Also see Ardeshir Salehpour, *Taranah'i namayish-ha-yi pishpardahkhani dar iran, 1320–1332* [The lyrics of the *pishpardahkhani* in Iran, 1941–53] (Tehran: Namayish, 2009), 14, 17.

11 Examples of famed cinema actors who were graduates of the Acting College include Majid Moshini, Rafi' Halati, Hushang Sarang, Hamid Qanbari, and Taqi Zuhuri. See Haydari, *Filmshinakht*, 21.

12 See Mir-Ansari and Ziaii, eds, *Guzidah'i asnad-i namayish dar iran* [Selected records of drama in Iran] vol. 2, 21; Haydari, *Filmshinakht*, 26.

13 This includes Haideh Akhundzadeh and Nejad Ahmadzadeh, who acted and choreographed for a few early films including the *Sharmsar* (Ashamed, 1950), *Zindani-i Amir* (1948), and *Shahin-i Tus* (The falcon of Tus, 1954) before founding the Iranian National Ballet Academy, as well as Muhammad-Ali Zarandi and Husayn Danishvar, who became actors afterwards. In the 1960s film *Vampiyar, Zan-i Khun Asham* (Vampiress, the bloodsucking woman), Akhundzadeh, the then director of the Iran Ballet Academy, choreographed some scenes that were to be performed by the company in a harem setting.

14 As my interviewee Shahin—the famed actress of 1950s who tangoed in a segment of *Mademoiselle Khalah* (Mademoiselle Auntie, 1957)—states, in such scenes the actors only knew one easy step and hence kept repeating it. For instance, in *Payman-i Dusti*, several European dances including Mambo, Swing, and Rock 'n' Roll were showcased.

15 Another example is *Tufan dar Shahr-i Ma* (Turmoil in our city, 1958), in which Rock 'n' Roll represented the transgressive behavior of nouveau-riche urban youth. The Rock 'n' Roll scene also included a rural couple's astonishment when witnessing this dance for the first time, and their humorous response when the man mocked the "foreign dance" with his wife and his donkey.

16 "Az raqs-i zamin bitarsid" [Beware of the earth-rattling dance], *Nida-yi Haq*, 19 Tir 1336/30 June 1957, 1, 2. The government's negative stance towards this dance is also manifested in the banning of this genre in Tehran's nightclubs in the 1950s. See Amir Khalil Yahyavi, "Sanad-i shumarah'i 153" [Document number 153], 15 Day 1337/5 January 1959, in *Asnadi az musiqi*, 2: 730–34.

17 Images of "modernist" cosmopolitan Tehranis skiing are depicted in *Payman-i Dusti*. Presenting bodies in swimsuits poolside or on the shore of the Caspian Sea in films of this era signified upper-class "*mutajaddid*" urban activities, as featured in *Lat-i Javanmard* (The manly *jahil*, 1958), directed by Muhsini. Further, the 1953 film *Chihirah Ashina* (The familiar face) made extensive use of a poolside

setting, featuring the famed Iranian (jazz) singer Vigen and his mixed audiences all in swimsuits, continued by another dance segment by a group of young men and women. The excitement about the presence of these anonymous actors was conveyed in their being announced in the credits as "the swimming beauties" (*mahruyan-i shinagar*).

18   See "Dawr, dawr-i six ast" [Sex is trendy], *Film va Hunar*, 26 Mihr 1347/18 October 1968, 25.

19   For instance, Gilani dance was shown in *'Arus-i Farari* (The runaway bride, 1958) and the films *Murad* (1954) and *Bulbul-i Mazra'ah* (The nightingale of the farm, 1957) showcased dances from the province of Luristan.

20   This is possibly due to the fact that, in these dances, the social practice of dance is more important than the spectatorship, and the audience members could become momentary dancing participants if they so wished. Director Ali Hatami's *Hasan Kachal* (The bald Hasan, 1970) and *Murchah Darah* (Ants in the pants, 1969) made use of such scenes for showcasing Tehrani folk customs and women's theatrical games for female audiences of home-based ceremonies.

21   "Third gaze" as identified by Laura Mulvey, "Visual Pleasure and Narrative Cinema," in *The Routledge Reader in Gender and Performance*, ed. Lizbeth Goodman and Jane de Gay (New York: Routledge, 1998), 270–75.

22   In some films the audiences were presented as solely interested in the artistry of the performance, but in the majority of films the spectators were sexually motivated men.

23   In the 1970s, group dances of national dance lineage were also featured in films; they appeared in the form of Broadway musicals, showcasing stylized versions of Iranian dances only for the camera and without the presence of intradiegetic viewers. The director Ali Hatami especially made use of these dances in his film *Baba Shamal* (1971).

24   For instance, in *Dukhtari az Shiraz*, the film's leads attended the performance of Sarkis Djanbzaian's Tehran Ballet Academy. Several sequences of that company's ballet-influenced dances on the stage of an amphitheater were inserted in the film.

25   An early instance of such a scene is the hysterical dance of the theater actress, Asiya Qustaniyan in the silent 1933 production *Haji Aqa Aktor-i Sinama*: dancing with live Persian music on a theatrical stage—with the audience only watching through a third wall—Qustaniyan entertained the king on the theater stage with a hybrid of ballet, Iranian, and oriental-style dances.

26   Other examples include *Khabha-yi Tala'i* (The golden dreams, 1951), *'Arus-i Dijlah* (the Tigris bride, 1954), *Shahin-i Tus* (1954), and *Rustam va Suhrab* (1957).

27   The initial name of the film was *Raqs-i Intiqam* (Vengeful dance), as reported in "Dar istudiu-ha-yi filmbardari-i iran chah miguzarad" [What is going on in Iranian recording studios?], *Sitarah'i Sinama*, no. 49, 17 Day 1334/8 January 1956, 13, 20. It was later called *Buhlul Divanah'i 'Aqil*. Also see M. Afruzah, "Darbarah'i film-i buhlul" [About the film Buhlul], *Pust-i Tihran-i Sinamayi*, no. 10, 21 Azar 1336/12 December 1957, 14–15; Khosrow Parvizi, "Dar dawr va baristudiyu-ha-yi iran" [Around Iran's film studios], *Sitarah'i Sinama*, no.143, 1336/1957, 6.

28   For statistical reports on the number of Egyptian films shown in Iran, see Hamid Shu'a'i, ed., *Farhang-i Sinama-yi Iran* [Iran's cinematic culture] (Tehran: Hirminku, 1354/1975), 51–8; see also Hamid Naficy, *The Social History of Iranian Cinema: The Industrializing Years, 1941–1978* (Durham, NC: Duke University Press, 2011), 160; Muhammad Tahaminejad, *Sinama-yi raw'ya pardaz-i iran* [The escapist cinema of Iran] ('Aks-i Mu'asir, 1364/1986), 46.

29   Rebecca Stone interprets the (balletic) appropriations of belly dance in Hollywood— with the increased mobility and foot work, as well as the toning down of the

body part isolations of the shoulders, ribcage, and hips—as a director's way of sidestepping the moral code laws of Hollywood in the 1940s; see Rebecca Stone, "Reverse Imagery, Middle Eastern Themes in Hollywood," in *Images of Enchantment, Visual and Performing Arts of the Middle East*, ed. Shrifa Zuhur (Cairo: The American University in Cairo Press, 1997), 242–63, 257. A case in point, when appearing in non-Egyptian orientalist cinematic productions, including *Ali Baba and the Forty Thieves* (1954), Samia Gamal's dance resembles the Hollywood harem scene, where her limbs lead her dance, and she de-emphasizes her core movements.

30 Other Hollywood films of this genre shown in Iran include *Son of Ali Baba* (1952) and *Slaves of Babylon* (1953), shown in 1957. For the former see "Pisar-i Ali Baba ... yik film-i sharqi-i digar" [Ali Baba's Son ... Another eastern/oriental film], *Sitarah'i Sinama*, no.3, 1332/1954, 22; and "Barnamah'i ayandah'i sinama riks, sinama dayana" [The next screenings of Rex Cinema, Dayana Cinema], *Sitarah'i Sinama*, no. 61, 9 Urdibihisht 1335/29 April 1956, 22. For the latter, see "Dar sinama humay-sinama taj" [In Cinema Humay and Cinema Taj], *Sitarah'i Sinama*, no. 106, 18 Farvardin 1336/7 April 1957.

31 "Duzd-i damishq" [Thief of Damascus], *Sitarah'i Sinama*, no. 3, 1332/1954, 7.

32 "Sinama-ha-yi riks-plaza-taj, i'shq-ha-y-i 'pisar-i sandbad va khayyam" [Rex, Plaza, and Taj Cinemas, the loves of Sandbad's son and Khayyam], *Sitarah'i Sinama*, no. 105, Nawruz 1336/March 1957, 24.

33 Dancing for the kings and sultans was a segment prevalent in *ruhawzi* performances. Also, the concept of oriental dance was in use in the modernist theatrical sphere of the 1920s, linked to the transnational orientalism of the early twentieth century. Aqabayov's "dance of the seven veils" (*raqs-i haft hijab*) in *Salomé* is one example of such works; see "Talar-i madrasah'i aramanah" [The venue of the Armenian School], *Iran*, no. 834, 20 Jumadi al-avval 1339/9 Feb. 1921, 4. As a style, *raqs-i sharqi* remained prevalent in the historical plays of Lalehzar and Sipahan (a theater in Isphahan) where the dancers and musicians would be asked to entertain the kings. Firishtah, interview with the author.

34 Such a scene was also featured in the first Persian talkie, *Dukhtar-i Lur* (1933), taking place in a Qhavah-khanah setting in the south of Iran.

35 These include Haideh Akhundzadeh in *Sharmsar* and Tamara in *Laghzish* (Slippage, 1953).

36 Dressed in 1950s-style identical floral dresses, the dancers appear to be interpreting a form of Western social dance quite similar to the 1950s "cheesecake dance." Their second piece is a fan dance to a Ukrainian/Russian tune and the dancers are wearing navy-style dresses.

37 Some films to feature belly dance in the 1950s are *Birahnah'i Khushhal* (The happy nude, 1957), *Payman-i Dusti*, and *Jahil Mahal* (1964). The attire of the performers appears to be regular belly dance clothing. In the first, Mahvash performed an Iranian-style belly dance, while in the third, Shahin performed the belly dance right after a segment where she appeared as a singer. Both performers' interpretations of belly dance differed: for her Iranian-style dance, Mahvash used shimmy movements initiated from her shoulder, while exaggerating her torso *qirs* to Persian *mutribi* music; in her execution of belly dance, Shahin's movements were very fast and sharp. Appearing in more than fifty films, and moving in the manner of musicals in some, Shahin only performed *raqs-i 'arabi* in *Jahil Mahal*.

38 The same dancer appears to have performed in the critically acclaimed film *Junub-i Shahr* (South of the city, 1958).

39 *Junub-i Shahr* and *Khisht va Aynah* (Brick and mirror, 1965) are examples of other films containing examples of these dances. The actress Taji Ahmadi also performed a regular solo-improvised dance in *Avval Haykal* (Looks first, 1960).

Accompanying the pop singer Puran, she holds a see-through fabric, resembling the bridal lace that Puran refers to in her lyrics.

40 For such instances, see *Usta Karim Nawkaritim* (Lord, I am at your service!, 1974) and *Duktur va Raqqasah* (The Doctor and the dancer, 1974).

41 Performing to a Persian tune, Furuzan's dance scene began with an Indian dance in sari, with "nihi nihi" in the lyrics of the chorus, signifying Indianness. Then she switches to a Persian dance accompanied by affectionate Persian song lyrics, originally sung by the famed pop singer Ilahah. Another famous dance segment in *Ganj-i Qarun* is Fardin's new rendition of the *ruhawzi* dance, *raqs-i haji*.

42 See *Usta Karim Nawkaritim* (1974), *Raqqasah'i Shahr* (The city's dancer, 1970), and especially *Mutrib* (1972), where the lead male character has daydreams of the dancer-character using seductive moves and gestures; these moves were enacted by the famous cabaret dancer, Nadiya.

43 These include *Murgh-i Hamsayah* (Neighbor's hem, 1974), *Mitris* (Mistress, 1974) and *Gulpari Jun* (Dear Gulpari, 1974).

44 In the opening dance segment of *Dalahu*, Furuzan sings in a car, "I have a lot of groove in my hips, I don't know where to pour it!" (*qir tu kamaram faravunah, nemidunam kuja birizam*). She then stops the car and starts dancing in a desert.

45 Mas'ud Mihrabi, *Tarikh-i sinama-yi Iran, az aghaz ta sal-i 1357* [History of Iranian cinema: From its beginnings to 1979] (Mahnamah'i Sinama'i-i Film, 1363/1984), 60.

46 Tahaminejad, *Sinama-yi raw'ya.*

47 Sasan Fatemi, *Jashn va musiqi dar farhang-ha-yi shahri-i iran* [Festivity and music in the urban musical cultures] (Tehran: Mahoor Institute of Culture and Arts, 1393/2014), 203. Examples of these films include *Madmazil Khalah* and *Payman-i Dusti.*

48 See Naficy, *The Social History of Iranian Cinema*, 277–308.

49 As featured in the films *Junub-i Shahr* and *Payman-i Dusti.*

50 See Hamid Shu'a'i, *Namavaran-i sinama dar iran: Fraydun rahnama* [Notable figures of cinema in Iran: Firaydun Rahnama] (Tehran: Hirminko, 1355/1976), 9–10.

51 Tughrul Afshar, *Dar kaman-i ranginkaman-i sinama* [In the bow of the rainbow of cinema] (Tehran: Mas'ud-i Sa'd, 1333/1954), 7.

52 Hasan Shirvani, "Hunar va san'at-i filmbardari dar Iran-2" [The art and technology of cinematography in Iran, pt. 2], *Sitarah'i Sinama*, no. 19, 1333/1954, 6–7; 6; Samuel Khachikian, "Chigunah mitavan navaqis-i film-ha-yi farsiva raf' kard?" [How can we eliminate the short comings of Farsi films?], *Sitarah'i Sinama*, no. 29, 1333/1954.

53 Khachikian, "Chigunah"; Afshar, *Dar Kaman-i*, 6–7.

54 Mihrabi, *Tarikh*, 60.

55 Examples include Lala and Tata in *Laghzish* (1953), Jadu in *Murad* (1953), and Shirin in *Jahil va Raqqasah* (1976). Jadu in *Murad* is a dissolute woman offstage; she is an urban femme fatale and malicious woman who has a secret relationship with the married male character of the film (Kamran), dancing tango and drinking wine with him. She also goes to a "rendez-vous" with a man at Kamran's home. This characterization was different from female performers of gypsy (*kawli*) background, as they were often cast as not overtly sexual, but rather pure, organic, obstinate, and entertaining. Examples of this include the lead female characters in *'Ishq-i Kawli* (Gypsy's love, 1969), and *Gulpari Jun.*

56 The main characters in *Usta Karim Nawkaritim* (1974), *Junub-i Shahr* (1958), and *Tigh-i Aftab* (The peak of sun, 1973) are instances of such characterization.

57 This stereotyping is manifested in *Gulpari Jun* where a character states: "anybody who goes to the city becomes a dancer." For an instance of a character coming from a poor and broken family, in *Randah Shudah* (Rejected, 1975), the mother (a former dancer) tells the judge that her dancer daughter who was charged with murder "grew up with no father, that's why she lost her way."

58 Marjan in *Harja'i* (The mobile harlot, 1974) is an example of such a portrayal.
59 For instance, Sitarah in *Kaj Kulah Khan* (1973) states that she has no one; a successful performer onstage, the dancer in *Duktur va Raqqasah* commits suicide for being forlorn.
60 The common corporeal and behavioral characteristic of the cabaret-owner-as-villain stereotype remained in Iranian media culture for a decade after the revolution, this time to represent those who were associated closely with the Shah and SAVAK (Pahlavi's intelligence and national security organization).
61 This theme is portrayed in *Mitris* (1973), *Khushgiltarin Zan-i 'Alam* (The most beautiful woman on earth, 1972), *Ruspi* (1969), *Usta Karim Nawkaritim* (1974), *Kaj Kulah Khan* (1953), and *Mutrib* (1972).
62 Another cabaret related issue was *fishkhuri*, which was understated in films; for instance, in *Mitris* and *Raqqasah'i Shahr* (1970), the dancers are depicted as drinking with the customers.
63 This theme is depicted in *Randah Shudah* and *Usta Karim Nawkaritim*.
64 As exemplified in *Raqqasah'i Shahr* and *Duktur va Raqqasah*. The co-worker is portrayed as jealous in the former and is sympathetic in the latter.
65 This was depicted in *Randah Shudah*.
66 For instance, in *Birahnah'i Khushhal*, in addition to enthusiastic male audiences, two of Mahvash's accidental audience members—who entered the café seeking jobs—reacted differently: one laughed hysterically while the male hero (Murad) spat as a sign of disdain for the dance.
67 The first type was depicted in *Mitris*, while in *Birahnah'i Khushhal*, an audience member—portrayed as a rich married man—approached Mahvash outside the café after being rejected by her and physically attacked her.
68 Examples include *Mutrib* and *Jahil va Raqqasah*.
69 For instance, in *Khushgiltarin Zan-i 'Alam*, there were a number of references to the ways an intimate relationship with the cabaret owner could help a performer in finding a job and progressing in it. Such relationships were also depicted in *Dalahu* and *Mitris*.
70 Examples include *Dash Akul* (1971), *Bihijab* (The unveiled, 1973), *Mitris*, and *Randah Shudah*; the last two hints at the involvement of the cabaret-owner in that trade.
71 Such association is evident especially in *Tigh-i Aftab* (1973), where the leading female character who works in a prostitution house (*najibkhanah*) in Shiraz also performed as a dancer with a *mutribi* troupe to entertain the customers in the location. Immediately after her performance, she got naked to sleep with the customer/audience member.
72 An early example is *Birahnah'i Khushhal*. In one scene, Mahvash unexpectedly appeared in her underwear to seduce Murad, who had saved her earlier; she was rejected by the male hero. A similar relationship—a seducing dancer and a rejecting male hero (often a *jahil*)—is portrayed in *Qaisar* (1969), *Dash Akul*, and *Mutrib*. In *Mutrib*, (the dancer) Nadiya enacted a flirtatious dancer with the same name. She seduced the leading man of the film with her sensual movements in a dreamlike scene that the man recalled several times throughout the film, telling him "spend the night with me." When the male hero marries, she tells him "I normally don't hang out with married men, but I can sleep with you as you are my friend." In contrast, in *Jahil va Raqqasah*, the *jahil* falls for the lustful *raqqasah* who is determined to get revenge on him by seducing him, stating "I will drag him from the 'prayer rug' (*sajjadah*) to the *kafah* stage."
73 Such a relationship was depicted in *Bihijab* and to some extent in *Junub-i Shahr* (1958).
74 This was a common theme in Egyptian dance films as well. See Roberta L. Dougherty, "Dance and Dancer in Egyptian Films," in *Belly Dance,*

Orientalism, Transnationalism and Harem Fantasy, Anthony Shay and Barbara Sellers Young, eds (Costa Mesa, CA: Mazda, 2005), 145–71; 152.

75 Two of the common terminologies used in this respect were "putting her back in her place" (*binshunadish*), meaning disciplining her, and "pouring the water of redemption (on her head)" (*ab-i tawbah rikhtan*), to imply purification.

76 Examples include *Raqqasah'i Shahr* and *Duktur va Raqqasah*. The film *Badkaran* (The Queans, 1973), however, went further by inventing an onscreen literal *ab-i tawbah* ritual, when the husband-to-be took the dancer to a clergy man to pour drops of water onto her head, a process that resembled Christian baptism.

77 In *Pashnah Tala* (The golden heeled, 1975), the film ends in the critical moment when the dancer (enacted by Shurangiz Tabataba'i) agrees to leave her career when she receives a marriage proposal onstage.

78 This is the theme of several films including *Mitris, Usta Karim Nawkaritim*, and *Duktur va Raqqasah*. Dougherty identifies this as "don't make me go back there" in Egyptian dance films; Dougherty, "Dance and Dancer," 166.

79 As happened in *Duktur va Raqqasah* and *Usta Karim Nawkaritim*.

80 I use "mobile harlot" for the translation of *harja'i* to emphasize the spatial dimension of the term. Similar plots occurred in *Duktur va Raqqasah, Usta Karim Nawkaritim, Randah Shudah*, and *Mitris*.

81 In *Mitris* and *Harja'i*, the leading roles went back to their cabaret-dancing career. In *Duktur va Raqqasah*, the lead character found a "proper" job—working in a factory—to raise her child. Dancing was not portrayed as a proper job in this context.

82 Occasionally, in some films of the last decade of the Pahlavi era, the dancers appeared scantily clad. An instance of this is a scene in *Badkaran*, where the dancer stripped onstage, though her dancing style and quality appeared "foreign." *Ruspi* even began by zooming in on the moving buttocks of a dancer—who only appeared to be wearing decorative underwear.

83 An example of this was Shahrzad's dance segment on a *kafah* stage in *Qaisar*. Wearing a 1960s Western-style short dress popular during this era, the film camera zoomed in on her torso and legs. Her dance consisted of exaggerated *qir*s, shimmies, and some interaction with the onstage musicians as well as the audience. Her performance had nuances of *mutribi* dances, including the dance of the *haji*.

84 For instance, the songs accompanying the dance piece in *Raqqasah'i Shahr, Gulpari Jun*, and *Jahil va Raqqasah* include such lyrics.

85 This attitude can be observed in films such as *Birahnah'i Khushhal, Duktur va Raqqasah*, and *Gulpari Jun*. In *Duktur va Raqqasah*, the dancer asserted that most people have prejudice against her job, thinking that all singers and dancers are "lewd" (*nanajib*). In *Gulpari Jun*, the *mutrib* Gulpari describes her twin sister: "She has everything, but I am nobody, I am a wandering dancer."

86 Enacting 'Iffat, Fakhri Khurvash executes amateur dance movements onstage (maybe intentionally).

87 The leading raqqas in *Kaj Kulah Khan* (1973) was slapped by the dissatisfied cabaret owner; in *Birahnah'i Khushal* (1957), she was slapped by an angry audience member; in *Gulpari Jun*, the dancer was slapped by a disappointed lover; and in *Usta Karim Nawkaritim*, the violent slap came from a revengeful husband.

88 "Mobile harlot" (*harja'i*) in *Usta Karim Nawkaritim*, "quean" (*badkarah*) in *Mitris*, "prostitute" (*ruspi*) in *Ruspi* (1969), and "*kafah* woman" (*zan-i kafah'i*) in *Jahil va Raqqasah*. Examples of other terms that were deployed to describe or refer to the dancers in demeaning ways were "the dancing jezebel" (*salitah'i raqqas*) and "the dancing bitch" (*maddah sag-i raqqas*) in *Dash Akul* (1971), and "*kafah* singer" (*avazah khun-i kafah*) in *Jahil va Raqqasah*.

89 For instance, Shahnaz Muradi described the role of Shahrzad in *Tangna* as a "dancer" (*raqqasah*) in one article, while in another essay identified Shahrzad's occupation in that film as a "prostitute" (*fahishah*); see Shahnaz Muradi, "Zan dar sinama-yi nadiri" [Women in Nadiri's cinema], in *Mu'arrifi va Naqd-i Film-ha-yi Amir Nadiri* [An introduction and critique of Amir Nadiri's films], ed. Ghulam Haydari (Tehran: Intisharat-i Suhayl, 1370/1991), 115–19; 118; Shahnaz Muradi Kuchi, "Jaygah-i zan dar film-ha-yi irani" [Depictions and roles of women in Iranian films], *Namah'i Filmakhanah'i Milli-i Iran* 1, no.4 (Summer 1369/1990), 68–91; 85.

90 "Falgush, majara-yi raqs-ha-yi film-ha-yi irani" [Eavesdropper, the story of Iranian films' dances], *Sitarah'i Sinama,* 18 Farvardin 1336/7 April 1957, 3; Samuel Khachikian, "In pardah'i jandar" [This living curtain], *Sitarah'i Sinama,* 18 Farvardin 1336/7 April 1957, 16; Khachikian made fun of Mahvash, calling her "the woman who has a slanted body part," referring to her famous song. Though, she not only danced and sang in films but also acted in some of them.

91 For the film *Hifdah Ruz Bah I'dam* (Seventeen days to the gallows, 1956), mentioned in Tahaminejad, *Sinama-yi Raw'ya,* 38.

92 "Rifrandum-i 'asr-i tala'" [The referendum of 'Asr-i Tala'i], *Pust-i Tihran-i Sinama'i,* 1, 20 Tir 1341/11 July 1962, 17; "Natijah'i rifrandum-i film-i gul-i gumshudah" [The results of the referendum for the film Lost Flower], *Pust-i Tihran-i Sinama'i,* no. 5, 17 Murdad 1341/8 August 1962, 17.

93 In her dancing, Jamileh switched her movements to double-time: she moved her body twice as quickly but still coordinated with the main musical beat. For her martial-arts-like fights, see especially *Gulpari Jun,* where she acted in the role of twin sisters who had been separated from each other at birth; in this film, she constantly engaged in physical fights for self-defense.

94 Guftigu'i ba jamilah, tajali-i hunar dar raqs" [A conversation with Jamileh, the manifestation of art in dance], *Ittila'at-i Salanah* 12 (Tehran: Mu'assisah'i Ittila'at, 1350/1971), 680–81, 680.

95 These include *Khushgiltarin Zan-i 'Alam, Zan-i Vahshi-i Vahshi* (The wild, wild woman, 1969), *Dukhtar-i Zalim Bala* (The beautiful tyrant of a girl, 1970), and *'Arus-i Pabirahnah* (The barefoot bride, 1974).

96 In the film, Sitarah not only avoided paying promissory notes to the cabaret owner; she also managed to receive her salary before performances.

97 Jamileh's role here is reminiscent of Samia Gamal's in *Nashshalah Hanim* (Miss Cutpurse, 1953), a film classified as a crime film in the Egyptian dance films described by Dougherty in "Dance and Dancer."

98 In *Mitris,* when her former husband accused her of corruption and criminality, a witness explained "she is pure and clean like an angel."

99 For example, see Hushang Gulmakani, *Tangna* [Impasse] (Tehran: Ruzanah Kar, 1385/2006), 118.

100 "Jamilah, zani keh bah ziba'iyash maghrur nist" [Jamileh, the women who is not boastful of her beauty], *Film va Hunar,* no. 48, 7 Isfand 1347/26 February 1969, 5.

101 For an example, see Alireza Nourizadeh, "Zani kah az zulamat miayad" [The woman who comes from the darkness], *Firdawsi,* no. 1033, 12 Mihr 1350/4 October 1971, 12–14.

102 For Hierarchy of Feeling see, Erin Hurley, *Theatre and Feeling* (London: Palgrave McMillan, 2010), 52.

103 "Furuzan: man digar giryah nakham kard" [Furuzan: I won't cry anymore], *Film va Hunar,* 17 Tir 1344/8 July 1965; "Ava-yi ashina" [The familiar voice], *Film va Hunar,* 3 Shahrivar 1345/25 August 1966.

104 Quoted from *Ittila'at-i Haftigi,* no. 1617, 76, in Mustafa Izadi, *Tamasha-yi Manfiha* [Viewing the negatives] (Tabriz: Sa'di, 1353/1974), 43.

105 See "Sar-i sahnah" [On filmset], *Film va Hunar,* 9 Tir 1345/30 June 1966.

106   For instance, see "Sarguzasht-i haghighi-i khanum-i zi" [The real account on
       Mrs. Z], *Film va Hunar*, no.465, 18 Bahman1352/7 February 1974, 16–17, 35;
       "Fattanah-ha-yi 'alam-i hunar," *Film va Hunar*, no. 463, 5 Bahman 1352/25
       January 1974, 5.
107   "Khanum-i puri bana'i, chira jilu-yi durbin birahnah shudid?" [Ms. Puri Bana'i,
       why did you get naked in front of the camera?], *Film va Hunar*, no. 463, 5
       Bahman 1352/25 January 1974, 222; "Khanum-i farzanah ta'idi, chira birahnah
       shudid" [Ms. Farzanah Ta'idi, why did you get naked?], *Film va Hunar*, no. 476,
       Khurdad 1353/May 1974, 7.
108   Among the most famous actresses to leave the cinema industry was Azar Shiva,
       who acted as the leading character in *Ruspi* (1969). See "Siks ya harf" [Sex or
       speech],*Film va Hunar*, no. 462, Day 1352/ January 1974, 14.
109   For one instance, see the interview with actress Halah Nazari, "Digar dar film-
       ha-yi siksi bazi nimikunam" [I won't act in erotic films anymore], *Film va Hunar*,
       no. 472, 24 Farvardin 1353/13 April 1974, 42.
110   M. Alkhass, "Ya'qub-i Laith," *Sitarah'i Sinama*, no. 128, 31 Shahrivar 1336/22
       September 1957, 36.
111   Siamak Pourzand, "Sinama dar Iran" [Cinema in Iran], *Sitarah'i Sinama*, no. 105,
       Nawruz 1336/March 1957, 14, 60; 14.
112   Ella Shohat, "Gender in Hollywood," *Middle East Report*, no. 162, January–
       February 1990, 40–42.
113   Afshar, *Dar Kaman-i*, 8.
114   For instance, see "Chihrah-ha-yi jadid-i muvaffaq" [The new faces of success],
       Sitarah'i Sinama 1, no. 2, 1332/1954, 65–8, which described Dalilah and Faranak
       as controversial figures who danced. The article interprets the latter's involve-
       ment in *raqs-i 'arabi* as her attempt to attract the media's attention. Similar assertions
       were made about Surayya Bihishti in "Surayya Bihishti, yik nu' siks-i idi'al!"
       [Surayya Bihishti, an ideal sex type], *Film va Hunar*, 1 Khurdad 1347/22 May 1968.
115   "Qabil-i tavajjuh-i vizarat-i muhtaram-i kishvar" [Addressed to the honorable
       ministry of interior], *Sitarah'i Sinama*, 14 Mihr 1336/6 October 1957, 2.
116   "Pursish-namah darbarah'i sinama va ta'lim va tarbiyat" [About cinema and its
       role in education], *Danish-sara-yi 'Ali, Sipidah'i Farda*, Khurdad va Tir 1339/
       June–July 1960, 8–15; 12.
117   Khosrow Parvizi, "Didar-i haftah" [Meet of the week], *Sitarah'i Sinama*, no. 116,
       26 Khurdad 1336/16 June 1957, 8.
118   See Parvizi, "Didar-i," 8; *Lat-i Javanmard* featured several clips of dance in a
       cabaret setting.
119   As described in "Dawr, dawr-i," 25, in *Qasid-i Bihisht* (1958), the actress Irin
       appeared in a bikini, which arguably was more revealing than the dancers of
       earlier eras.
120   For the term *vamp*, see "Dawr, dwar-i," 24–5, 42. A similar observation regard-
       ing the transformation of representation of women in pre-revolutionary cinema
       was attested by the film scholar, Parviz Jahid. See Ihsan Ibadi, "Zanan-i bir-
       ahnah dar sinama-yi iran, guftugu ba parviz-i jahid" [Nude women in Iranian
       cinema: In conversation with Parviz Jahid], *Shahrgon*, 21 Bahman 1390/10 Feb-
       ruary 2012, shahrgon.com/2012/02/10/گفت-ایران-سینمای-در-هنهبر-زنان%E2%80%
       8Cگوگوبا/.
121   For instance, in *Tigh-i Aftab*, the actresses appeared topless in some scenes.
122   "A'in-namah'i sinama-ha va mu'assisat-i namayishi, musavvab-i khurdad 1329"
       [The Regulations of cinema and dramatic institutions, passed in June 1950], in
       Shu'a'i, ed., *Farhang*, 5–15; 12.
123   "Iqdam-i vizarat-i farhang va hunar dar murid-i man'i tamasha-yi film-ha baray-
       i kamtar az 18 sal" [Measures taken by ministry of arts and culture to prevent
       underage viewings of films], *Film va Hunar*, 6 Murdad 1345/28 July 1966.

124 "Sukhani ba idarah'i kull-i namayishat" [A word with the cinema administration], *Film va Hunar*, no. 461, 30 Day 1352/20 January 1974, 10.

125 See Parviz Ijlali, *Digarguni-i ijtima'i va film-ha-yi sinama'i: Jami'ah-shinasi-i film-ha-yi ammah-pasand dar iran 1309–1357* [Films and social transformations: The sociology of popular films in Iran 1930–79] (Farhang va Andishah, 1383/2004), 272; "Dawr, dawr-i," 24–5, 42; "Buhran dar sinama-yi iran-2" [The crisis in Iranian cinema-2], *Film va Hunar*, 24 Urdibihisht 1348/14 May 1969; this last one describes a case showing the cleavage of a women's breasts that was eliminated from an Iranian film for being unchaste, while a foreign film in which only the breasts and hips of a woman were covered received screening permission; "Sanad-i shumarah'i 256/4"[Document number 256/4], 19 Bahman 1354/8 February 1976, in *Asnadi az musiqi*, 3: 1304–08; 1305.

126 Jamal Umid, "Film va Fardin" [Film and Fardin], *Film va Hunar*, 4 Shahrivar 1344/26 August 1965.

127 Tughrul Afshar, *Dar Kaman-i Ranginkaman-i Sinama* [Under the arch of the cinematic rainbow] (Tehran: Mas 'ud-i Sa'd Publications, 1954), 3.

128 Ibid., 1–3.

129 "Mas'alah'i sinama-yi farsi: aya raqs va avaz ba'is-i ibtizal ast?" [The problem of Farsi cinema: Do dancing and singing result in degeneration?], *Film va Hunar*, 11 Khurdad 1346/1 June 1967.

130 See Afshar, *Dar Kaman-i*, 7; Amir-Husayn Aryanpour quoted in Muradi Kuchi, "Jaygah-i zan dar film-ha-yi irani," 86; and Mihrabi, *Tarikh*, 60.

131 "Siks ya harf" [Sex or speech],*Film va Hunar*, no. 462, Day 1352/January 1974, 14; "Tahiyah-kunndigan-i film-ha-yi farsi muqassirand" [It is the *film-i farsi* producers' fault], *Film va Hunar*, no. 466, 25 Bahman 1352/14 February 1974, 20; Muhammad Javad Kaziruni, "Tark-i 'adat mujib-i maraz ast" [Old habits die hard], *Film va Hunar*, no. 467, 2 Isfand 1352/21 February 1974, 21; Samad Sa'i-var, "Bayad jilu-yi film-ha-yi mubtazal ra girift" [The degenerate films must be banned], *Film va Hunar*, no. 464, 9 Isfand 1352/28 February 1974, 14.

132 "Tamashachi-i junub-i shahri va shumal-i shahri" [South of town audience vs. north of town], *Film va Hunar*, no. 462, Day 1352/January 1974, 37; "Tahiyah-kunndigan-i", 20; Iraj Jamshidi, "Baray-i pishraft-i sinama-yi iran chah bayad kard...?" [What should be done for the progress of Iranian cinema?], *Tihran-i Musavvar*, no. 1057.

133 Ali-Akbar Akbari, "Darbarah'i sinama-yi farsi" [About Farsi cinema], *Arash* 20 (Bahman 1349/February 1960), 41–59; the author further expanded his idea in a book, *Ali-akbar Akbari, Lumpanizm* (Tehran: Sipihr, 1352/1973).

134 "Dast-ha-yi marmuzi kah mani'-i takamul-i san'at-i sinama-yi iranast" [Mysterious hands that block the progress of Iranian cinema], *Sitarah'i Sinama*, no. 118, 9 Tir 1336/30 June 1957, 8.

135 Ijlali also speculates that the audiences were more attracted to dance sequences than to explicit nudity; see Ijlali, *Digarguni-i Ijtima'i*, 372.

136 "Sanad-i shumarah'i 186" [Document number 186], 9 Khurdad 1341/30 May 1962, in *Asnadi az musiqi*, 2: 866–70; 866–7. As an editorial in *Sitarah'i Sinama* reveals, a few wealthy investors approached the Iranian film studios, encouraging them to insert seductive dance scenes into their films in exchange for more money (20,000 toman [approximately $US 22,681 today]) so they could sell them in neighboring countries. The article described those as "scenes of dance and seductions by prostitutes"; see "Qabil-i tavajjuh-i vizarat-i," 2.

137 "Va inha chihrah-ha-yi dirakhshan-i sinama-yi farsi hastand" [And these are the shinning stars of Iranian cinema], *Film va Hunar*, 9 Day 1345/30 December 1966; "Marz-ha-yi andishah, guftiguba Siamak Yasimi-2" [The frontiers of thought: A conversation with Siamak Yasimi], *Film va Hunar*, 12 Khurdad 1345/2 June 1966.

138 Naficy, *Social History of Iranian Cinema*, 149.
139 See Erin Hurley, *Theatre and Feeling*, 43; John Mercer and Martin Shingler, *Melodrama: Genre, Style and Sensibility* (London: Wallflower, 2005).
140 Ann Ubersfeld, "The Pleasure of the Spectator," *Modern Drama*, no. 25 (1982): 127–39.
141 Tahaminejad, *Sinama-yi Raw'ya*. Also see "Guriz az 'ishq" [Escape from love], *Film va Hunar*, 29 Khurdad 1347/19 June 1968, which describes the fantasy world of the audience that became so important that in the late Pahlavi era, the actresses put off marriage in order to keep their appeal.
142 This was described by Abbas Baharloo in an interview. Abbas Baharloo, interview with the author, Tehran, Shahrivar 1393/August 2011. Also see, Muhammad Zarghami and Muhammad-Reza Kazimi, "Irutism dar sinama-yi iran" [Eroticism in Iranian cinema], Nigah-i Tazah (New perspective [radio show]), *Radio Farda*, 9 Azar 1388/30 November 2009, http://www.radiofarda.com/con tent/f35_Eroticism_in_Iranian_Cinema/1891057.html.
143 See "Bazar-i ashuftah'i," 56.
144 See Naficy, *Social History of Iranian Cinema*, 160.
145 Hollywood-style ballet-inspired harem dances can be found in the Iranian films. These include *Buhlul* (1958) and *Rustam va Suhrab* (1957).
146 In Egypt, belly dancing, which was considered risqué and of lower class, was an established occupation in Cairo; but, the filmic representation of belly dancers included a more complex range of characters than Iranian *raqqas*-centered films. See Dougherty, "Dance and Dancer," 153. Dougherty maintains that the portrayals of female dancers were not always negative, but, depending on the theme of the film and (the power of) the actress, some groups of films, including backstage musicals, represented the dancers positively. In Bollywood films, the dancer was also more revered. In Iran, cabaret dancing was a career created in a short period of time.
147 The family pressure on female performers due to the stigma of performance was also expressed by well-known actresses including Shahin and Fakhri Khurvash; Fakhri Khurvash, in interview with Parviz Qarib Afshar, www.youtube.com/wa tch?v=8lbWsy-WIs0 (accessed 15 June 2013).
148 "Shahin, davam-i yik sitarah" [Shahin, the perpetuity of a star], *Film va Hunar*, 19 Aban 1345/10 November 1966; "Sinama chihrah-ha-yi mashhur-i musiqi ra bah dam mikashad" [Cinema is trapping the popular faces of music], *Film va Hunar*, 22 Farvardin 1347/15 April 1968, 26.

6 The dancing body in the anti-obscenity discourse of the Islamic press in pre-revolutionary Iran

The expansion of new sites of sociability, the permeation of new communication media, and the transformation of the public sphere prompted a politically conscious religiously oriented press of the Pahlavi era to reflect on the socio-political refashioning of the country. The result was the formation of a moralizing discourse that associated a cluster of practices, spaces, and mediums with "eroticism" (*shahvat*), one I here dub "the anti-obscenity discourse."[1] This discourse consisted of recognition of and objection to those erotic zones, which were deemed to be undermining public and familial "chastity" (*'iffat*) and causing a "disorder" in the society. In this context, the public dancing body, especially in the popular scene, was a pivotal element of this anti-obscenity discourse.

While sharing some similarities with the nationalist and Marxist-inspired discourses on art, a key distinguishing feature of the pre-revolutionary Islamic anti-obscenity discourse was its rejection of all performing art forms. This was mainly due to the fact that the Islamic authors were not engaged in the newly emerged performing arts spheres, and did not differentiate between generic categories of art while reacting to them. As I demonstrate in this chapter, during the four decades leading up to the 1979 Revolution—along with the growth of leisure, media, and political and cultural transformations of the press—the constituents and meanings ascribed to the "erotic zones" were transformed. Using the Marxist theater and national(ist) art discourses as a backdrop, this chapter focuses on the ways the politically motivated Islamic press reacted to the female public (performing) body, crafting it as a driving force in the revolutionary process.

The dancing body in twentieth-century anti-obscenity discourse

The emergence of a discourse sensitive to the new performing arts and media is evident in the religiously oriented press of the 1930s. Classified as and opposed to disseminating immoral behaviors and eliciting the "fire of sexual desire" (*atash-i shahvat*) and "sexual attraction" (*jazbah'i jinsi*) in their participants and audiences, cinema, theater, the gramophone, and novels were all grouped into one cluster.[2] The Islamic press identified sexual stimulation as a consequence of entering these erotic zones, which could lead to "illicit" (*namashru'*) sexual encounters and to the diffusion of venereal diseases.

After the abdication of Reza Shah in August 1941, the religiously oriented periodicals found more freedom to condemn the first Pahlavi's secularizing policies. The unveiling of women in 1936, a centerpiece in the Women's Emancipation programs, was the prime target for these criticisms, making the term "unveiling" (*kashf-i hijab*) another component of the anti-obscenity discourse of the time. Concerned with the social consequence of unveiling, religiously oriented authors' anxieties over the presence and sexual affects of the unveiled female bodies in public led to the emergence of a new meaning for "prostitution" (*fahsha*) that linked venereal diseases to unveiled public female bodies.[3] In this context, where the unveiled women were viewed as the main initiators of social corruption, *fahsha* did not denote only the act of prostitution. The public practices, spaces, and media that presumably sexually affected the participants, leading to unbridled interaction with the opposite sex, as well as those acts that resembled the performance or exhibition of *fahsha* and "sinful actions" (*munkir*), were also perceived as *fahsha*.[4]

Additionally, the presence of unveiled women as viewers, participants, and performers in the then-expanding sites of leisure, including cafés, broadened the previously formed cluster of erotic zones aligning its constituents with prostitution—and labeling them the "foci of prostitution" (*kanun-i fahsha*) and "centers of corruption" (*marakiz-i fisad*).[5] Grouped into one cluster, theater, cinema, cafés, (mass-printed) paintings, photographic studios, radio, and the press, as well as cocktail parties, "ballroom dancing events" (*majlis-i bal*), and dance classes, were deemed "foci of erotic production" (*kanun-i shahvat-za'i*) and agents of "arousing sexual desire" (*biadri-i shahvat*), through which the youngsters learned to make love and were incited to "home-wrecking" and life-ruining (*khaniman-suz*) activities.[6] While the collective participation and public nature of these mediums and sites appear to have directed the anxiety towards them, the commercialization and expansion of these "institutions of erotic provision" (*mu'assiat-i ta'min-i shavat*) exacerbated these tensions.[7]

Other components of this discourse, closely linked to the erotic zones in the 1940s, were "modernity" (*tajaddud*) and the "modern person" (*mutajaddid*). A *mutajaddid* was assumed to be either a participant or a consumer in these zones or alternatively an actor/policy maker promoting them. For instance, a pro-unveiling parliament member and a minister of culture who backed a school performance were ridiculed as *mutajaddid*. *Mutajaddid* women were identified as members of a "class" who were consumers of fashion, luxury, and the culture of unveiling, and who abused their illegitimate freedom to hang out in the sites associated with the eroticism.[8] Moreover, they were accused of spending their days and nights in "dancing houses" (*raqqas-khanah*), cinemas, and the streets, selling their "chastity" (*'iffat*).[9] A *mutajaddid* male participant of these practices, spaces, and media was identified as giving away his wife to dance with strangers, as he was assumed to be a socialist.[10] This was in contrast to the men of the Qom Seminary School (Hawzah'i 'Ilmiyyah'i Qum), who were described as zealous, brave, and intelligent and as never entering the cinema or theater.[11]

The anti-obscenity discourse did not display much change in the 1950s. The zones associated with *shahvat* were regularly labeled "centres for prostitution and immorality."[12] These sites included theaters, cinemas, bars, cabarets, dancing houses, coed swimming pools, and prostitution houses, and were in addition to promoters of "promiscuity" (*shahvat-rani*), such as the press's depiction of under-clad women, misleading films, alcohol, romantic novels, and ogling.[13] The constituency of the erotic zones in the 1960s and 1970s remained nearly unchanged from those of the 1950s. Like the more dominant nationalist discourse of the 1950s, reflected in the periodicals with varying ideological persuasions, the religiously inclined authors criticized the performances of the "foreign" dancers in venues associated with nightlife.[14] However, their stance towards ballet was contrary to the more dominant nationalist discourse that revered ballet as an artistic form (as described in Chapter 2). The anti-obscenity discourse reproached all forms of dance blaming ballet schools for encouraging dance and immoral behavior among the children. Indeed dance was identified as "religion destroying" (*din kharab kun*) and "Islam-killing" (*islam kush*) performance.[15]

The societal affects of the erotic zones

The "promoters" of erotic zones were regularly condemned for corrupting society by sexually affecting the participants while instructing immoralities. Dance, music, cinema, and theater were all seen as mediums of sexual desire in this discourse. The body of a female café dancer was purported to incite evil when captivating the souls and hearts of the youth, who would lose themselves in watching dance and "coquetry" (*qammazi*).[16] The café dancers were accused of making the youth hate marriage, and thus causing the extinction of the human race.[17] Comparably, the café dancers were regarded as disseminators of immorality also in the more dominant social discourse (as discussed in Chapter 4).[18]

Music was no better off. It was similarly considered to be responsible for exciting the sexual instinct: it was accused of filling the heart of the listener with *shahvat* and a desire for "lovemaking" ('*ishq bazi*).[19] The music vibrations were thought to provoke dancing, the mingling of men and women, the drinking of alcohol, and the damaging of the nerves and ultimately the human psyche.[20] Not surprising, film was also considered a medium of sexual stimulation that could transform the youth into unchaste and irreligious beings.[21] In the same vein, theater was associated with sexual pleasure and its claim to moral edification constantly questioned.[22] However, this stance was in contrast to that of the nationalist (art) movement that advocated for moral theater, nationalist operettas, classical music, and ballet. It also differed from the discourse on Marxist theater that viewed art as a medium for class struggle.

The spaces associated with the erotic zones were themselves seen as sites for immoral instruction, where not only were the attendants active participants, but also (through imitation) the appearances of their bodies were in danger of being transformed into those of superstars.[23] Cinema and cabaret, especially, were viewed as having the potential to convert women into prostitutes.[24] In contrast, those who attended spaces such as the Qom Seminary School were presumed to be embodying the light of spirituality, and thus never committed crimes or were infected by venereal diseases.[25]

Due to the presence of women and the public display of practices identified as evoking *shahvat* in the erotic zones, the participants' bodies were perceived by these authors as a mode of uncontrolled, hyper-exaggerated, and almost grotesque sexuality—one that resonates with the Russian literary critic Mikhail Bakhtin's notion of the carnivalesque body.[26] Additionally, these spaces provided an easier setting for the mingling of men and women, where the intrusion of one sex into another's bodily zone frequently occurred, as was manifested in the nearness of the male and female bodies who sat in the dark theaters.[27] Since the sexual attraction between men and women was viewed as a "strong electricity" (*iliktirisitah'i qavi*), the mingling was imagined to result in immediate "unauthorized" sexual interaction that discouraged marriage.[28]

Physical proximity was most apparent in the popular European social dancing scene (regularly referred to as *dans*). Here, men and women danced in close physical contact with each other in public. As in the aesthetics of Western social dance, it was common for a person to engage physically with another person in public. The display of this bodily closeness in partner dancing provoked the most severe reactions in these periodicals, to the extent that these corporeal practices were described as "new masturbation" (*istimna'-i nuzuhur*) and "civilized onanism" (*unanism-i mutamaddinanah*).[29] In one instance, Rock 'n' Roll was reported as a dance in which the female dancer loses her virginity.[30] Similarly, partner dancing prompted anxieties in the dominant press discourse of the era.[31]

In medieval Islamic classifications, "sexual desire" (*shahvat*) and "carnal desires" (*hava va havas*) of the illicit kind were associated with the "evil-inciting self" (*nafs-i ammarah*) and animalistic instincts, while "intellect"/ "reason" (*'aql*) was ascribed to angels. Thus, following *shahvat* aligned an individual with animals, and following reason affiliated a person with angels.[32] In this hierarchy of faculties, to be moral also meant to control *shahvat* with wisdom. Adapting these notions to the context of the twentieth century, the authors recognized those who were attuned to the erotically charged media, practices, and spaces as "following their evil-inciting selves," and imagined those who were not attentive to media, practices, and spaces of the erotic zones as "following their wisdom."[33]

With the ascription of *shahvat* to a cluster of media, practices, and spaces, "chastity" (*'iffat*) also became infused with new meanings.[34] This is exemplified in a 1959 article which, corresponding to the social circumstances of urban life of the time, defined an array of chastities: a person with "chastity of step" (*'iffat-i qadam*) did not attend those spaces associated with the erotic zones, a person with "chastity of pen" (*'iffat-i qalam*) did not write erotic novels or amorous stories, and a person with "chastity of tongue" (*'iffat-i zaban*) did not sing or utter stimulating words.[35]

In the case of women, chastity and veiling seemed to be closely allied: the veil was the foremost physical marker of the ideal woman, who was imagined as the living "embodiment of chastity" (*mujassamah'i 'iffat*). In contrast, unveiling was viewed as the starting point of "absence of chastity" that led to "revealing the private areas" (*kashf-i 'urat*) of women's bodies and was viewed as the cause of social absence of chastity and the mal-behavior of Iranian men.[36]

The presence of unveiled women in public was supposed to have societal sexual affects: while hanging out on streets, the unveiled women's eyes and gazes had the power to drag youth to *shahvat*, as their hearts desired what they saw.[37] This interpretation drew on the medieval Islamic conception of unrestrained gazing for the purpose of sexual desire as a consequence of following the evil-inciting self.[38] The veiled/ideal women, however, were characterized as wise and embodying modesty, chastity, and purity. These periodicals described the veiled (ideal) woman as being obedient to her husband and as capable of raising healthy children.[39]

If unveiled women were "promiscuous" (*shahvatran*) and "capricious" (*havasbaz*), their presence on the street had the capacity to disseminate *fahsha*.[40] Those women were identified as "demons" and not "angels."[41] Moreover, the "exhibitionism" (*jilvahgari*) of unveiled women was considered to be feeding the prostitution business.[42] According to this view, the fire of the "absence of chastity" (*bi-'iffati*) of "promiscuous" unveiled women threatened the Iranian lineage as well as "several thousand years of Arian chastity."[43] While the nationalist discourse often collided with the religiously inclined authors over women's veiling, the two shared the view that associated the nightlife industry as well as the cinema with the propagation of *fahsha* and un-chasitity.[44] Furthermore, terms such as "public chastity" (*'iffat-i 'umumi*) and "public morality" had legal applications and were in use in national legislations.[45] Nevertheless, the interpretations of such notions by these religiously oriented authors and the state appeared to have distinct differences.[46]

Corruption, absence of chastity, and prostitution were not viewed as the only consequences of entering the erotic zones. Perceiving the mediums, practices, and spaces associated with *shahvat* as negative aspects of European civilizations, the associated recreational activities were regarded as endangering human beings by drowning them in "eroto-worshipping" (*shahvat-parasti*) and "loosing sanity" (*ikhtilal-i havass*).[47] While overstimulation of the sexual drive was regarded as a health-endangering issue associated with the erotic zones, mental and corporeal diseases were the other consequences of the mechanized life's recreations, for which people harmed their bodies by staying awake at night.[48] To warn people of these dangers, in 1975 the periodical *Masjid-i A'zam* disseminated translations of Koranic verses to encourage sleeping at night and working during the day and avoiding sinful sites.[49]

There were other social consequences to entering the erotic zones, besides *fahsha,* debated in the anti-obscenity discourse. These included discouraging marriage, loosening family ties, and an increased divorce rate.[50] Similar ideas are also discussed in periodicals which do not necessarily display religious tendencies, where "nudity" (*birahnigi*) in cinema and the nightlife were recognized as influences of a Western lifestyle that damaged family ties.[51]

Othering and resistance in the anti-obscenity discourse

In their discursive practices, the Islamic authors identified a cluster of mediums, practices, and spaces as erotic and corrupting. Ascribing those to the "other" *mutajaddid* (as well as a range of others in society), these authors were able to define themselves in the process of prefiguring an ideal society.[52] In the meantime, through casting the bodies of their others as "pariah bodies," the authors justified the need for a form of social control and disciplining.[53] These spectators of society subjected the bodies of the participants of the erotic zones to a controlling, curious, and corrective gaze, aiming to normalize and regulate them. These authors not only tried to personally regulate the public's behavior, they invited other Muslims to join them in this task, citing the responsibility of each individual Muslim to "command right and forbid wrong" (*amr-i bah ma'ruf va nahy-i az munkar*).[54] Likewise, they tried to expand the Muslim power network and create a web of control in which each individual Muslim would police both the self and others during social interactions.[55] This network of surveillance, comprised of a collective of individual corrective gazes, would take action against the corruption disseminated by the "others" and their mediums, practices, and spaces.

Furthermore, through contesting the erotic zones in their discourse, the authors were able to express dissidence and to pressure the government. Since the 1940s, the ministries of culture and education, the parliamentary members, the City Police (*Sharhrbani*), and later, the state institutions, including the national radio and television, were under criticism for sanctioning or planning activities associated with the erotic zones which occurred in their domain. While most often these institutions or individual politicians were blamed for promoting *tajaddud*, depending on the daily political circumstances they were also associated with (other) internal others, including Baha'is and Tudeh Party members (especially after the coup d'état of 1953).[56] Occasionally, those participating in the erotic zones were accused of promoting the ideologies of the "other," including Bahaism, and communism.[57]

The purveyors of culture were especially under attack for "turning angels into demons," while the education system was constantly criticized in regards to the physical education and extracurricular activities for girls, which included dance and music (especially in the 1940s).[58] The notions of dance and *tajaddud* were so negatively intertwined that to humiliate a *mutajaddid* politician, he would be identified as "a good dancer" (*khush-raqs*).[59] In a similar vein, the terms *sar-i mutrib-ha* ("head of *mutribs*") and *raqqas* were used to demean parliamentary members and journalists who took sides with the ministry of education in regards to girls' attire and physical education in schools.[60] Those politicians who sanctioned children's exposure to plays (e.g., by Molière)—instead of the Koran—were also seen as traitors.[61] Dance and theater training in kindergartens were linked to communists and Jews, and the education system was criticized for primarily producing dancers and singers.[62] Meanwhile, as noted in Chapter 2, the nationalist discourse highly endorsed certain types of dance and the physical education of girls.

These religiously oriented authors pressured the state to shut down the performing arts programs supported by the ministry of education, including balletic and sportive performances, and even moral plays.[63] Additionally, the state and its related institutions, such as the city police, were persuaded to call for the closure of "sites of corruption" with performance or exhibitions of irreligiosity, impurity, and immorality. This especially included venues that featured dance performances, such as cafés, which were viewed as centres of prostitution.[64]

The public presence of unveiled women and the expansion and popular reception of the erotic zones in Tehran made the city the locus of these authors' attacks. Tehran was labeled the "focus of womenizers" (*kanun-i zanparastan*), where images of *raqqas* and actresses were visible on every corner, and the "city of catastrophes" (*shahr-i fajayi'*) where people lost themselves watching café and partner dancing.[65] Tehran was deemed the "cemetery of purity" (*qabristan-i pakdamani*), a "school for imitation" (*madrasah'i taqlid*), and the "marketplace of modesty" (*jaygah-i furush-i hujb va haya*); drowning in dance, *dans,* and alcohol, Tehran was perceived to be burning in the fire of corruption, *shahvat,* and crime.[66] Even though the city had a designated prostitution district (Shahr-i Naw), the spaces associated with the erotica cluster, its highly concentrated streets with a visible presence of unveiled women (such as Lalehzar, Nadiri, Istambul, and Sipah Square), were also held to be "centres of prostitution."[67]

Viewing the "correction of environment" (*islah-i muhit*) as a prerequisite for practicing Islam and "nurturing the intellects"(*tarbiyat-i afkar*), some authors proposed plans that included not allowing women to enter public sites of sociability, as well as banning dance and music.[68] These authors' tendencies towards controlling and regulating public urban spaces resonate with Foucault's notion of spatial ordering for the purpose of subjugating individuals to discipline and controlling society.[69]

In the meantime, an anti-colonial trope had been shaping in the anti-obscenity discourse of the Islamic press since the 1940s that linked the mediums, practices, and spaces associated with eroticism to Western imperialism and colonialism.[70] Identifying the foreign hands behind the expansion of Tehran's recreational centers and larger cultural programming, the goal of the enemy was perceived to be destroying the Iranian soul as well as the religion of Islam.[71] Recreational means and "corrupting elements" associated with the erotic zones were viewed as colonialism's indirect attack on Islam for the purposes of converting the dynamic Islamic nation to a "static" (*ista*) one, and killing the spirits of "valiance" (*shahamat*), "bravery" (*shuja'at*), and "struggle" (*talash*).[72] In a similar vein, movie stars and cabaret dancers were viewed as servants to colonialism who led the society to corruption and propagated *bi'iffati*.[73]

A parallel narrative associated the origin of mediums, activities, and spaces with the feudalists and millionaires, whose culture had also contaminated the middle class.[74] The anti-colonial and anti-imperialist trend, however, continued to permeate the anti-obscenity discourse of these press. An example of this attitude is reflected in an article that recognized sex, dance, alcohol, and drugs as weapons with which US imperialism held back and weakened "disinherited" (*mustaz'af*) countries.[75] Similarly, cinema was perceived as "an imperialist medium" for its portrayal of "eroticized" women, and as a "Western weapon" against Islam that employed sex and crime instead of opium to defeat people of the East.[76]

Similar to the discourse of Marxist theater which I explored in Chapter 3, the Islamic discourse of obscenity embodied resistance. It did, however, display a major difference: while the former largely blamed the state for the "degeneration" (*ibtizal*) of the arts, the Islamic press linked the expansion of erotic zones to colonialism. In the last years of the Pahlavi era, the anti-obscenity discourse became a constituent of the larger anti-imperialist Islamic revolutionary discourse. The notion of committed art, and art as a medium for class struggle which was originally a leftist construction, also entered into the Islamic revolutionary realm, especially through the teachings of Ali Shari'ati (1933–77), the Islamic-Marxist ideologue of the revolution. The plays *Abuzar*, inspired by an early Islamic historical character, and *Sarbidaran* (Those who were hung), a revolutionary play about Shi'i Iranian's struggle during Mongol rule in the fourteenth century, are early instances of such attempts that were staged between 1969 to 1972 in the city of Mashhad as well as the religious venue Husayniyah'i Irshad in Tehran.[77]

With the Revolution of 1979, the erotic zones went through major transformations. The cabarets were shut down for being deemed centers for corruption and prostitution, while their owners' wealth was confiscated—a fate experienced by other groups including the employees of SAVAK (Pahlavi era's Organization of Intelligence and National Security) as well as owners of cinematic and theatrical venues.[78] The propositions formerly suggested in the anti-obscenity discourse were realized when purging of the environment became a part of the post-revolutionary agenda: to confront "sexual deviations" (*inhiraf-i jinsi*) in society, men and women's intermixing in public, "sexually stimulating" (*shahvat-barangiz*) get-togethers and spaces of "revelry" ('*ayyashi*), and "illegitimate" ogling and gazing by men at women became prohibited. What's more, veiling became the utmost solution for preventing women's exhibitionism and the performance of femininity/coquettishness ('*ishvahgari*).[79] This included the banning of the public female dancing body. For at least a decade afterwards, the erotic zones remained a cluster of issues in relation to the pre-revolutionary "social corruption," evident in the debates which occurred in the Islamic Parliament of Iran.[80]

Conclusion

Reacting to the social and political re-fashioning of the country, an anti-obscenity discourse emerged in the religiously oriented press of pre-revolutionary Iran. Constructing a binary opposition between the "erotic" (*shahvat*) and the "chaste" (*'iffat*), the anti-obscenity discourse provided the grounds of intelligibility between the licit and the illicit; the moral and the immoral; and the Islamic and the un-Islamic norms, conducts, and practices. This moralizing discourse was used effectively in construing public spheres of entertainment and male–female interaction as sites of "promiscuity."

The contestations against the popular female performances in the Islamic anti-obscenity discourse shared similarities with the contending nationalist and Marxist ideologies, especially when introducing the corporeal characteristics of vice. Moreover, the anti-obscenity Islamic discourse was not just moralizing, it was imbued with a sense of identity formation and resistance towards the Others, who needed to be regulated, as well as a prefiguration of an ideal society.[81] This moralizing anti-imperialist discourse later converged into a revolutionary driving force, and its predispositions were realized when the Islamists consolidated power as the new government to establish the Islamic Republic of Iran.

Notes

1 The term "*shahvat*" is often translated as "lust" and "passion" in English. As my discussion was merely about the discourse addressing sexual desire, I chose a vocabulary rooted in "eros," as it better captured the meanings of *shahvat* in this context. Moreover, the term "*shahvat*" corresponds historically and spatially to the term "eroticism": as argued by Lynn Hunt, the definition of the term "erotic" was at its base "private" and concerned with love; but with the intrusion of female eroticized bodies into the public sphere, eroticism was viewed as a source of corruption. This is quite similar to the case of *shahvat* in pre-revolutionary Iran, where the public presence of unveiled female bodies and erotic mediums caused critical reactions in the Islamic press. See Lynn Hunt's introduction in *Eroticism and the Body Politic*, ed. Lynn Hunt (Baltimore: Johns Hopkins University Press, 1991), 1–13.
2 "Tabliqat" [Advocacy], *Humayun*, Mihr 1313/September–October 1934, 25; "Tabliqat," *Humayun*, Isfand 1313/February–March 1935, 25; "Tabliqat," *Humayun*, Fravardin 1314/March–April 1935, 31–2.
3 For instances see, "Dar atraf-i bi-hijabi" [Around unveiledness], *A'in-i Islam*, 27 Murdad 1323/18 August 1944, 3; Muhammad-Ali Ansari, "Parah sazid ayah-ha-yi hijab" [Tear apart the implications of veiling], *Dunya-yi Islam*, 28 Azar 1326/20 December 1947, 1–2; 2; Nuryani, "Ma tarafdar-i islam va ijra-yi ahkam-i an hastim" [We support Islam and the execution of its laws], *A'in-i Islam*, 27 Murdad 1323/18 August 1944, 2.
4 A. Madani, "Atash-i bi 'iffati va bi-namusi dudman-i irani ra tahdid mikunad" [The fire of immodesty and immorality is threatening the Iranian lineage], *Dunya-yi*

Islam, 17 Bhaman 1326/7 February 1948, 1–2; Khuldi, "Az bara-yi 'iffat va pak-damani-i zanan luzum-i hijab yik amr-i musallam va tabi'i ast" [The enforcement of veiling is necessary and natural for the safekeeping of women's chastity and morality], *Dunya-yi Islam*, 11 Urdibihisht 1327/1 May 1948, 1–2; 2; "Chigunah az fahsha mitavan jilawgiri nimud?" [How to prevent prostitution?], *A'in-i Islam*, 22 Shahrivar 1325/13 September 1946, 1–2; 2; "Islam va banuvan-i imruz" [Islam and the women of today], *A'in-i Islam*, 31 Shahrivar 1323/22 September 1944, 5.

5   "Dar atraf-i bi-hijabi," 3.

6   "Sinama va andishah-ha-yi mardum" [Cinema and the people's thoughts], *A'in-i Islam*, 23 Isfand 1325/14 March 1947, 12; Munsif Yaraqchi, "Azadi-i zanan, 3" [Women's emancipation, 3], *Dunya-yi Islam*, 1 Isfand 1326/21 February 1948, 1–2: 2; Munsif Yaraqchi, "Sukhani dar piramun-i hijab" [Some words on veiling], *Dunya-yi Islam*, 12 Farvardin 1327/1 April 1948, 1–2; Shir-khuda'i, "Shahr-i fajayi'" [The city of catastrophe], *Parcham-i Islam*, 26 Azar 1325/17 December 1946, 3; Faqihi-Shirazi,"Ghugha-yi raqs" [The uproar of dance], *Parcham-i Islam*, 3 Urdibihisht 1326/24 April 1947, 1–2; H. Karbasi, "Salun-i raqs, kilas-i dars" [Dance room, the classroom], *Parcham-i Islam*, 2 Urdibihisht 1324/22 April 1945, 2, 4.

7   "Chigunah yik millati mimirad?" [How does a nation die?], *Parcham-i Islam*, 16 Farvardin 1325/5 April 1946, 3; Muhammad Jinabzadah, "Aya fahsha faqat marbut bah shahr-i naw ast?" [Is prostitution limited to Shahr-i Naw?], *Nida-yi Haq*, 18 Mihr 1335/10 October 1956, 1, 3.

8   Yaraqchi, "Azadi-i zanan, 3," 2; Faqihi-Shirazi, "Aya nabayad ba mafasid-i ijtima'i mubarizah nimud?" [Don't we have to fight the social corruptions?], *Parcham-i Islam*, 6 Aban 1327/28 October 1948, 1–2; 2; Sayyad-Jalal Kashani, "Shahr-i khuda-parastan ast ya kanun-i zanparastan" [Is this the city of god worshippers or women worshippers?], *Dunya-yi Islam*, 1 Khurdad 1327/22 May 1948, 1, 4; 4.

9   Yaraqchi, "Azadi-i zanan, 3," 2; Faqihi-Shirazi, "Aya nabayad ba mafasid," 2; Shir-khuda'i, "Shahr-i fajayi'," 3.

10   Kashani, "Shahr-i khuda-parastan," 4; "Fisad-i akhlaq" [Moral decay], *Parcham-i Islam*, 3 Azar 1328/24 November 1949, 1, 4; 4.

11   Muhammad-Taqi Ishraqi, "Hawzah'i 'ilmiyah'i qum" [Qum Seminary School], *Parcham-i Islam*, 10 Bahman 1325/30 January 1947, 1, 3; 3; "Asarat-i ruz-i tarikhi …" [The consequences of this historic day], *Nida-yi Haq*, 27 Bahman 1333/16 February 1955, 2, 4; 4.

12   Fakhruldin Burqi'i, "Az khud shinasi ta khuda shinasi" [From knowing thyself to knowing thy god], *Majmu'ah'i Hikmat*, Tir 1338/June–July 1959, 41–2; quote on 42.

13   Burqi'i, "Az khud shinasi," 42; "In hamah fisad-i matbu'at az chist?" [What causes such corruption of the press?], *Maktab-i Islam* 2, no. 12, Day 1339/December 1960–January 1961, 96.

14   For instance, see "Dar hutil ivirist" [In Everest Hotel], *Nida-yi Haq*, no. 294, Tir 1335/June–July 1956, 1, 4; 4; Imadzadah, "Mubarizah ba fahsha ya 'iffat-i ijtima'" [Battle with social vices or the social chastity], *Nida-yi Haq*, 1 Isfand 1335/20 February 1957, 1–2.

15   "Hunaristan-i 'ali balit, tarbiyat-i atfal bah raqs va fisad-i akhalq" [Academy of Ballet, children's education with dance and the decay of morality], *Nida-yi Haq*, 2 Tir 1333/23 June 1954, 1, 3; 1.

16   "Fisad-i akhlaq," 4; H. Karbasi,"Awza'i ijtima'i az darichah'i intiqad" [The social situation from the viewpoint of a critic], *Parcham-i Islam*, 19 Farvardin 1327/8 April 1948, 3–4; 4; Shir-khuda'i, "Shahr-i fajayi'," 3; "Raqs va shahvat, rah-i jadid-i tabligh-i masihiyat" [Dance and eroticism: The newest form of Christianity's preaching], *Maktab-i Islam* 4, no. 11, Azar 1341/November–December 1962, 43–4; 43.

17 H. Karbasi, "Tihran dar atash-i fisad misuzad" [Tehran is burning in the fire of immorality], *Parcham-i Islam*, 2 Azar 1326/4 December 1947, 1–2; 2.
18 See Husayn Shahzaydi, "Muravvijin-i fisad" [Disseminators of immorality], *Khandaniha*, 27, no. 65, 13.
19 Nurildin Varzani, "Musiqi va saz va avaz dar gumrahi va fisad-i mardum asar-i bah siza'i darad" [Music and dance and singing have a significant effect on leading the population astray and to immorality], *Nida-yi Haq*, 3 Mihr 1336/25 September 1957, 1, 4; 1.
20 Muhammad Mujtahidzadah, "Ta'min-i salamati-i jism va jan dar islam" [Securing the health of body and soul in Islam], *Jahan-i Danish,* no. 1, Farvardin 1339/March–April 1960, 190–200; 192; Riza Gulisurkhi-Kashani, "Pasukh bah mush-kilat-i khanandigan" [A response to the problems of readers], *Maktab-i Islam* 10, no. 1, Day 1347/December 1968–January 1969, 50–52; 52.
21 Mujtahidzadah, "Ta'min-i salamati-i jism," 192; Husayn Haqqani, "Aman az fisad-i muhit" [Alas! The corruption of the environment], *Maktab-i Islam* 2, no. 9, Mihr 1339/September–October 1960, 58–9; 59.
22 For instance see, "Dar hutil ivirist," 4; Zabiullah As'di, "Va inham film-i 'ilmi baray-i danishamuzan" [And here is a scientific film for children ...], *Maktab-i Islam*, no. 4, Farvardin 1349/March–April 1970, 67–9.
23 See "Tabliqat," *Humayun*, Mihr 1313/September–October 1934, 25; Dariush Asadpur-Bushihri, "Sitarigan-i sinama va javanan-i muqalid" [Stars of cinema and the mimicking youth], *Nur-i Danish* 4, no. 3, 115.
24 Mili Jami', "'Illat-i harj va marj-i fikri va akhlaqi-i irani chist?" [What is the underlying reason of Iranians' disarray of thought and morality?], *Parcham-i Islam*, 10 Bahman 1325/30 January 1947, 2. The collective participation of a "community of taste," leading to the creation of a sense of a new collective morality as well as the physical presence of large audiences also confirmed the status and popularity of these newly developed secular erotic zones, which were perhaps threatening from the authors' perspectives.
25 Ishraqi, "Hawzah'i 'ilmiyah'i," 3.
26 The carnivalesque moment, as described by Ruth Holiday and Graham Thomson, features characteristic scenes in which "women's breasts and buttocks are accen-tuated and exposed, along with some of men's genitalia... and the bodily repre-sentations are the antithesis of the 'perfect body.'" See Holiday and Thomson's description of the office party in Ruth Holiday and Graham Thomson, "A Body of Work," in R. Holiday and D. Hassard, eds., *Contested Bodies* (London: Routledge, 1997), 127.
27 See Asadpur-Bushihri, "Sitarigan-i sinama va javanan-i muqalid," 115.
28 Yaraqchi "Sukhani dar piramun-i hijab," 2; Husayn Haqqani-Zanjani, "Zanashu'i vasilah ast na hadaf" [Marriage is a means and not an end], *Maktab-i Islam* 9, no. 8, Murdad 1346/July–August 1967, 64–7; 67.
29 Munsif Yaraqchi "Azadi-i zanan, 2" [Women's emancipation, 2], *Dunya-yi Islam*, 24 Bahman 1326/14 February 1948, 1–2: 1; Yaraqchi, "Sukhani dar piramun-i hijab," 2.
30 "Az raqs-i zamin bitarsid" [Beware of the earth-rattling dance], *Nida-yi Haq*, 19 Tir 1336/30 June 1957, 1–2.
31 For example, Surur Afkhami, "Man baray-i suing mimiram, shuma chitur?" [I die for swing, how about you?], *Taraqqi* 8, no. 16, 28 Shahrivar 1329/19 September 1950, 11, 21.
32 See Faqihi-Shirazi's translation of an article published in *Al-'Irfan* for a description of ethics (*akhlaq*) and the ways in which an individual's "reason" ('*aql*) should control his/her anger (*ghazab*) and sexual desires (*shahvat*). Faqihi-Shirazi, trans., "Akhlaq" [Morality], *Parcham-i Islam*, 26 Day 1325/16 January 1947, 1,2; 2.

33 Abulqasim Danish-Ashtiyani, "Maktab-i Parsa'i va parhizkari" [The school of chastity and piety], *Masjid-i A'zam* 2, no. 8, Aban 1345/October–November 1966, 2–8; 8; Burqi'i, "Az khud-shinasi," 42.

34 A'rabi, "Mafhum-i kalamah'i 'iffat dar qadim chah budah va hala chist?" [What was the meaning of the term chastity in older times and what is its meaning now?], *Nida-yi Haq*, 17 Mihr 1336/9 October 1957, 1–2.

35 Zaynul'abidin Qurbani, "'Iffat chist? Afif kist?" [What is chastity? Who is chaste?], *Ru'in*, Farvardin 1337/March–April 1958, 38–9.

36 Nuriyani, "Zanan va hijab" [Women and veiling], *A'in-i Islam*, 9 Tir 1323/30 June 1944, 1; Sayyad Jalal-Kashani, "A'uz-u billah min-al shaytan-i rajim" [I seek refuge in God from the accursed Satan], transcribed lecture, *Dunya-yi Islam*, 26 Day 1326/17 January 1948, 1, 3; 3.

37 One finds evidence of this voyeuristic male gaze in the repetition of the eleventh-century Persian poet Baba Tahir's verse by the religiously inclined authors, emphasizing the importance of *hijab* for women: "cry from the eyes and from the heart, 'cause what the eyes see, the heart remembers" (*Zi dast-i didah va dil har du faryad, kah har chah didah binad dil kunad yad*).The major claim behind the usage of this verse in these writings was that if the eyes of a man were to see the unveiled body of a woman, he could get sexually aroused; and this is the first step towards immorality. For example, see Ni'matullah Faturichi, "Dukhtaran va pisarn-i javan bikhanand" [Young men and women, read this!], *A'in-i Islam*, 6 Mihr 1324/28 September 1945, 4; Nuriyani, "Zanan va hijab," 1; Karbasi, "Awza'i ijtima'az darichah'i intiqad," 4.

38 See, for instance, Sayyad-Mujtaba Husayni, *Ahkam-i nigah va pushish, mutabiq ba nazar-i dah tan az marajai'i 'uzzam* [The laws of gaze and clothing according to ten religious authorities] (Qom: Daftar-i Nashr-i Ma'arif, 1389/2010), 111–15; Ya'qub-'ali Burji, "Chishmandaz-i fiqh bar namayish" [The perspective of religion on performance], *Fiqh*, nos. 4–5, Tabistan va Pa'iz 1374/Summer and Fall 1996, 283–326.

39 Hidayatullah Hatami, "Khahran-i musalman" [The Muslim sisters], *Nur-i Danish*, 3 Day 1326/25 December 1947, 366.

40 See H. Karbasi, "Fahsha ma ra bih kuja sawq midahad?" [Where is *fahsha* taking us?], *Parcham-i Islam*, 26 Azar 1326/18 December 1947, 1–2; 2.

41 "Zan, ruh-i mard, qalb-i mard, sahib-i dil-i mard ast" [A woman is the soul of a man, the heart of a man, and the owner of the man's love], *Nida-yi Haq*, no. 292, Tir 1335/June–July 1956, 1, 4; 4.

42 Qurbani, "'Iffat chist? 'Afif kist?," 38–9.

43 Madani, "Atash-i bi 'iffati," 1–2; Khuldi, "Az bara-i 'iffat va pakdamani-i zanan," 2.

44 See the Islamic author, Sayyad Jalal Kashani's opposition to the justification of unveiling in *Ragbar* by Sayyad Ha'iriniya: Sayyad-Jalal Kashani, "Munafiqin ra ham bishinasid" [Recognize the infidels too], *Dunya-yi Islam*, 21 Azar 1326/13 December 1947, 1–2.

45 See, for instance, "Qanun-i islah-i mavadd-i 207 ila 214 qanun-i mujazat-i 'umumi" [Amendment to laws numbers 207 to 214 of the law of public punishment], *Mamjmu'ah'i Ruzanamah'i Rasmi* [*Iran Official Gazette*] 4621, 29 Shahrivar 1312/ 20 September 1933, dastour.ir/brows/?lid=18868.

46 Imadzadah, "Husn va qubh chist? 'Iffat-i 'umumi" [What is virtue and indecency? Public chastity], *Nida-yi Haq*, 3 Mihr 1336/25 September 1957, 1–2.

47 Abulqasim Ashtiyani, "Intikhab-i aslah" [The advisable choice], *Masjid-i A'zam*, no.13, Urdibihisht 1345/April–May 1966, 2–6; 3; Jami', "'Illat-i harj va marj-i fikri," 2.

48 Mujtahidzadah, "Ta'min-i salamati-i jism," 192.

49 Mansur Amini, "Sayah-ha-yi mutaharrik nishanah'i az qudrat-i ust" [Moving shadows are tokens of his power], *Maktab-i Islam* 16, no. 9, Shahrivar 1354/

August–September 1975, 4–8; 7; "Duri az majlis-i gunah" [Avoiding sinful gatherings], *Maktab-i Islam* 17, no. 10, Mihr 1355/September–October 1976, 4–7; 4.

50 Husayn Haqqani-Zanjani, "Huquq-i khanivadah dar Islam, 53" [Islamic laws of family, 53], *Maktab-i Islam* 14, no. 1, Bahman 1351/January–February 1973, 66–8; Haqqani Zanjani, "Zanashu'i vasilah," 67.

51 For instance, see "Qabil-i tavajjuh-i vizarat-i muhtaram-i kishvar" [Addressed to the honorable ministry of the interior], *Sitarah'i Sinama*, 14 Mihr 1336/6 October 1957, 2.

52 Stuart Hall, "The Spectacle of the 'Other,'" in S. Hall, ed., *Representation: Cultural Representation and Signifying Practices* (London: Sage, 1997), 249.

53 Following Bakhtin's notion of the grotesque body, Holiday and Thomson describe the pariah body as "a body that is associated with loss of control, is relived and deintegrated," starkly contrasting with Foucault's disciplined body, which is "connected intimately with the mind." The pariah bodies are "othered bodies," bodies which "provoke disgust and dread" while at the same time inciting "fascination and desire." Like the pariah bodies, the *mutajaddid* bodies in the Islamic periodicals represented uncontrolled sexuality, in contrast to the disciplined Muslims who were depicted as representatives of rationality. See Holiday and Thomson's description of pariah bodies in Ruth Holiday and Graham Thomson, "A Body of Work," in R. Holiday and D. Hassard, eds., *Contested Bodies* (London: Routledge, 1997), 9–10.

54 For example, see "Rah-i islah-i bishtari az mafassid amr-i bah ma'ruf va nahy-i az munkar ast" [Best means to correct social corruption is to command right and forbid wrong], *Nida-yi Haq*, 6 Murdad 1333/28 July 1954, 1, 4; "Amr-i bah ma'ruf va nahy-i az munkar vaizifah'i har musalmani ast" [Every Muslim is responsible to command right and forbid wrong], *Nida-yi Haq*, 18 Murdad 1334/10 August 1955, 1, 4.

55 In her speech published in *Nur-i Danish*, 'Izzat Girami refers to faith as an internal police; see 'Izzat Girami, "Sukhani chand ba banuvan" [A few words with ladies], *Nur-i Danish*, 16 Mihr 1326/9 October 1947, 75.

56 Sayyad-Muhammad-Hasan Sayf, "Pishbini-ha-yi pishvayan-i din" [The foresight of religious leaders], transcribed lecture, *Dunya-yi Islam*, 12 Day 1326/3 January 1948, 4; "Chigunah yik millati mimirad?," 3; Ali Dava'i, "Farhang?" [Culture?], *Nida-yi Haq*, 16 Mihr 1331/8 October 1952, 1,4; 4; Imadzadah, "Fiqdan-i 'alim va faqr-i 'ilmi" [The lack of learned men and the theoretical poverty], *Nida-yi Haq*, 8 Bahman 1331/28 January 1953, 1–2; 2; Ghulam-Husayn Jami, "Kashf-i Hijab ya 'amil-i fitnah va fisad" [Unveiling and the agents of sedition and corruption], *Nida-yi Haq*, 6 Isfand 1331/25 February 1953, 1,3; 3; "Aqa-yi vazir-i farhang" [Mr. Cultural Minister], *Nida-yi Haq*, 9 Tir 1333/30 June 1954, 1.

57 "Ittihad va ittifaq-i Islam" [The union and alliance of Islam], *Majmu'ah'i Hikmat*, 13 Azar 1331/4 December 1952, 16–17; 17.

58 A. Darakah'i, "Aya farhang-i ma firishtah ra ahriman nimikunad?" [Doesn't our culture turn angels into demons?], *Dunya-yi Islam*, 22 Khurdad 1327/12 June 1948, 1–2; Ghulam-Husayn Jami, "Farhang bayad az ru-yi mabani-i dini islah shavad" [Our culture must be reformed according to the religious bases], *Nida-yi Haq*, 20 Isfand 1331/11 March 1953, 2; Muhammad Mukhtarzadah, "Farhang ra daryabid" [Mind the culture!], *Nida-yi Haq*, 21 Murdad 1332/12 August 1953, 1–2; 2; "Aqa-yi vazir-i farhang," 2.

59 See "Shab-i nur-afshani-i islam" [The night of Islam's luminosity], *Dunya-yi Islam*, 19 Bahman 1325/8 February 1947, 4; Muhammad-Ali Taqavi, "Millat-i dindar 'alaqahmand bah hifz-i namus-i khud mibashad" [A religious nation is interested in safeguarding its honor], *Dunya-yi Islam*, 16 Aban 1326/8 November 1947, 1,4; 4.

60 "Bikhanid vizvizahkishi-ha'i ra kah ..."[Read the buzzings of ...], *Dunya-yi Islam*, 14 Azar 1326/6 December 1947, 1, 4; 4.

61 See Sayyad-Jalal Kashani, "Bismillah-i rahman-i Rahim" [In the name of God, the Merciful, the Compassionate], transcribed lecture, *Dunya-yi Islam*, 12 Day 1326/3 January 1948, 1, 4; 4.
62 Mukhtarzadah, "Farhang ra daryabid," 2.
63 Muhsin Mir I'timadi, "Chishm-i awlia-yi umur rawshan" [The authorities must be proud!], *A'in-i Islam*, 1 Khurdad 1326/23 May 1947, 13.
64 Faqihi-Shirazi, "Dawlat-i ayandah?!" [The next government?!], *Parcham-i Islam*, 12 Shahrivar 1326/4 September 1947, 1; "Chira shahrbani tavajjuh nimkunad va lanah-ha-yi fisad va fahsha ra nimibandad?" [Why is it that the police don't close the kennels of corruption and prostitution?], *Nida-yi Haq*, 2 Tir 1332/23 June 1953, 1, 4; 4; "In yiki nist" [This is not the only one], *Nida-yi Haq*, 17 Tir 1332/8 July 1953, 1, 2; Jinabzadah, "Aya fahsha faqat marbut bah shahr-i naw ast," 1, 3; Sayyad-Murtiza Khalkhali and Abdulhusayn Mu'tazidi, "Namah'i sargushadah" [An open letter], *A'in-i Islam*, 23 Bahman 1326/13 February 1948, 14–15.
65 Kashani, "Shahr-i khuda-parastan ast ya kanun-i zanparastan," 4; Shir-khuda'i, "Shahr-i fajayi'," 3.
66 Karbasi, "Tihran dar atash-i," 1–2.
67 Karbasi,"Fahsha ma ra bih kuja suq midahad," 2; Jinabzadah, "Aya fahsha faqat marbut bah shahr-i naw ast," 1, 3.
68 Haqqani, "Aman az fisad-i muhit," 59; "Luzum-i tavajuh-i daqiq bar amakin-i 'umumi" [The necessity of close attention to the public spaces], *Nida-yi Haq*, 22 Mihr 1332/14 October 1954, 1, 3; "Dar muqabil-i har maykadah, yik masjid bana kunid" [Open a mosque in front of every winery], *Parcham-i Islam*, 20 Farvardin 1326/10 April 1947, 1, 3.
69 Michel Foucault, Michel Senellart, François Ewald, and Alessandro Fontana, *Security, Territory, Population: Lectures at the Collège de France, 1977–78* (Basingstoke: Palgrave Macmillan, 2007), 26.
70 See Kashani, "Bismillah-i rahman-i Rahim," 4.
71 Imadzadah, "Dalai'l-i zindah dar ist'imari budan-i barnamah'i farhang" [The real reasons for the colonialist nature of cultural programming], *Nida-yi Haq*, 9 Mihr 1331/1 October 1952, 1–2; Hasan Nik-khu, "Aksariyat-i mardum dar in kishvar vazifah'i khud ra anjam nimidahand" [Most people in this country run away from their responsibilities], *A'in-i Islam*, no. 21, 3 Day 1327/24 December 1948, 19.
72 Zaynul'abidin Qurbani, "Ilal-i pishraft-i islam va inhitat-i muslimin" [The reasons for progress of Islam and decay of Muslims], *Maktab-i Islam* 18, no. 12, Isfand 1357/February–March 1979, 40–43; 42–3.
73 Ghulam-Husayn Jami, "Sitarah-ha-yi sinama va raqqas-ha-yi kabarah" [Stars of cinema and cabaret dancers], *Nida-yi Haq*, 8 Bahman 1332/28 January 1954, 1–2; 1; Ali-Akbar Hasani, "Ulgu-ha-yi jahad va taqva" [The role models of piety and jihad], *Maktab-i Islam* 18, no. 2, Urdibisht 1357/April–May 1978, 40–42; 40.
74 Haqqani Zanjani, "Huquq-i khanivadah," 66–8.
75 Ahmad Bihishti, "Mustaz'af kist?" [Who is the disinherited?], *Maktab-i Islam* 20, no. 2, Urdibisht 1359/April–May 1980, 22–8; 25.
76 Muhammad Salar Simnani, *Naqsh-i Sinama dar 'Asr-i Ma* [The role of cinema in our times] (Sa'id-i Naw, 2556/1978), 84.
77 "Bazi dar mashhad, kargardani dar tihran" [Acting in Mashhad, directing in Tehran], *Zamimah'i Farhangi-i Ruznamah'i Khurasan* 1, Bahman 1391/February 2012, 38–9; Muhammad-Husayn Badri, "Sarbidaran, dastan-i inqilabi pish az piruzi" Sarbidaran, the story of a revolution before victory], *Surah*, no. 33, Tir va Murdad 1386/July–August 2007, 104–107; "Duktur shari'ati yik hadisah va yik jarayan ast" [Dr. Shari'ati is a phenomenon and a flow], *Khabarguzari-i Miras-i Farhangi*, 4 Khurdad 1383/24 May 2004, www.chn.ir/NSite/FullStory/?Id=86195.
78 Islamic Consultative Assembly, Majlis 1, 19 Bahman 1362/8 February 1984, *Official Gazette*, no. 10824, retrieved from the DVD *Parliamentary Proceedings*

(Mashruh-i Muzakirat-i Majlis) published by Kitabkhanah, Muzah va Markaz-i Asnad-i Majlis-i Shawra-yi Islami [The Library, museum, and document center of Iran's parliament].

79 Ali-Akbar Hasani, "Nazari bah qavanin-i jaza'i-i Islami" [A brief look at the laws of Islamic punishment], *Maktab-i Islam* 20, no. 2, Urdibisht 1359/April–May 1980, 106–10; 107.

80 For instance, Islamic Consultative Assembly, Majlis 1, 5 Tir 1362/26 June 1983, *Official Gazette*, no. 9005; Islamic Consultative Assembly, Majlis 1, 19 Khurdad 1362/9 June 1984, *Official Gazette*, no. 8859; Islamic Consultative Assembly, Majlis 2, 26 Urdibisht 1364/16 May 1985, *Official Gazette*, no. 2827.

81 Stuart Hall, "Spectacle of the 'Other,'" 249.

7   *Harikat-i mawzun*
The post-revolutionary Iranian theatrical dance*

Within a few years after "dance" (*raqs*) was banned for being an immoral cultural practice, a new mode of performance appeared on the theatrical stage in post-revolutionary Iran. Cast as "rhythmic movements" (*harikat-i mawzun*), this new genre soon became a vehicle embodying the Islamic government's religious and political ideologies. Appropriated through the renaming and reshaping of the dancing subject, the genre of rhythmic movements was constructed to counter the previous associations of "dance" with immorality, corruption, "eroticism", and "degeneration", largely instigated by the image of the "enticing" dancing subject of the popular entertainment scene of cabaret. Embodying chastity, modesty, and spirituality, the dancing subject of *harikat-i mawzun* has been enacting the narratives of Islam and the revolution.

Scrutinizing the dancing subject of the post-revolutionary theater stage, this chapter traces the genealogy of rhythmic movements to the pre-revolutionary "national dance" (*raqs-i milli*), and explores its theatricalization of Islamic and mystical themes and performative motifs. Moreover, situating the genre in the post-revolutionary cultural context and in relation to the discourse of "committed" arts, I here study the ways this genre became a vehicle for visualizing holy figures, and realizing religious and revolutionary narratives. Investigating the corporeal purging process and the politics of aesthetics of this genre, in this chapter I also explore the discourses surrounding the dancing body on the post-revolutionary stage.

Terms, themes, and performing subject in post-revolutionary Iranian theatrical dance

With the advent of the revolution, there was an immediate disruption of the performing art forms and venues that were deemed to be improper, or that signified "prostitution" (*fahsha*), "eroticism" (*shahvat*), and "degeneration" (*ibtizal*)—most of which involved women's bodies. These included the cabaret scene; Lalehzar theaters featuring dance and music, pop music, and women's solo voice; as well as all forms of public dancing. Consequently, the former state-sponsored National Ballet Company and National Dance

Company (Iran National Folklore Organization) were also dissolved, and their members were dismissed or offered work within the Ministry of Culture as actors or office employees.[1] After a few years of struggle and the trial and error of those dancers who stayed in the theatrical milieu, a new form of dance appeared on the theater stage. Defamiliarized by being renamed as *harikat-i mawzun* and relocated to the theatrical stage, the post-revolutionary genre introduced a new performing body to the Iranian stage, one which shared continuity with pre-revolutionary national dance.

Coming to replace *raqs* on the post-revolutionary stage, the term *harikat-i mawzan* had been in use in reference to movements in theatrical and sportive contexts from the early twentieth century. An early instance was used in 1928 by a critic who valorized the dance and movements of Pari Aqababov in an operetta from the early modernist-nationalist scene.[2] The term also described the marching and acrobatic movements of female students in the grand celebration, Jashn-i Duvvum-i Urdibisht, that occurred in 1939 in the presence of the Crown Prince and his Egyptian wife—a spectacle that exhibited a variety of "national" cultural forms.[3] As with the above mentioned instances, and unlike the term *raqs* that could also imply negative meanings, *harikat-i mawzun* have had only positive connotations even prior to the revolution.

Similarly, the post-revolutionary return of the term was meant to ascribe a different meaning to the movement-based performances that were happening on the theater stage. Starting in 1983, early rhythmic movements were often segments of plays with diverse themes, ranging from international plays to those written by Iranian playwrights on vernacular literary, mystical, and religious and revolutionary themes.[4] Regarded as "designers" (*tarrah*) of *harikat-i mawzun*, most choreographers in these plays were former dancers with the major dance companies prior to the revolution.[5] The genre had also been referred to with alternative terms including "structured movements" (*harikat-i furm*), "expressive movements" (*harikat-i bayani*), and "ritual movements" (*harikat a'ini*), and its performers were interchangeably referred to as "actors of form" (*bazigar-i furm*), "performer" (*namayishgar*), and "choir" (*hamsurayan*).

As sequences within the plays, *harikat-i mawzun* gradually found more dominance. This was especially seen in the prevalence of mystical plays that provided the groundwork for a combination of Iranian mystical music, poetry, and dance. In the absence of a distinct dance scene, such combination had a popular reception, exemplified in the works of the theater director Pari Saberi, who aimed at staging operettas based on Iranian literary themes reminiscent of those staged in the early modernist-nationalist performing arts scene.[6] Instances of her mystical-inspired works include *Man bah Bagh-i 'Irfan* (Me in the garden of mysticism, 1988), *Haft Shahr-i 'Ishq* (The seven cities of love, 1995), and *Shams-i Parandah* (The flying shams, 2000). Firdawsi's *Shahnamah* (Book of the kings) was also the source of inspiration for Saberi's *Bijan va Manijah* (1997), *Haft-Khan-i Rustam* (The seven adventures

Figure 7.1 Shams-i Parandah (The Flying Shams), directed by Pari Saberi
Photo by Farshid Saffari.

Figure 7.2 Zal va Rudabah, directed by Nadir Rajabpur
Photo by Farshid Saffari.

of Rustam, 2009) as well as *Rustam va Isfandiyar* (2010).[7] (See Figure 7.1 for
an image of *Shams-i Parandah*)

Similar to pre-revolutionary *raqs-i milli*, poetry and mythology have
remained prevalent themes in the full-length movement-based productions
that have been staged since 2000. Examples of works produced by two former
soloists of the National Dance Company include *Simurgh* (Phoenix, 2002) by

Farzanah Kabuli, and *Haft-Iqlim* (The seven regions, 2003) and *Zal va Rudabah* (2009) by Nadir Rajabpur. (See Figure 7.2 for an image of *Zal va Rudabah*.) The movement styles of these productions were a combination of easily traceable balletic movements with vernacular Iranian performances—a blend reminiscent of the pre-revolutionary national dance.

As described, mystical themes have been central in the post-revolutionary genre. In addition to the appropriation of mystical movements, the Sufi ritual *sama'* has served as a source for the legitimatization of dance in Iran: as a midpoint between the worldly practice of dance for the single purpose of entertainment and the strict interpretations of Islam which fully reject dance, *sama'* has helped in justifying *harikat-i mawzun* as a spiritual dance. In the early 2000s, when this performance genre was receiving more attention, several authors emphasized the significance of *sama'* as a performance for the divine, rejecting worldly dances which serve no purpose but pleasure.[8]

Concurrently, some producers of *harikat-i mawzun*, struggling to stage their work, widely related their dance to *sama'* and the philosophy behind it, or emphasized dance and other rituals as national art forms. For instance, in an interview about the *Jashnvarah'i Amin* (Amen Festival)—a narrative-based full-length rhythmic movements production that featured several regional folk dances—the director described those dances as "a means for praying to God." Furthermore, she stated that the last scene of the work, in which multiple groups simultaneously performed various folk dances to the same music, represented a communal prayer of the "nation" of Iran consisting of many ethnicities and cultures including Kurdish, Turkish, Khurasani, and Gilaki.[9] The attempt to associate all types of dance with the "mystical" or the "religious" was also evident in an article published in 2001 in the monthly *Hamshahri-i Mah*. Interviewing several active dance artists, and reporting on the present-day activities that related to this art form in society, the author emphasized the importance of the "preservation of this religious-national art form [*raqs*]."[10]

Besides mystical themes, religious narratives have also been dominant in rhythmic movement productions, to the extent that this genre has widely been used as a means to stage stories of 'Ashura, and those of the holy figures of Shi'i Islam (such as Zaynab, Fatimah, Husayn, and Ali), as well as those of Muslim Ibn-i 'Aqil and Hurr. All of these productions have been categorized as "religious theater" (*namayish-i mazhabi*).[11] Often identified as "committed art" (*hunar-i muti'ahhid*), movement-based performances enacting the narratives related to the Iran–Iraq war (1980–88) have also become a recurring element of the "Holy Defense Theater" (*ti'atr-i difa'-i muqaddas*) (see Figures 7.3 and 7.4).[12] Produced in varying lengths, these performances have also been commissioned for different purposes by governmental organizations. Intifada and the Israel–Palestine conflict have been inspiring works in this genre, including the full-length rhythmic movements production *Hamasah'i Inqilab-i Sang* (The epic of the rock revolution, 2000) (see Figure 7.5). This work was identified as the first Islamic ballet.[13]

Figure 7.3 Flyer of *In Fasl ra ba Man Bikhan* (Sing this season together with me! 2009)

Figure 7.4 In Fasl ra ba Man Bikhan (Sing this season together with me! 2009)
Photo by Farshid Saffari.

Figure 7.5 Hamasah'i inqilab-i sang (The Epic of the Rock Revolution, 2000)
Photo by Omid Salehi.

The staged body in rhythmic movements

A major transformation of dance in this post-revolutionary genre was its relocation to the theater stage—a space that itself was converted from a secular theatrical space into a sphere governed by Islamic biopolitics, also enforcing a major alteration of the performing body. Aiming to justify this dance as mystic or religious and its performer as a chaste subject, the themes, music, costuming, and performer's appearance and actions in rhythmic movements all defamiliarized *raqs*. A key to this restaging of dance was removing the corporeal signifying elements of *raqs* and *shahvat*.

To obscure the shape of the body, loosely fitted costumes in black, white, or other muted tones have often been used in rhythmic movements. Sometimes, in mixed performances, both men and women have similar costuming which occasionally also covers the face, thereby practicing a strategy of de-gendering to reduce the sensitivity towards the public female dancing body (see Figure 7.6).[14] As depicted in Figures 7.1, 7.2 and 7.5, the costumes of both male and female performers in the rhythmic movements genre often have not represented any regional culture of Iran or any traditional Iranian clothing, but have followed a style developed for this particular performance genre. They, in fact, give much more coverage than the regular clothing one would wear in public in post-revolutionary Iran. Arguably, this kind of costuming has not only aimed to prevent sexual connotations of the performing body on stage; it has also reinforced the Islamic bio-ideology.

Figure 7.6 Raz-i Sarzamin-i Man (The secret of my land, 2004), directed by Nadir
        Rajabpur
Photo by Farshid Saffari.

The movements of *harikat-i mawzun* have often been a theatrical blend of ballet, stylized folk dances mainly from men's Bauluchi and Khurasani dances, the Sufi ritual of *sama'* (including the movements of swaying, swiveling, and whirling), and the Shi'i ritual of *ta'ziyah*. Added to this blend are the movements associated with the mourning of Imam Husayn, including "beating the chest" (*sinah-zani*), "beating oneself with chains" (*zanjir-zani*), and "self-flagellation with swords" (*qamah-zani*). In constructing the female chaste dancers, meanwhile, certain key signifiers of Iranian dance, including free-flowing wrist rotation and hip movements, have been eliminated. Instead, women mostly have been moving their arms for a defined purpose in a way that resembles prayer, or for the carriage of props such as books, candleholders, flowers, and fabrics.

The stage depictions of celebrations have been completely transformed in post-revolutionary performances through the implementation of mystical elements, occasionally creating a contradiction between the theme and style of these dances. An example of this can be seen in the depiction of love scenes between a man and a woman where the dancers also communicate with God by performing movements of *sama'* in addition to showing affection to each other.[15] In addition, in depictions of secular celebrations, where one would expect to see Persian classical or national dance, the post-revolutionary productions instead employ elements of the *sama'*.[16]

The post-revolutionary societal restrictions on gender relations have been manifested and rather exaggerated in theatrical performances. In particular, depicting a love relationship between a husband and a wife is quite challenging as both performers are mute and sometimes it is impossible to see the facial expressions of the female dancer's covered face. In this situation, the pauses between movements to express doubt or affection have become a key channel of communication for the dancers depicting love.[17] The exchange of props is also metaphorically employed to depict the sexual scenes, since the performers are not allowed to touch each other.[18]

Within the religious and revolutionary works, women have been widely staged as angels dressed in white.[19] This archetype is genealogically related to the dancing bodies developed in the early twentieth-century nationalist-modernist theater scene in Iran and its byproduct, the Iranian national dance genre. Similar to the early twentieth-century situation discussed in Chapter 2, the casting of women as desexualized angels on the post-revolutionary stage has been a legitimate means for the staging of female bodies, where engaging female performers has been very difficult. In contrast to the exaggerated performance of sexuality by the cabaret *raqqas*, the dominant characteristic of the female performer of *harikat-i mawzun* has been the embodiment and performance of the expressions of heaviness, modesty, chastity, and austerity.

Rhythmic movements as a committed art

The transformation of dance and its resurfacing on the theater stage must be viewed within the larger cultural context of the post-revolutionary era.

Although after the revolution some performance forms, including dance, were eliminated immediately from the public stage, the purging of the theater stage was a longer process.[20] In the meantime, in the politically active theatrical milieu of the immediate post-revolution era, themes reflecting the socio-politics of the day, including the "revolution" (*inqilab*), anti-imperialism, and Islam, as well as the Iran–Iraq war, became inspirations for artistic endeavors.[21]

With the settling of the new Islamic state, and the purging of the art sphere in the process of cultural revolution, the question of the ways the arts could serve the revolution—meaning the new state—came to the foreground of the new government's cultural planning. Arts and culture were identified as the means for "eternalizing" (*javidanah kardan*) the revolution—which later materialized as the state.[22] The pre-revolutionary concept of committed art was also integrated into the state's discourse. While a range of terms, including "religious art" (*hunar-i dini*), "Islamic art" (*hunar-i islami*), and "doctorinaire art" (*hunar-i maktabi*), were used in this discourse, the new committed art was positioned to merge and depict Islam as both a religious and political ideology.[23] As described in Chapter 6, such fusion of Islam, politics, and the arts was a pre-revolutionary phenomenon largely ascribed to Ali Shari'ati's followers.[24] Nevertheless, the post-revolutionary notion of committed art promoted by the state had to embody and promote the state's ideology, instead of subverting the power.[25] In this historical context, the notion of "art for art's sake," and indeed all other performing-art forms of the pre-revolutionary era, were distrusted as "degenerate" (*mubtazal*).[26]

In this discourse, theater was especially found to be an appropriate and effective medium for visualizing and eternalizing the narratives of the revolution, and the Iran–Iraq war, as well as a means for exporting the revolution and for awakening the impoverished nations of the world (*millat-ha-yi mahrum-i jahan*).[27] The ritualistic roots of theater were used to justify its religious functions, while *ta'ziyah*—the Iranian religious performative form—further vindicated the theater's capacities for fostering the state ideology, revolution, and the war, all of which discursively deployed Shi'i metaphors and motifs.[28]

Adopting revolutionary values was regarded as a means for "popularizing" theater, and to make peace between traditional and religious sectors of the society with actors—who were prior to the revolution regarded with negativity.[29] Women's recruitment to the stage in this discourse was to "create awareness" (*agahi-afarini*) and showcase "healthy" (*salim*) arts instead of depicting corruption and "lewdness" (*harzigi*)—a term used to refer to the representation of women in the pre-revolutionary era.[30] Women's presence onstage was linked to their participation in the revolutionary scene and the post-revolutionary society; thus, as articulated by the Mahdi Hujjat, a state authority in arts, the "cabaret dancers" (*raqqas*) could not be shown onstage as no *raqqas* existed in the society anymore.[31]

Within a few years religious theater and the Holy Defense (referring to the Iran–Iraq war) became established genres with festivals, expertise, and publications. In the meantime, now tasked as a committed art, rhythmic movements permeated these scenes. With this new status, and after years of attempts at staging religious narratives, theorization of these themes and characters became a new venture for committed scholars and practitioners. One of the main issues was to adapt traditional and community-based performances to the contemporary stage setting for an audience more adept to contemporary technology. Such a problem was said to have been intensified by the temporal and technological disruption between contemporary times and the "golden era" of religious theater in Iran—often perceived as the Qajar era.[32]

The topics and questions prevalent in this discourse include: (1) What is religious theater?[33] (2) What topics and historical periods can it cover? (3) What is the purpose of it? (Is it to commemorate the heroes? Or does it presume to create heightened emotion and thus purification in the audience?)[34] (4) How can Koranic narratives be translated to the stage?[35] (5) What are the dramatic capacities of the stage for presenting unearthly characters? and (6) How might one make these themes accessible and attract younger audiences through the use of contemporary theatrics?[36]

Among such theoretically inclined writers, Hasan Bayanlu viewed the element of "wonder" (*shigifti*) as a commonality between religious narratives and the performance stage.[37] He argued that the stage can enhance time and space between the other, invisible world (*'alam-i ghayb*) and the material world, both of which are embedded in religious narratives.[38] He attested that the stage can be used to present religious plots, superhumans, and "invisible" (*qaybi*) beings, such as angels and Satan; the "forcible" (*qahir*) manifestation of God on earth; and those "hyper-real" (*fara-vaqi'yat*) and mystery elements of religious narratives.[39] To him, the holy figures embodied wonder and drama: they seldom made mistakes, they were aware of the invisible and unknown and communicated with angels, and they suppressed their "evil-inciting sel [ves]" (*nafs-i ammarah*). Their prayers, mortification, and self-disciplining exceeded those of regular people.[40]

Other writers discussed the ways stage design can enhance presenting the metaphysical and spiritual aspects of religion and improve audience responses by triggering their potential sensitivity towards religious performative forms and symbols.[41] For instance, Sirus Kahurinezhad, a stage designer who worked in this genre, asserted that the design for these performances should include both a physical image onstage and a mental image in the audience members' minds, especially when depicting a metaphysical character such as the Prophet, whose face may not be illustrated.[42]

It is within this discourse that the rhythmic movements genre has become an essential element of contemporary religious theatrical stagings. Being deployed as a mobile set, rhythmic movements genre has been enhancing the scenic affects of the plays. In the meantime, acting as a chorus, it has been contributing to mood creation and intensification of the emotional response in the audience, especially in scenes that require "mystical" or "heroic" ambience.[43] Moreover, it has improved the presentation and sensory appeal of holy figures and other-worldly beings, such as Satan and angels in religious narratives, as well as the scenes pertaining to the (Iran–Iraq) War and the Revolution.[44] Meanwhile, in the absence of a distinct dance scene, the rhythmic movements genre has been presenting dancing bodies onstage, thereby attracting audiences.[45]

Such incentives have been evident in the works of Husayn Musafir-Astanah, a prolific director in the genres of religious and Holy War theater, who directs movement-based works. Recognizing the need for change in the presentation of these genres of theater and aiming to make these themes more accessible to the general audience in Iran and abroad, as well as to attract the younger generations, his works have often featured a contemporary combination of various theatrical elements, including movements, video projection, and sound effects.[46]

Rhythmic movements and staging religious and revolutionary themes

The recurrence in contemporary stagings of religious and revolutionary themes include the *ta'ziyah*, Shi'i Islamic history, and the Iran–Iraq war. Two of the main inspirational and performative sources for these contemporary stagings of religious narratives have been *ta'ziyah* and Muharran mourning rituals, to the extent that in narrating the Iran–Iraq war, sometimes the Battle of Karbala on the Day of 'Ashura has been merged into a stage scene.[47] It is important to note that like the Iran–Iraq war, along with the religious aspect of the form, *ta'ziyah* has had great (secular) nationalist appeal.[48]

In these productions, a variety of contemporary techniques and mediums, including video projection, lighting, stage machinery, as well as music and sound effects, are also deployed. As in *ta'ziyah*, the use of props and stage sets in these contemporary productions has been symbolic. Imaginary sceneries of seventh-century Arabia have often been created by the use of elements assumed to have existed in the everyday life of the early Islamic era.[49] These include palm trees and items such as swords, flags, daggers, and tents. Candles and lanterns are often used to imply waiting, especially in regards to the twelfth Imam, Mahdi. The shi'i symbolic colors black, green, and red have also been enhanced to distinguish between the protagonists' roles of Husayn supporters (who are represented with green) and Husayn enemies, the antagonists signified by red. The depiction of Iran–Iraq war scenes is achieved through weapons, military clothing, as well as video projection of images of the war and the martyrs.

Sound signifiers have also contributed to the narration of the story. For instance, in enacting historic religious narratives, horse-riding sounds and military-like music have often signaled the arriving of an army, and romantic choral music has accompanied the protagonists. In *Dar Qab-i Mah*, the rhythmic Arabic music—often used for belly dance—accompanied the antagonists. Narration in the form of poetry broadcast from a house speaker has been used to represent and accompany movements of an actor onstage or to explain the story behind the movements of the performers.

The female performers in religious *harikat-i mawzun* have been cast as angels, an archetype present in the Koranic narratives as well as in *ta'ziyah* performances.[50] Acting as the mediators between God and earth, the white-dressed angels appear in a variety of themes including the contemporary stagings of *ta'ziyah* and revolutionary themes.[51] Additionally, other key roles at work have included sacred figures such as Fatima and Zaynab, as well as pedestrian women engaged in praying, mourning, or escaping the war. The predominant male actions, with the exception of the sacred figures, have involved participating in war, praying, or moving in celebratory scenes or in simple scenes of daily life.

While traditionally the depiction of the key protagonists in *ta'ziyah* required certain corporeal specifications in appearance and actions, the representation of the sacred figures on the contemporary stage has been greatly enhanced by the combination of stage technology and rhythmic movements. If appearing onstage, their faces are covered, as most interpretations of Islam prohibit the depiction of holy figures.[52] Their costumes fully cover their bodies and include long robes and loose pants, as well as head-scarves. On top of these articles of clothing, women wear additional swaths of long fabric.

The actors playing the holy figures have been positioned upstage behind the cyclorama curtain, where the audience only sees their silhouettes.[53] When appearing on stage, a spotlight follows them to create a mystical aura usually associated with holy figures. Their voices have often been heard from the house speakers, separating the voice from the performing body, as if an otherworldly message is being transmitted via the medium of the performing body.[54] These actors' holy figure presence onstage has also been signified by the way they move, at a much slower pace than the other performers. Their signature movement has been to open their arms, with face and palms facing upwards, to resemble prayer. Such codification in movements has also been drawn from *ta'ziyah* conventions.[55]

By using technology and rhythmic movements, the personification of religious characters has reached a new level of distantiating the actor's body from that of the (holy) character. This perhaps has answered some of the original clerical issues with the impersonation of holy figures by earthly human bodies in the traditional *ta'ziyah* performances.[56] Moreover, the recruitment of women in these contemporary productions has also resolved the clerical issues with the cross-dressing in the original *ta'ziyah* performances where male actors performed the female roles.[57]

The main difference between the pre-revolutionary secular national dance and "religious" rhythmic movements lies in the intention behind the performance. Presumably the recent religious productions—just like the "traditional" religious performances, including the *ta'ziyah*—have aimed to create a uniform emotional response in the audience by purifying their souls when they mourn for the martyrs. Some scholars view the message behind the religious performances as rather universal, standing for the ongoing battle between purity and impurity, virtue and vice, and for human resistance against tyranny.[58] A similar notion has also been expressed by the dancers enacting such performances: the aim was not the exact religious ideology, but the spiritual message behind those narratives.[59]

While these performers have often been trained as national dancers in secular settings, they have been transforming into new spiritual performing selves when on the religious stage. As they themselves report, this transformation has not been just a regulatory process. Several characteristics of performance have been providing the foundation for epiphanic and other-worldly experiences for performers: the situation of high emotionality embedded in the narrative, the witnessing of the audience members' responses (which often include bursting into tears), and the enacting of sacred characters by moving slowly with a covered face while possessing a technologically produced aura.[60] While these onstage "dancer-believers" could be identified as having a "contented self"(*nafs-i mutma'innah*)—as opposed to the "evil-inciting self" associated with the common notion of *raqs*—state scrutiny has nevertheless been fully exerted against these stagings of movement-based works, in a similar (or even more formidable) manner as that against all other theatrical performances.

Rhythmic movements under the correctional gaze

A condition for staging performances of rhythmic movements has been their acceptance in a preview process held by an inspection and evaluation committee. Responsible for deciding whether a work is suitable for public staging, the committee has to ensure that no component of a performance, including its theme and performers' appearances and actions, is against Islam and the government's policies. One main responsibility of this committee is to verify that the performers' appearance and actions onstage do not provoke sexual desires in the audience.

Due to sensitivities towards (female) dancing bodies, the preview and permission process for the movement-based works, especially the full-length rhythmic movements productions, have been more challenging compared to regular plays.[61] While the process of previewing has been crucial in staging a work, its regulatory mechanism has also been functioning effectively in its absence: in an internalized manner, the corrective gaze of this committee has been subjugating the performers to constant self-monitoring even before the preview session begins.[62] This gaze—identifiable with Foucault's notion of correctional gaze—has been a key constituent of a network of power that has been regulating the theatrical sphere in post-revolutionary Iran.[63]

Moreover, the members of the committee not only have been gazing at theatrical productions for surveillance, but also have had the power to decide whether the public should be able to watch the work. In the subjective process of inspection, movements and other visual aspects of the stage—which could possibly signify unacceptable semiotic meanings and aesthetics, or bear a sexual undertone and affect—could get eliminated or cause the elimination of an entire work. The committee has often expressed over-sensitivity towards women's bodies and their affects—including instances when the profile of their figure became visible under multiple layers of fabric due to lighting. Similarly, the committee's hyper-sensitivity towards female body parts has forced the female performers to use wide elastic garments to flatten their breasts.[64] Movements that are not considered expressions of a proper Muslim, and/or resemble lightness, carefreeness, or spontaneity, have also raised red flags for the committee.[65] These have included manners of walking or small gestures that could be read as flirtatious.

Another requirement, as articulated by one of my interviewees, has been the elimination of movements that involve rotations of the wrist, hip, and/or chest, as these are thought to signify *raqs* for the public.[66] While a spectator's interpretation of a dance performance significantly relies on his or her own personal history, understanding, and knowledge, as Alexandra Carter has suggested, "the interpretation of dance is also necessarily contingent upon the recognition of common cultural meanings ascribed to signs, symbols, patterns, structures, etc."[67] Renamed *harikat-i mawzun*, a stage performance merely concerned with body movements still could be interpreted as "dance" (*raqs*). The sensitivity of the inspection committee members towards *raqs* possibly relates to their exposure to the common discourses that associated the dancing body with *shahvat* and the behavior of the unconstrained body of a Pahlavi-era cabaret dancer.

Since an inspector's decision about the suitability of a particular public performance can be read as the government's statement on the performance, I can hypothesize that the inspectors exercise a great deal of caution and care to not be too permissive. Arguably, a main function of the preview process has been to eradicate "eroticism" from female performers' bodies. Another "aesthetic" outcome of this process has been tasking staged female bodies with immediate functions, including carrying various props. This has been done to represent the female performing bodies and their movements as purposeful and thus "committed," rather than merely exhibitionist and entertaining for the gaze of the spectators; to differentiate them from the pre-revolutionary cabaret dancers who were associated with "degeneration".

Post-revolutionary counter-dance discourse

As has been discussed, despite having undergone the de-familiarization process, the genre of rhythmic movements continues to remain under the shadow of the immorality associated with the "evil-inciting" *raqs*. This has not just been the case with the preview sessions, but also has been evident in discourses around the term, exemplified in a major choreographer of this genre's call for a differentiation between the virtue-based (*khub*) and vice-based (*bad*) forms of *harikat-i mawzun*.[68] Referring to the diversity of Iran's time-honored regional folk dances and movement-based rituals (which have been popular among Iran's Muslim populations, including the *sama'* and *zurkhanah*), Jahansuz Fuladi, a former soloist of the Iran National Folklore Organization, emphasized the affinity of these performances with Islam.[69]

The ongoing dispute over *harikat-i mawzun* and its association with *raqs* manifested in the conflicts over the opening ceremony of the Fourth Women's Islamic Games in 2005. While its director had previously clarified that the ceremony included "only *harikat-i mawzun* and not *raqs*," the event was widely criticized by some factions of society for showcasing dance.[70] Reflecting on the same event, the author of the blog *Raz-i Khun* questioned *harikat-i mawzun*, calling it "*raqs* according to kindergarten artsy fartsies."[71] While the creation of an association for *harikat-i mawzun* in 2005 was a sign of its official acceptance, its renaming to the Association for "Mute Performances" (Namayish-i Bidun-i Kalam) in 2007 to imply mime rather than dance testifies to the uncertain situation of this genre.[72]

The notion of *sama'* as a mystical ritual, which has been invoked to legitimize rhythmic movements, has also been rejected by the more conservative circles. An example of this attitude can be found in an account by Hamidullah Rafi'i, a contributor to *Andishah'i Qum* in response to the Rumi scholar Sayyad Salman Safavi, who argued that Islam has to be presented in ways appealing to youth, recommending *sama'*, as an appropriate spiritual (*ma'navi*) means to this end.[73] Emphasizing the prohibition of dance in Islam for arousing sexual and sensual passion, Rafi'i asserted that the only dance allowed in Islam is the dance of a wife for her husband. Rafi'i denounced the idea of *sama'* as a way of getting closer to God, proclaiming: "Dance is dance, and there is no such thing as spiritual dance ... Dance distances the man from God, and, in particular, leads the youth to sensuality and sex."[74]

Similarly, the post-revolutionary forms have their own opponents within the system. For instance, the carrying of the Koran in an official ceremony by a woman with a rhythmic walk who was also accompanied by a dozen female drum players was a serious predicament for the organizing institution in 2008, as her walking was read as dance.[75]

Conclusion

The term *rhythmic movements* legitimized dance to return to the post-revolutionary stage, introducing a dancing body that defamiliarized the corporeal characteristics of the "eroticism" and "degeneration" associated with the cabaret dancer. This resurgence was the product of the negotiations between the dance artists who remained in the theatrical milieu, as well as a post-revolutionary quest for new forms of committed performances. Similar to its predecessor *raqs-i milli*, the post-revolutionary genre of rhythmic movements distantiated itself from the signifiers associated with the dancing subject of the popular scene, *raqqas*. A hybrid dance form, the rhythmic movements genre has also been borrowing heavily from performative elements of Iranian culture, but with a greater emphasis on the religious rituals and performances.

Desexualized and controlled, the performer of this genre embodies the virtues of an Iranian Muslim, conveying a message often related to God and revolutionary values. Through connecting to God and overcoming the evil-inciting self, as in the Sufi ritual of *sama'*, the performing subject in rhythmic movements correlates with the "contented self."[76] Reinforcing the image of a "proper" Muslim through embodying the expressions of heaviness, chastity, purity, and spirituality, the "purified body" of this subject continues to enact the bio-ideology of the government. Contributing to the reception of religious performances, the genre has also resolved some of the contested issues related to the presentation of body within the traditional religious performances.

Similar to popular performative forms of Islam, including *ta'ziyah*, as well as secular performances, the new stagings have provoked negative responses from the more conformist interpreters of Islam. Nevertheless, with all contestations—and similar to the Pahlavi state—the Islamic government of Iran has deployed movement-based performance as part of its ideological state apparatus, particularly useful for fostering its domestic and foreign policies. The theatrical movement-based productions on themes of the Iranian Revolution, the Iran–Iraq war, and the holy figures of Islam are only a few of the productions commissioned by the state. Even within this governmental system, the issue of mute female performing bodies remains one of the most challenging problems of the theatrical stage in Iran.

Notes

* A different version of this chapter is published in *Muslim Rap, Halal Soaps, and Revolutionary Theater: Artistic Developments in the Muslim Cultural Sphere*, ed. Karin Van Nieuwkerk (Austin: University of Texas Press, 2011), and the forthcoming *Islam, Popular Culture and Art*, ed. Karin Van Nieuwkerk, Martin Stokes, and Mark LeVine (Austin: University of Texas Press, 2016. I would like to thank the editors for their comments on them.

1 See Paula Citron, "Ali Pourfarrokh Remembers Iran," *Dance Magazine* 63, no. 9, September 1989, 20; Hasan Shirvani, "Anchah ra ma az dast midahim" [What we are losing], *Khurus Jangi*, 12 Khurdad 1358/2 June 1979, 1–2.

2 Unnamed critic, quoted in Mas'ud Kouhestaninejad, "Dar takapuy-i tajaddud" [In search of modernity], *Faslnamah'i Ti'atr*, no. 36, Pa'iz 1382/Fall 2003, 23–112; 46.

3 "Guzarish-i jashn-i duvvum-i urdibihisht" [Report of the 23 April ceremonies], *Ta'lim va Tarbiyat* 9, no. 2, Urdibihisht 1318/April–May 1939, 4–24; 13.

4 See Mansurah Shuja'i and Shu'lah Pakravan, "Kitabshinasi-i sahnah'i namayish" [Bibliography of performance/theater], *Faslnamah'i Ti'atr*, nos. 6–8, Tabistan, Pa'iz, Zimistan 1368/Summer, Fall, Winter 1989, 337–452. This published report listed the plays performed in the first decade of the revolution. According to this document, early instances of the usage of the term *harikat-i mawzun* were specifically for the play *Zar* staged in 1982; written by Hasan Zerehi and choreographed by Manizhah Gulchin, the play was inspired by the ritual of *zar*. Gulchin also choreographed *Rakhsh, Dilam Juz Bar-i Muhabtat Nakhahd Burd* [Rakhsh, my

heart would only carry your love] inspired by Firdawsi's *Shahnamah* in 1983. Based on the theme of the Iranian Revolution, *Shakib* was staged in 1983; the choreographer was Nadir Rajabpur.

5 Some of the most active choreographers included Nadir Rajabpur, Farzanah Kabuli, and Asghar Faridi Masulah.

6 "Pari Sabiri ba haft khan-i rustam miyayad" [Pari Saberi returns with seven adventures of Rustam], *I'timad-i Milli*, 28 Khurdad 1388/18 June 2009, 7.

7 For a list of Saberi's plays, see her Web page on the Iran Theater website, www. theater.ir/fa/artists.php?id=592.

8 See for example Ahmadriza As'adi, "Raqs-i jan" [The dance of the soul], *Maqam-i Musiqa'i* 8, 1382/2003, 144–5; Lina Sajjadifar, "Paykubi va sama" [Dance and *sama*'], *Hunar-pu*, Zimistan 1381/Winter 2003, 9; Lina Sajjadifar,"Sama-yi Daravish" [*Sama*' of dervishes], *Hunar-pu*, Bahar 1383/Spring 2004, 12; "Raqs baray-i khuda" [Dancing for God], trans. Mas'ud Faryamanish, *Iran*, 10 Day 1383/30 December 2004.

9 Farzanah Kabuli, quoted in Nigar Babakhani, "Zani kah az ghurub amad" [The woman who came from the sunset], *Hambastigi*, 8 Bahman 1381/31 January 2003.

10 Sam Farzanah, "Raqs dar chand qadami-i marg" [Dancing a few steps away from death], *Hamshahri-i Mah*, Khurdad 1380/May–June 2001, 22–3.

11 Examples include *Tajrubah'i bar Namayish-i Muslim* (Experiments with performing Muslim (Ibn-i 'Aqil), 1988), *Hamsara'i-i Mukhtar* (Mukhtar's choir, 1993), *Zaynab* (1999), *Hurr* (2000), by Mahmud Azizi; *Ghazal-i Kufr* (The poem for blasphemy, 2006) and *Dar Qab-i Mah* (In the moon's frame, 2008) by Husayn Musafir-Astanah. *Mir-i 'Ishq* (The prince of love, 2001), about Imam Ali, by Hadi Marzban; and *Rasul-i 'Ishq va Umid* (The messenger of love and hope, 2007) on Prophet Muhammad are some of the theatrical works narrated by religious stories.

12 These include *Pargar-i Mihr* (Compass of love, 1998), *Hamasah'i 'Ishq* (The saga of love, 1999), *Bahar-i Surkh* (The red spring, 2000), and *In Fasl ra ba Man Bikhan* (Read with me this chapter!, 2009).

13 Mihrdad Abulqasimi, "Goftigu ba Hadi Marzban, Farzanah Kabuli va Sa'id Nikpur" [A conversation with Hadi Marzban, Farzanah Kabuli, and Sa'id Nikpur], *I'timad-i Milli*, 10 Murdad 1386/1 August 2007, 7.

14 This is especially evident in *Raz-i Sarzamin-i Man* (The secret of my land, 2004) by Nadir Rajabpur and *Rastakhiz-i 'Ishq* (The resurrection of love, 2006) directed by Husayn Musafir-Astaneh.

15 This is especially evident in *Rastakhiz-i 'Ishq*.

16 *Haft Iqlim* (Seven regions, 2005) directed by Nadir Rajabpur is an example. The work was inspired by the thirteenth-century poet Nizami Ganjavi's *Haft Paykar*. When the main character, Bahram, arrives in Iran, a celebratory scene is performed by women only when they move to the music of Daf, a frame drum mostly associate with Sufi music.

17 An example is in *Rastakhiz-i 'Ishq*, when Rumi and his wife first enter a romantic relationship.

18 In the play *Shab ru-yi Sangfarsh-i Khis* (Nigh on the wet stone pavement, 1999) directed by Hadi Marzban, a red piece of fabric was used to depict rape.

19 Examples include Mahmud Azizi's *Sirisht-i Sugnak-i Zindigi* (The sorrowful nature of being, 1997) and Rajabur's *Milad-i Nur* (The birth of light, 1998).

20 Up until a few years after the revolution, some Marxist-driven plays were still being staged, including *Abbas Aqa Kargar-i Iran Nasiunal* (Mr. Abbas, the Iran-national labourer, 1980) by Sa'id Sultanpur.

21 For a list of these productions, see Shuja'i and Pakravan, "Kitabshinasi-i," 337–452.

22 Minister of Culture and Islamic Guidance Muhammad Khatami, "Natijah'i jash-navarah-ha-yi mantaqah'i mardumi kardan-i hunar ast" [The result of local festivals is the popularization of art], *Faslnamah'i Hunar*, no.13, Zimistan 1365/

Winter1987 and Bahar 1366/Spring1987, 522–31; 523; also see Rajab'ali Mazlumi, "Nigahi bah mazamin-i hunari dini" [A survey of religious art's topics], *Faslnamah'i Hunar*, no. 28, Bahar 1374/Spring 1996, 79–92; 80.

23 For instance, see Mazlumi, "Nigahi bah mazamin-i," 83. For a definition of "doctorinaire" (*maktabi*) in relation to literature, see Ali Gheissari, "Naqd-i adab-i id'iulujik, mururi bar adabiyat-i rawshanfikri va maktabi-i Iran" [A critique of ideological literature, a survey of intellectual and doctorinaire literature in Iran], *Iran nameh* 12, no. 2, Bahar 1373/Spring 1994: 233–58; 239.

24 See Nasrullah Qadiri, "Raz naguftah'i va surud nakhandahi" [You haven't told a secret and haven't sung a hymn], *Namayish,* Khurdad 1369/June 1990, 8–9, 49–50.

25 Ya'qub'ali Burji, "Chishmandaz-i fiqh bar namayish" [The perspective of religion on performance], *Fiqh*, nos. 4–5, Tabistan va Pa'iz 1374/Summer and Fall 1996, 283–326; 283; Mahdi Hujjat, "Jahanbini-i islami va hunar" [Religious worldview and art], *Faslnamah'i Hunar*, no. 1, Pa'iz 1360/Fall 1982, 352–5; quote on 354.

26 Hujjat, "Jahanbini," 355.

27 Transcribed lecture by the parliament member, Harati, in the Ninth Fajr Theater Festival, published in *Namayish* 4, nos. 40–41, Bahman va Isfand 1369/Winter 1991, 48–51; 49; Head of Parliament Ali-Akbar Hashimi- Rafsanjani, "Hunar-i ti'atr dar rasta-yi bidari-i millat-ha-yi mahrum-i jahan" [Theater in the service of awakening the impoverished nations of the world], *Faslnamah'i Hunar*, no. 13, Zimistan 1365 and Pa'iz 1366/Winter and Spring 1987, 520–47; 547.

28 Mustafa Mukhtabad, "Diram-i 'ibadi" [Drama for servitude], *Faslnamah'i Hunar*, no. 29, Tabistan va Pa'iz 1374/ Summer and Fall 1996, 373–84; 383.

29 Khatami, "Natijah'i," 527.

30 Burji, "Chishmandaz," 311.

31 Mahdi Hujjat,"Vaqi'yat-i rishah afarinish-i asar-i hunari" [The truth about the roots of artistic creation], *Faslnamah'i Hunar*, no. 3, Bahar 1362/Spring 1983, 42–61; 58.

32 Majid Sarsangi, *Muhit-i Ti'atri va Rabitah'i Bazigar va Tamashagar-i Namayish-i Dini* [The theatrical space and the relationship between performer and the audience in religious theater] (Tehran: Intisharat-i Afraz, 1389/2010), 23.

33 The notion of religious theater has been interpreted in two ways: some believed that most theaters are religious as they deal with human elements and thus godly roots; and some interpreted religious theater as that dealing with religious concepts and values, e.g., the lives of Imams and the Prophet, as well as religious narratives. But, it is the second interpretation that has commonly been used in the post-revolutionary era; see Payam Furutan, "Barrasi-i sahnah-pardazi dar namayish-i mazhabi" [An exploration of scenery design in religious performances], in *Namayish dar Harim-i Hashtum* [Theater in the eighth sanctuary], ed. Payam Furutan, et al. (Tehran: Intisharat-i Namayish, 1385/2006), 87.

34 Riza Abbasi, "Jilvah-ha-yi imam riza dar namayish-ha-yi dini-i iran" [The manifestations of Imam Riza in Iranian religious performances], in *Namayish dar Harim-i Hashtum*, 17.

35 See for instance, Muzaffar Salari, *Darun Mayah-ha va Dast-Mayah-ha-yi Namayishi dar Quran* [Dramatic themes and situations in the Koran] (Tehran: Intisharat-i Surah'i Mihr, 1387/2008); Ihsan Muqaddasi, "Janbah-ha-yi namayish dar quran" [The performative aspects of the Koran], in *Namayish dar Harim-i Hashtum*, 27–83.

36 Furutan, "Barrasi-i sahanah-pardazi", 91.

37 Hasan Bayanlu, *Vadi-i Hayrat: Namayish-i Dini va 'Unsur-i shigifti* [Territory of wonder: Religious dramas and wonder element: A collection of researches on religious theater] (Tehran: Intisharat-i Namayish, 1385/2006).

38 Bayanlu, *Vadi-i Hayrat*, 41.

39 Bayanlu, *Vadi-i Hayrat*, 142, 63.

40 Bayanlu, *Vadi-i Hayrat*, 72, 114, 82, 89, 86.

41 Furutan, "Barrasi-i sahanah-pardazi," 86.
42 Sirus Kahurinezhad, quoted in *Namayish dar Harim-i Hashtum*, 116.
43 This resembles Erin Hurley's description of the function of the chorus in tragedies. See Erin Hurley, *Theatre and Feeling* (New York: Palgrave and McMillan, 2010), 40–42.
44 See "Intiqad az bitavajjuhi-i mas'ulan bah harikat-i mawzun" [A critique of the responsible parties' neglect of the rhythmic movements genre], *Tasnim New Agency*, 18 Farvardin 1392/7 April 2013, www.tasnimnews.com/Home/Single/38777.
45 Qutb al-ddin Sadiqi, "Furmalism-i jahan, Iran diruz, imruz" [World's formalism, Iran of the past, Iran of today], transcribed lecture, *Namayish,* nos. 109–110, Mihr and Aban 1387/October and November 2008, 66–72; 71.
46 Omid Biniyaz, "Imruz ba Husayn Musafir-i Astanah" [Today with Husayn Musafir-Astanah], *Iran*, no. 3844, 3 Bahman 1386/23 January 2008, 24.
47 Furutan, "Barrasi-i sahanah-pardazi", 101.
48 Some scholars, including Muhammad-Husayn Nasirbakht, emphasize *ta'ziyah* as a national performative form, originally developed as a means for garnering national unity against the Ottoman Turks. Nasirbakht further related the historical interest of Iranians for the third Shi'i Imam Husayn to the Iranian background of his wife, Bibi Shahrbanu who was of Sassanid lineage. *Ta'ziyah* has regularly been regarded as a ritual ceremony with capacities for development to a national theatrical form. See Muhammad-Husayn Nasirbakht, *Naqshpushi dar Shabihkhani* [Wearing the character in Shahbihkhani] (Tehran: Intisharat-i Namayish, 1386/2007), 1, 12–13. The Marxist theater scholar Khosrow Shahriari also highlights *taziyah*'s correlation with Iranian identity, while interpreting Husayn as an allegorical figure of resistance, who stands for the possibility of social change and political reforms. Khosrow Shahriari, *A Different Approach to a Unique Theatre: Taziyeh in Iran* (Sweden: Kitab-i Arzan, 2008), 155, 163, 167.
49 This is observable in *Ghazal-i Kufr, Dar Qab-i Mah, Zaynab*, and *Hamsara'i-i Mukhtar*.
50 See Bayanlu, *Vadi-i Hayrat,* 63.
51 For instance in the 'Ashura scene in *Dar Qab-i Mah*, the angels carried Ali-Asghar, the infant son of the third Shi'i Imam, to his aunt Zaynab and father Husayn.
52 Examples of this include *Zaynab* and *Ghazal-i Kufr*.
53 *Tavallud ta Tavallud* (Birth by birth, 1996) directed by Nadir Rajabpur is an instance where Prophet Muhammad and other holy figures are only shown behind the cyclorama.
54 Instances of this include *Sirisht-i Sugnak-i Zindigi, Dar Qab-i Mah*, and *Tavallud ta Tavallud*.
55 Nasirbakht, *Naqshpushi,* 77.
56 See, for instance, "Nazar-i maraji' nisbat bah nishan dadan-i chirah'i hazrat-i 'abbas" [Religious authorities' opinion on showing the face of Hazrat-i Abbas], *Paygah-i Hunari-Tahlili-i Hunar-i Muti'ali*, 14 Tir 1389/5 July 2010, honaremotaali.org/NewsDetail.aspx?itemid=201.
57 See Sayyad Mujtaba Husayni, *Ahkam-i Nigah va Pushish, Mutabiq ba Nazar-i Dah Tan az Maraji'-i 'Uzzam* [The laws of gaze and attire according to ten religious authorities] (Qom: Daftar-i nashr-i ma'arif, 1389/2010), 111–15; Burji, "Chishmandaz," 287–305; Shahriari, *A Different Approach*, 34.
58 Sarsangi, *Muhit-i Ti'atri*, 203; Shahriari, *A Different Approach*, 18.
59 Ali, interview with the author, Tehran, 2 Tir 1389/23 June 2010.
60 Ali, interview with the author.
61 For men, there have been fewer limitations, but still not total freedom in movements and costuming. Occasionally, during the preview sessions by an inspection committee, some movements of the male performers have been identified as

improper and hence have had to be eliminated. For instance, in an all-male commissioned work in 2006, the inspection committee requested the elimination of ballet's *step-jeté* movement from the choreography, presumably because they identified the movement as inappropriate. Lalah, interview with the author, 4 Tir 1386/25 July 2007.

62 For mechanisms of correctional gaze, see Margaret McLaren, *Feminism, Foucault, and Embodied Subjectivity* (Albany, NY: State University of New York Press, 2002).

63 Michel Foucault, "The Eye of Power," in *Power/Knowledge: Selected Interviews and Other Writings, 1972–1977*, ed. C. Gordon (New York: Pantheon, 1980), 146–65.

64 Maryam, interview with the author, Tehran, 14 Murdad 1389/5 August 2010.

65 For a discussion of expressions of a proper Muslim, see Asef Bayat, "Islamism and the Politics of Fun," *Public Culture* 19, no. 3 (2007): 433–59.

66 Guli, interview with the author, Tehran, 19 Tir 1389/10 July 2010.

67 Alexandra Carter, "Feminist Strategies for the Study of Dance," in *The Routledge Reader in Gender and Performance*, L. Goodman and J. De Gay, eds (New York: Routledge, 1998), 247–50.

68 Farzanah Kabuli, "Ja-i khali-i harikat" [The empty space of movement], *Iran*, 18 Khurdad 1381/8 June 2002, 13; Muhammad Chaharduli, "Ta'sir-i harikat dar namayish-i simurgh" [The effect of movement in the play *Simurgh*], *Abrar*, 26 Isfand 1380/17 March 2002.

69 Farzanah, "Raqs dar chand," 2. *Zurkhanah* is a vernacular Iranian martial arts form.

70 "Pasukh-ha-yi fa'izah hashimi bah su'alat-i bishumar-i khabarnigaran" [Fa'izeh Hashimi's response to numerous questions posed by the journalists], *Baztab*, 26 Shahrivar 1384/17 September 2005, www.baztab.com/news/29121.php (accessed 30 January 2009).

71 "Varzish-ha-yi banuvan-i kishvar-ha-yi Islami" [The sports of the women of Islamic countries], *Raz-i Khun*, www.razekhoon.parsiblog.com/-25541.htm (accessed 30 January 2009).

72 See Manuchihr Akbarlu, *Yik dahah khanah'i Ti'atr* [House of theater, a decade] (Tehran: Mu'assisah'i Farhangi-i Khanah'i Ti'atr, 1388/2009), 441.

73 *Andishah'i Qum* is the website of the Center for Religious Studies and Research in Qom (Markaz-i Mutali'at va Pazhuhish-ha-yi Dini Hawzah'i 'Ilmiyah'i Qum), dedicated to answering questions related to religious matters.

74 Hamidullah Rafi'i, "Islam, din-i shari'at va ma'naviyat" [Islam is the religion of Shari'a and spirituality], *Andishah'i Qum*, www.andisheqom.com/Files/shobheinternet.php?idVeiw=30514&level=4&subid=30514 (accessed 31 August 2009).

75 The organizing institution was Iran's Cultural Heritage, Handcrafts, and Tourism Organization (Sazaman-i Miras-i Farhangi, Sanayi'-i Dasti va Gardishgari). See Edmund Blair, "Iran Vice-President Under Fire over Koran 'Dance'," Reuters, 16 November 2008, www.reuters.com/article/2008/11/16/us-iran-politics-ahmadinejad-idUSTRE4AF1E620081116 (accessed 31 August 2009).

76 Through *sama'*, the Sufis are believed to overcome their evil-inciting selves and unite with God.

8 Dance, body, space, and subjectivity on the twentieth-century Iranian stage

This chapter examines the ways the three different dancing subjects of twentieth-century Iran—the *raqqas*, or cabaret dancer; the national dancer (*raqsandah*); and the "performer" (*namayishgar*) of rhythmic movements—have been constructed onstage.[1] It explores the ways in which, according to the biopolitics of the stage and the discursive construction of performance, the onstage (female) performer in each genre constitutes a differing dancing self through choice of movement, costume, music, sensory appeal, appearance, behavior, as well as gender performativity and relations. This phenomenological analysis examines the theatrical process through which the female dancing self of the pre-revolutionary cabaret scene—one associated with enticing *shahvat* and the "evil-inciting self" (*nafs-i ammarah*)—was sublimated to correspond with a respectable "contented self" (*nafs-i mutma'innah*) to conform to her role on the post-revolutionary theatrical stage.

While focusing on semiotic and sensory examinations of these bodies on stage, this analysis relies on the socio-historical study of dance in Iran explored throughout this book. For the purpose of this analysis, I deploy Islamic law (*ahkam*) as well as contemporary clerical reactions to the "veil" (hijab), Muslim behavior, gazing, dance, music, and performance. I also make reference to the religiously oriented anti-obscenity discourses of the pre-revolutionary era. I do this because (1) they encompassed detailed responses to actual practices of public performances that involved women, and (2) the Pahlavi-era public performances and the discourses surrounding them have largely informed the collective imagination and knowledge of art practitioners, audiences, and regulators of theatrical space in the post-revolutionary period.[2]

The performing body on stage is a physical symbol, one reflecting various complex meanings through both its appearance and actions and interacting with various stage signifiers such as costume, and more importantly, the audience.[3] The explored dance genres were performed in three drastically different milieus: the cabaret stage and the *mutribi* scene were the main venues for cabaret dancing, while the Pahlavi-era theatrical stage was the sphere of performance of the national dancer. The performer of *harikat-i mawzun* also performed on the theater stage but on one that has been governed by post-revolutionary Islamic regulations. This variation of performance space has not only affected the dance genres, it has also changed the performer–audience relationship in each genre.

As interpreted by the journalist Farrukh Safavi, the transferring of dancing bodies from the traditional *hawz* stage, as well as the popular cabaret stage, to the Western-style proscenium theatrical space elevated the status of dance to a high art form in the Pahlavi era, as this transition forced the audience to sit and watch dance in silence.[4] As Safavi pointed out, the performer–audience relationship in the traditional *ruhawzi* sphere and the cabaret space was more direct, since the audience could utter their verbal reactions. In the case of *raqqas*, the environment of the cabaret (as reconstructed in films) allowed the audience members to express their sexual interest and to approach the performers for *fishkhuri* as described in Chapter 4. Due to this unregulated intermingling of men and women, cabaret was charged with *shahvat* in the pre-revolutionary Islamic discourse. The proscenium stage of national dance and its stage lighting created a distance between the audience and the performer, while presumably its rather elitist environment regulated the audience's response.

The transition from the pre-revolutionary national dance to the rhythmic movements genre was made possible by the conversion of the theatrical space, and by obliging four elements of performance—theme, message, structure, and the performer—to follow Islamic regulations and values.[5] While the theme, message, and structure of rhythmic movements have appeared to be easily adaptable and to even reflect the ideology of the state, creating a chaste (de-eroticized) dancer appears to be an impossible task. As Laurence Senelick indicates, the stage, and the staged body as a "commodity for strangers' gaze," are both essentially imbued with eroticism.[6] Not only do most contemporary clerics identify dance with *shahvat*—only allowing a woman to dance for her husband—but a close examination of the pre-revolutionary discourse of the Islamic press (in Chapter 6) indicates that the public dancing body was associated with *shahvat*, exhibitionism, *fahsha*, and evoking *nafs-i ammarah* then too.[7]

Moreover, while those texts largely reflected details of the corporeal characteristics of unveiled *mutajaddid* women, ideal Muslim women were identified as embodying "chastity" (*'iffat*) and veiling. Ideal Muslim women were described as following their wisdom, obeying their husbands, and raising healthy children. The actual corporeal characteristics and behavior of these women, however, were largely invisible in society for the Islamic writers, and thus in their texts. Additionally, as the recent compilation and interpretations of Islamic jurisprudence on women's behavior indicates, women have been encouraged to practice the "veiling of behavior" (*hijab-i raftar*) through chaste and "wise" movements and have been prohibited from exhibitionism and "flirtatious" (*'ighva-garanah*) movements that lead to sexual arousal in men. These sources, however, do not provide further details on specifically what movements are considered chaste and wise.[8]

This dichotomy of eroticism associated with the dancing body and the invisibility of (the corporeal characteristics of) a chaste Muslim female body have posed a challenge in the construction of a theatrical chaste dancing body, as dancing after all is a corporeal performance. To overcome the difficult task of sublimating the dancing subject into a chaste performer, a range of techniques and stage elements have been deployed. It is important to note that this sublimation process is perhaps more difficult for a dancer than it would be for a regular actor, as the task of speaking by itself distantiates the notion of exhibitionism associated with the performing body.

A performance costume is the most obvious signifier for framing the performing body. As Helen Gilbert and Joan Tompkins assert, the "costume's simultaneous specificity and versatility makes it an unstable sign/site of power," which can be deployed to "(mis) identify race, gender, class and creed, and make visible the status associated with such markers of difference."[9] The body of a *raqqas* on the cabaret stage was constructed to reflect her discursive associations with *shahvat*, nakedness, and *fashsha* to attract male audiences. As described, "nakedness" was a temporal discursive notion that was echoed by the costuming of the dancer: while in the 1950s her costume consisted of pants or a midi-skirt, in the 1970s, her low-cut mini-dress exposed and accentuated her hips and breasts.

Embodying the aesthetics of Iranian modernity, the national dancer looked distinctly different from the cabaret *raqqas*. The national dancer's body was often fully covered with vivid clothing inspired mostly by Persian miniature paintings, in which the curves of her body were apparent. In contrast, the costumes used in performances of rhythmic movements have been mostly black, white, or other muted tones, and loosely fitted so as to obscure the shape of the body. This multi-layered costuming has not only been working to cover female bodies, but also to de-eroticize them: by covering the feminine curve and flattening the breasts, the costumes have been used as a strategy of distantiating the dancer's body from a woman's body.[10]

The cyclorama has also been functioning as a device for de-eroticizing the body, as women have been able to move rather freely behind it, and the audience can only view their flat silhouettes. Another means of reducing the sensitivity towards the female public dancing body, as explained in Chapter 7, has been de-gendering strategies, such as similar costuming for men and women as well as the occasional coverage of the face or head for both sexes.[11] Arguably, this absence of gendered female bodies on stage correlates with the invisibility of the bodies of the ideal veiled women described in the Islamic sources. Another consequence of eliminating women's corporeal characteristics has been the occasional adopting of "female" aesthetic features by men in these settings: this is especially evident in the long hairstyle trend for men in rhythmic movements.[12]

Music has also been used to de-eroticize the performer of rhythmic movements. On the cabaret stage, dancers performed with belly dance music or with Iranian 6/8 (an upbeat, rapid time signature) popular urban music, often lip-synching the explicit lyrics that usually introduced her as an attractive "commodity" for the other's gaze. As discussed in Chapter 6, these types of music were identified as evoking dance, *shahvat*, and lovemaking. The national dancers often performed to traditional Persian music, regional folk music, and sometimes contemporary and classical Western art music. While the goblet drum *zarb* was dominant in the music used for national dance, the circular drum *daf*, which is usually associated with mystical music, has accompanied the post-revolutionary rhythmic movements. Furthermore, to keep these performances from becoming "celebratory," romantic choral music with slow rhythms has been deployed. This has also been to de-eroticize the performance, as, according to my interviewee Guli, an upbeat environment is considered to be imbued with eroticism in the post-revolutionary context.[13]

Another main difference between cabaret dancing on the one hand, and national dance and rhythmic movements on the other, is the improvisational nature of the movements of the former genre. Nevertheless, through adjustment and modification of movements, the choreographers and performers have endeavoured to adapt dances to the socio-political milieu. The Iranian solo improvised dance which adapted to a cabaret situation stands in contrast with the more stylized version of this dance employed in national dance or Persian classical dance. In the creation of national dances, choreographic units of the solo improvised dance, as well as the movement vocabulary of Iranian regional folk dances and rituals, were employed. This includes the rotation of wrists, triplet steps, some movements of the arms and shoulders, and, occasionally, minor hip movements.

The most important movement that seems to play a crucial role in characterizing the dance styles is *qir*. The free-flow rotation of hips, *qir* has both a sexual (for its accentuated hips) and a comedic affect (as it creates a sense of elation in the audience). Both *qir* and the shimmy-like movements of shoulders are commonly used in the solo improvised Iranian dance, while exaggerated adaptations of them were widely used in cabaret styles to highlight sexuality. Depicting an "unrestrained" character and enacting a performer with sexual agency, the cabaret dancer improvised and exaggerated the sexual movements of the body parts according to her onstage mood. These hip and shoulder movements, however, were not absorbed into the often-choreographed national dances, perhaps because of their sexual resemblance and presumed connection to cabaret style dances.

Although appropriated to fit the biopolitics of the time, movement is still the most obvious element shared by the (docile) dancing bodies of pre-revolutionary national dance and post-revolutionary rhythmic movements.[14] The choreographed genre of *harikat-i mawzun* is likewise predictable and can be previewed and controlled. Contrasting with the "unrestrained" *raqqas*, this predictability of the performer of rhythmic movements creates an image of a chaste subject who submits to her wisdom—as has been discussed, following wisdom is considered a prerequisite for chastity.

A major distinction between the pre-revolutionary and post-revolutionary genres is the absence of movements that signify the solo improvised dance, as these movements would connote *raqs* for the public. Especially to distantiate women's movements of *harikat-i mawzun* from *raqs*, the free-flowing rotation of the wrists, triplet steps, and delicate shoulder movements borrowed from the solo improvised Iranian dance are either less emphasized or completely non-existent. This is also evident in the performances of the Khurasan folk dance in which the *bishkan* have been replaced by clapping.[15] Instead, in *harikat-i mawzun*, women mostly move their arms for a defined purpose in a way that resembles prayer, or for carrying props such as books, candleholders, flowers, and fabrics. As discussed in Chapter 7, the use of props implies that female bodies are not exhibitionist, but are performing a task.[16] Otherwise, the movements of *harikat-i mawzun* are often a theatrical hybrid of ballet and a variety of vernacular movements with an emphasis on religious and mystic themes.

Unlike cabaret dancing, the choreographed national dance and rhythmic movements both rely on ballet aesthetics: this has emphasized a straight spine and thus given a verticality to performers in both genres, with restrictions in the horizontal movements of the hips and chest. This verticality in national dance created a sense of lightness, delicacy, and pride in the performers and helped with the elimination of *qir*. Using Andrée Grau's explanation of the correlation between ballet and spirituality, I argue that this verticality in rhythmic movement has helped the ascending image of the performer who, in communication with heaven, danced upward.[17] This verticality in rhythmic movements also matches Mohamad Tavakoli-Targhi's observation of ascendance (*'uruj*)—a vertical movement towards heaven and God—in Iran–Iraq war paintings that aimed to promote "martyrdom" (*shahadat*) as a result of participation in war.[18]

While performers of both national dance and rhythmic movements have exhibited balletic bodies, the movements of the female dancer in national dance were light, sustained, free-floating, and expanding, while the movements of rhythmic movements performances are binding and shrink towards the centre. The spatial focus in national dance was more sagittal, as the dancers used their trunk in shoulder-opposite-hip relationships, whereas in rhythmic movements, the dancer's stress is on remaining neutral and erect as the head, neck, and trunk are fairly fixed around the vertical midline of the body.

The female performer in rhythmic movements often cautiously crosses the stage, making separate lines upstage and keeping a gap with her male colleagues. Her positioning onstage is meant to consciously emphasize a distance between men's and women's bodily zones. In contrast, as was depicted in the *film-i farsi* genre, the cabaret dancer was usually confident in crossing her stage. She moved in proximity to the musicians on stage, and directly asked audiences to adore her sexuality. A certainty and freedom were also evident in the movements of the national dancer, who traveled freely across the stage. While keeping a distance from the bodily zones of her male co-performers, the female dancer of the national dance often acted playfully, teasing the men onstage and unreservedly communicating with them. The post-revolutionary productions do not present such self-assurance and liberty in women's movements.

The behavior of the performers is another area of contrast between pre-revolutionary and post-revolutionary dance. The *raqqas* enacted a confident performance of sexuality, gazing directly at the audience, and enacted gestures with sexual undertones (such as blinking) with which she invited customers to offstage interactions. Such unrestrained gazing on the part of women was associated with *shahvat* and evoking *nafs-i ammarah* in the pre-revolutionary discourse on obscenity and was discouraged by Islamic law.[19] In *raqs-i milli*, while the image of both men and women presented on stage was physically fit, healthy, confident, joyful, and active, displaying a sense of pride in their behavior, the female national dancer enacted a controlled femininity and charm.

The dominant characteristic of the female performer of *harikat-i mawzun* has been her embodiment and performance of the expressions of heaviness, modesty, chastity, and austerity. To remove the connotations of unrestrained gazing, the *harikat-i mawzun* performer has had to control her gaze and smile when facing an audience, especially in celebratory occasions. The combination of controlled facial features and her exceedingly covered body, at times has created a certain image: it is as if the head of a doll has been placed on the body of a life-size puppet, whose expression of sexuality is mediated through other means. With the exception of some performances and key roles, including Zaynab who not only is a holy character but is also a religious symbol of agency and resistance, the construction of dancing women on stage has been mostly passive and obedient, contrasting to men's more active and strong roles, especially in terms of expressing sexuality. The recurring appearance of women angels is an example of such characterizations.

Unlike the cabaret setting, the performance space of the proscenium stage has restricted a direct relation between the audience and performers in rhythmic movements. The post-revolutionary societal restrictions on gender relations have manifested in a rather exaggerated way onstage, especially when the script requires a female character to be in a romantic or sexual relationship with her male counterpart. Since the mute performers of the post-revolutionary stage have not been allowed to touch each other, expressions of sexuality have been mediated through other methods, including pauses between movements to express doubt or affection, the exchange of props, the use of fabric, and gestural hints of lovemaking while the bodies of the performers are apart from each other.[20] Arguably, not only has the eroticism of female bodies been eliminated by the mediation of gender through other means, but the depiction and sensory experience of *shahvat* has been reconfigured to be transmitted through other mediums, leading to the establishment of a new aesthetics regime for gender representation on the post-revolutionary stage.[21] Such restrictions on gender performativity and relations have been less visible in puppetry, which has managed to provide a more natural sense of sexual encounters than human body does.[22] Another means to overcome the situation has been the recent resurgence of *zanupush*, the cross-dressing male performers who are able to enact female roles with less restrictions when depicting sexual relations.[23]

The resurrection of *zanpush* to the theater stage in the twenty-first century might signify an artistic revisiting of an older vernacular corporeal presentational style. It might also attest to the restrictions of the current theatrical milieu in the presentation of gender performativity and relations. Or it might be a way of challenging the new regime of gender aesthetics under the post-revolutionary theatrical culture of the Islamic Republic. It certainly, however, is reminiscent of the *zanpush* of the pre- and early twentieth-century performance sphere, when, in that very different environment, female sexuality was mediated through male bodies onstage.

The continuous presence of dancing angels on the post-revolutionary stage also hints back to an earlier time when non-Muslim women joined the stage to become the mediators of Iranian women's gendered bodies. Later, when Muslim women joined the stage in the Pahlavi era, they used stage names to avoid the social backlash, as if they mediated themselves through others' bodies. The bifurcation of dance scenes along with the emergence of an enticing cabaret dancer and a chaste self-reflexive national dancer with controlled sexuality was yet another phase of the process of staging female dancers. Although the Revolution of 1979 purged both the national dancer and her contrasting counterpart on the cabaret stage from the public stage, she has returned to the stage with a new dancing self—one whose corporeal characteristics were already prefigured in the collective imagination of the society.

At the same time, the cultural evaluation and aesthetics configuration of performing arts in Iran is still informed by the categorizations that emerged throughout the twentieth century, while as a consequence of the sociopolitical transformation of the cultural and artistic realms and the media, most of the "othered" cultural forms of the urban popular culture of the Pahlavi era have vanished, their descriptors—*mutrib, raqqas, ruhawzi*, and *Lalahzari*—have remained degrading within the discourse on contemporary art and culture and could be used as a means to humiliate an artist. The term *ibtizal*, along with the array of characteristics, signifiers, and/or emotions associated with it, has been transmitted to the contemporary cultural criticism and has been continuously applied applied to the new forms of urban popular culture and its audience, including the post-revolutionary popular music produced in Iran. The debates prompted after the death of the popular singer Morteza Pashaei in 2014 are a vivid example of the diligence of such conceptualizations in contemporary times, and are reminiscent of the debates about Mahvash's death five decades earlier.[24]

Notes

1 For this chapter, I have consulted available videos of national dance as well as recordings of post-revolutionary theatrical productions. For cabaret dancing, I have relied on the reconstructions of these dances and their audiences in

commercial cinema of *film-i farsi*. In this analysis, to provide a broader perspective, in addition to rhythmic movements, instances of other theatrical performances have been used.

2 This analysis is based on my observation of common representational styles that appear in these genres; of course, the stage presentations could have varied depending on the character roles as well as the day-to-day politics.

3 Helen Gilbert and Joan Tompkins, *Post-Colonial Drama: Theory, Practice, Politics* (London: Routledge, 1996), 203.

4 Farrukh Safavi, "Raqs dar jam'iah'i ma" [Dance in our society], *Iran-i Abad*, Azar 1339/November 1960, 69–72.

5 Ya'qub'ali Burji, "Chishmandaz-i fiqh bar namayish" [The perspective of religion on performance], *Fiqh*, nos. 4–5, Tabistan va Pa'iz 1374/Summer and Fall 1996, 283–326; 284.

6 Laurence Senelick, introduction to *Gender in Performance: The Presentation of Difference in the Performing Arts*, ed. Laurence Senelick (Hanover, NH: University Press of New England, 1992), xii.

7 See Sayyad Mujtaba Husayni, *Ahkam-i musiqi bah zamimah'i raqs va qumar, mutabiq ba nazar-i dah tan az maraji'* [The laws of music, dance, and gambling according to ten religious authorities] (Qom: Nahad-i Namayandigi-i Maqam-i Mu'azzam-i Rahbari Dar Danishgah-ha,1389/2010), 80–85.

8 See Muhammad-'Ali Karimniya, Hijab-i Dukhtaran, *Amuzish-i pushish bah zaban-i sadah* [Girl's veiling: Education on dressing in an easy language] (Qom: Kawsar-i Adab, 1383/2004), 25, 37; Muhammad-Taqi Rukni-Lamuki, *Ahkam-i arastigi-i zahiri* [The laws on adornment of the appearance] (Qom: Zamzam-i Hidayat, 1386/2007), 86.

9 Gilbert and Tompkins, *Post-Colonial Drama*, 244.

10 Referring to the heavy costuming of performers, the Europe-based dancer Shahrukh Mushkin-Qalam referred to post-revolutionary performances as "dance with fabrics" (*raqs-i parchah*). See Azadah Asadi, "Baray-i raqs jangidaham" [I fought for dance], *RadioZamaneh*, zamaaneh.com/azadeh/2007/08/post_56.html.

11 This is especially evident in *Rastakhiz-i 'Ishq* (The resurrection of love, 2006) directed by Husayn Musafir-Astanah as well as Nadir Rajabpur's *Raz-i Sarzamin-i Man* (The secret of my land, 2004).

12 That is, male dancers grow their hair long, as women cannot show their hair publicly.

13 Guli, interview with the author, Tehran, 19 Tir 1389/10 July 2010.

14 A main incentive for *harikat-i mawzun*'s deep reliance on the pre-revolutionary national dance is its corporeal transmission, passing on the embodied knowledge of its main choreographers and instructors, most of whom were formerly the dancers of pre-revolutionary dance companies.

15 *Bishkan* refers to Persian-style snapping employing both hands.

16 In a discussion with Raw'ya, an actress who regularly acts in television shows in Iran, she described similar situations in television productions where female actors are often being depicted as doing simple jobs. Raw'ya, interview with the author, Tehran, 25 July 2011.

17 See Andrée Grau, "Dancing bodies, spaces/places: A cross-cultural investigation," *Journal of Dance and Somatic Practices* 3, nos. 1–2, 3 Murdad 1390/April 2012, 5–24; 10.

18 Mohamad Tavakoli-Targhi, "Frontline Mysticism and Eastern Spirituality," *ISIM Newsletter* 9, no. 1, 2002, 13, 38.

19 See Sayyad-Mujtaba Husayni, *Ahkam-i nigah va pushish, mutabiq ba nazar-i dah tan az marajai'i 'Uzam* [The laws of gaze and clothing according to ten religious authorities] (Qom: Daftar-i Nashr-i Ma'arif, 1389/2010), 111–15; Ya'qub'ali Burji, "Chishmandaz-i fiqh bar namayish" [The perspective of religion on performance], *Fiqh*, nos. 4–5, Tabistan va Pa'iz 1374/Summer and Fall 1996, 283–326; Hamid

Ahmadi-Julfa'i, *Chihil Hadis piramun-i hijab va 'iffat-i zanan* [Forty Hadith on women's hijab and chastity] (Qom: Intisharat-i Za'ir, 1387/2008), 39–40.

20 In *Othello* (2011), directed by Atifah Tihrani, two columns were used as mediators in a sex scene: Desdemona was standing behind a column with her back to the audience; standing behind the next column while facing the audience, Cassio was pretending to be having sex. In another instance of an inspector's reaction during a preview session, the director Ahmad (pseud.) was asked to amend a metaphoric fencing scene between a man and a woman that stood for making love, as the inspector felt the scene was excessively erotic.

21 This resonates with Jacques Rancière's notion of "reconfiguring the distribution of the sensible." See Jacques Rancière, *The Politics of Aesthetics: The Distribution of the Sensible*, Gabriel Rockhill, trans. and intro. (London and New York: Continuum, 2004).

22 In the puppet operas of Behruz Qaribpur, including *Hafiz*, the male and female puppets get close and touch each other.

23 In a recent production of *Macbeth* (2012) by Riza Sirvati, Lady Macbeth was performed by a male actor who was described by a critic as "a man who surpassed women," as he could more easily express femininity and even seductiveness, make love to his partner, and have freedom in his movement; Sanaz Safa'i, "Mardi kah zanan ra pusht-i sar guzasht" [A man who surpassed women], *Tamasha*, 31 Khurdad 1391/20 June 2012, honaretamasha.blogfa.com/post-117.aspx (accessed 15 November 2012).

24 One instance is the recent lecture by a University of Tehran sociology professor Yousef Abazari at a session held there entitled, "The Cultural Phenomenology of a Death." Responding to the death of Pashaei, which drew hundreds of thousands of mourners to the streets of Tehran and other cities who recited the singer's songs, Abazari called his music "degenerate" and "worthless" for lacking any musical qualities, and his audience "idiots" (*ablah*) and new-day "*lumpan*" who have been trapped in the state's scheme of a depoliticizing of arts and culture. Making parallels between Pashaei's fans and those who attended Mahvash's funeral, he related the current growth of the popular music industry of Iran to the state's resolution to open the doors to popular entertainment in order to divert people from serious social and political issues. See Yousef Abazari, "Padidar shinasi-i farhangi-i yik marg" [The cultural phenomenology of a death], seminar, Macbeth 1391/2012/8 December 2014, http://simafekr.tv/0fa1026idattach.htm (accessed 15 January 2015).

Index